Pictures, Quotations, and Distinctions

Pictures, Quotations, and Distinctions

FOURTEEN ESSAYS IN PHENOMENOLOGY

ROBERT SOKOLOWSKI

Catholic University of America Press
University of Notre Dame Press
Notre Dame and London

Library of Congress Cataloging-in-Publication Data

Sokolowski, Robert.
   Pictures, quotations, and distinctions : fourteen essays in
phenomenology / Robert Sokolowski.
   p.   cm.
Includes index.
ISBN 978-0-8132-3518-9
1. Phenomenology.   I. Title.
B829.5.S577   1992
142′.7—dc20   91-50575
                                                                  CIP

To
Gian-Carlo Rota
In Friendship and Gratitude

Contents

Preface

The essays contained in this book were written over a period of some twelve years. After I had written my book, *Presence and Absence: A Philosophical Investigation of Language and Being* (Bloomington: Indiana University Press, 1978), I thought it would be good to attempt a series of phenomenological studies of various kinds of intentionality. *Presence and Absence* was very formal, a metaphysics of speech, appearance, and being; it would be desirable, I felt, to show how Husserl's style of philosophical thinking could illuminate a range of diverse and more concrete phenomena. The essay on picturing was the first to be written, and others followed as the occasion or the inclination prompted. The essays are examples of what one might call applied phenomenology. Husserl's way of thinking allows us to address the grand themes in Western philosophy, and I hope that these papers can serve as a modest contribution to that tradition.

I have received help and inspiration from many colleagues and friends, and I try to acknowledge my debt to them in particular passages in the essays. I would like here to express my thanks to Thomas Prufer, whose influence can be seen throughout the volume and whose comments have improved all of the papers. It is my pleasure to dedicate this book to Gian-Carlo Rota, who has made it possible for me to enter into discussion with contemporary science and mathematics, and whose generosity and friendship I have enjoyed for many years.

Provenance
of the Essays

The first three essays appeared in *The Review of Metaphysics*: "Picturing" in vol. 31 (1977), pp. 3–28; "Quotation" in vol. 37 (1984), pp. 699–723; and "Making Distinctions" in vol. 32 (1979), pp. 639–76. "Explaining" appeared in *Nature and Scientific Method: Festschrift for William A. Wallace*, edited by Daniel Dahlstrom (Washington: The Catholic University of America Press, 1991), pp. 37–50.

"Timing" appeared in *The Review of Metaphysics*, vol. 35 (1982), pp. 687–714. "Measurement" was published in the *American Philosophical Quarterly*, vol. 24 (1987), pp. 71–79; earlier versions were given as lectures at the Jagiellonian University in Cracow, Poland, in May 1985 and at The American University in October 1985. "Exact Science and the World in Which We Live" was first read at a conference at the Reimer Stiftung in Bad Homburg in November 1978; it was published in *Lebenswelt und Wissenschaft in der Philosophie Edmund Husserls*, edited by Elisabeth Ströker (Frankfurt: Klosterman, 1979), pp. 92–106.

"Exorcising Concepts" was published in *The Review of Metaphysics*, vol. 40 (1987), pp. 451–63, and earlier versions were given as papers at Yale University in February 1985 and to the Washington Philosophy Club at the University of Maryland during a conference on cognition and brain sciences in March 1985.

"Referring" appeared in *The Review of Metaphysics*, vol. 42 (1988), pp. 27–49. "Grammar and Thinking" was given as a lecture before the *Deutsche Gesellschaft für phänomenologische Forschung* in June 1987 and appeared as "Grammatik und Denken" in *Phänomenologische Forschungen*, vol. 21 (1988), pp. 31–50. "Tarskian Harmonies in Words and Pictures" has not been previously published.

"Moral Thinking" appeared in *Husserl and the Phenomenological Tradition*, edited by Robert Sokolowski (Washington: The Catholic University of America Press, 1988), pp. 235–48. An earlier version appeared in *Jagiellonian University Reports on Philosophy*, vol. 11 (1987), pp. 29–37, and earlier forms of the essay were presented as the Aron Gurwitsch Lecture in October 1984 at a meeting of the Society for Phenomenology and Existential Psychology, held in Atlanta, Georgia; as a lecture at the Jagiellonian University in Cracow in May 1985; and as a paper at The Catholic University of America in September 1985. "What Is Moral Action?" appeared in *The New Scholasticism*, vol. 63 (1989), pp. 18–37, and earlier versions were presented as the Suarez Lecture at Fordham University in April 1987, and also at Duquesne University in April 1988. "Knowing Natural Law" was published in *Tijdschrift voor Filosofie*, vol. 43 (1981), pp. 625–41, and earlier versions were presented at The Catholic University of America in October 1980, as the Cardinal Mercier Lecture at the University of Leuven, Belgium, in March 1981, and at the University of Texas at Austin in February 1982.

Introduction

We are generally not at ease with appearances. We tend to think that they are essentially deceptive, or at least essentially an obstacle, and that we must outwit them. We suppose that one of the services philosophy can provide to culture is to help us overcome the apparent and attain to things "as they really are." But appearances do not necessarily deceive. The things that are can also seem to be as they are. There are true as well as false appearances.

Instead of trying to navigate around appearances, we can, in our philosophy, think about appearances themselves and about what is disclosed in them. Once we stop being suspicious, we find that appearances come in a marvelous variety of forms and that they richly reward our philosophical curiosity. The essays in this book are attempts to describe various ways in which things can appear: as pictured, quoted, measured, distinguished, explained, meant, and referred to, and also as coming to light in moral conduct. The description of each of these forms is made more vivid and exact by being placed alongside the descriptions of the others. And because appearance always involves that which appears and the one to whom it appears, my essays are meant to be not only an analysis of appearance but also a venture into the question of being and a clarification of what we are. Although the primary inspiration for these studies comes from Husserl and the phenomenological tradition, the papers also reflect the influence of Frege and his philosophical progeny.

The fourteen essays can be grouped into pairs or triplets. "Picturing" and "Quotation" describe representation in image and in speech. "Making Distinctions" and "Explaining" discuss two ways in which we respond to issues that arise for thought. "Timing" and "Measurement" describe how two different kinds of wholes are articulated into parts, and "Exact Science and the World in Which We Live" further develops the theme of measurement. "Exorcising Concepts" and "Referring" are a phenomenological attempt to treat sense and reference. "Grammar and Thinking" and "Tarskian Harmonies in Words and Pictures" discuss the formal composition of sentences and images and its relationship to the way things are disclosed. The final three papers, "Moral Thinking," "What Is Moral Action?" and "Knowing Natural Law" are studies in the phenomenology of ethical performance.

Each of the essays tries to describe a form of appearance, but the issue of being as the origin of these forms remains a topic behind and in all the rest, always approached but only occasionally treated. Each essay makes a new attempt at access, a running start from a different direction, an effort to reveal another slant on the question that we never leave behind. If we were stringent enough, we might try to discuss the issue of being just by itself, but then we would not enjoy the color and diversity of the many forms through which being is diffracted at some distance from itself. Everything would be too tight and too abrupt. I would also like to think that some of the sentences in these essays are so put together that an insight into a form of appearing is not just discussed in them, but is actually accomplished when they are read.

I

1
Picturing

'Tis the eye of childhood
That fears a painted devil.
Macbeth, II 2

When we move from darkness into the light, it becomes possible for us to let many things appear that could not appear in the dark. The presence of light lets us see things like trees and tables, which we can touch but not see when there is no light, and it lets us see things like colors and pictures, which cannot be present at all while we remain in darkness. We are all familiar with light as that which lets such things appear to us. However, there is something besides light, something we can call, metaphorically, another kind of illumination, that is also at work when things appear to us; this is the achievement of letting things appear. It comes about in us, and if it did not take place, going from darkness into the light would not do us much good. Only because we are engaged in the achievement of letting things appear do we normally prefer light to darkness, and there are also times when we achieve manifestation better in darkness than in the light.

The achievement of letting things appear takes place in different ways. It occurs as perceiving and as picturing, as remembering and as imagining, as naming and as articulating, as registering what is before us and as reporting what is absent. These are all forms of the "other illumination" that makes being in the light desirable for us. They are achievements or activities, what Aristotle called *energeiai*. They are not simply organic tensions or processes that occur in us, like pains, the circulation of the blood, or electrical discharges in the nervous system. They are disclosures; they let things appear. Things could not appear unless we or someone like us permitted them to appear by serving as the datives of their manifestation; we serve in this capacity by our various activities of disclosure.

The various ways of allowing things to appear depend on one another. Things could not be named or articulated if they could not be pictured or recollected; things could not be pictured or recollected unless they could be named, registered, and reported. The various forms of manifestation are implicated with one another, and all contribute to the achievement of letting things appear. The activity of manifestation occurs inexorably within us—we do not seek it out, and only because it takes place in us can we seek anything out—and it establishes in us the possibility of being human.

We will explore the activity of letting things appear by exploring one of its forms, the activity of picturing. We will examine what it is for us to take something as a picture and what it is for something to be a picture. Inevitably, we will also examine what it is for us to take something as pictured and what it is for something to be pictured. Although the word *picture* usually refers to visual representations, we intend to speak about picturing in a wider sense, and will use the term, with appropriate qualifications, to cover auditory images like echoes or vocal imitations, as well as lively representations like mimicry and plays. The word *image* might have been a better term than *picture* to name what we wish to discuss, but *image* has acquired an intrusive flavor of the internal and the imaginary. It has lost the bodiliness and the publicness in the meaning of the Greek word *eikōn*; the phrase *graven images* harks back to an earlier usage of the English noun. Instead of running the risk that this spiritualized meaning of *image* might subvert what we wish to say, we will use the more solid term *picture* to name the kind of appearance we intend to describe.

When pictures were extremely rare, there would have been
something venerable in the captured, imaged presence of almost
any object. But we now live amid a proliferation of pictures of all
sorts, in newspapers and magazines, books, recordings, movies
and photographs, on television and on the radio. We are often
fascinated by what is presented in particular images, but picturing as such has become banal and we take it for granted. Because
pictures are no longer extraordinary, it has become more necessary to think about depiction itself in order to obtain some
distance toward the images that surround us, to keep ourselves
from getting so lost in what is pictured that we forget that there
is something at work in us that allows pictures to come to be.

1

Being a picture cannot be explained by similarity alone. Although John resembles his brother Paul, and although my car
is similar to yours, neither John nor my car are pictures, respectively, of Paul and of your car. There can be similarity without
picturing. Further, there can also be picturing without the normal similarity of one thing to another. There are pictures that
barely resemble what they picture: some sketches or statues, for
example, may be so contrived that we would never say that this
object resembles the thing it represents unless we knew that the
object is to be taken as a picture. Its being taken as a picture
allows us to find a similarity that we would not otherwise have
seen. Further, similarity is reciprocal but picturing is not: if my
car is similar to yours, yours is also similar to mine, but if this
object is a picture of Janet, Janet is not a picture of this object;
she would be a picture of this object if picturing were established only by being similar. Finally, in similarity we have two
distinct individuals that resemble each other, while in picturing
we have the same individual presented in two different ways; I
see Eisenhower when I see his picture, I do not see someone
or something that looks like Eisenhower. The last reason is an
explanation for the first three: it is because picturing is a different kind of presentation than similarity that similarity is insufficient to account for picturing, that pictures can be in many ways

dissimilar to what they portray, and that similarity is reciprocal while picturing is not.

How does picturing come about? It occurs when something is taken as a picture of something else: there must be an object taken as the picture; there must be something appreciated as pictured; and there must be somebody who takes the object as a picture. Picturing occurs at the intersection of these three elements. The one who takes the object as a picture brings about the achievement of picturing, but it is the object that actually becomes the picture; being a picture does not occur in the one who takes the object as a picture, it occurs in the picture itself. It takes place in the thing taken as a picture; that is "where" picturing happens. Moreover, the activity of being a picture is not the same as the activity of taking something as a picture, even though both achievements must occur together. What I do when I take this piece of variously colored paper as a picture is not the activity of being a picture, even though nothing could be a picture unless I or someone like me took it as such.

Some pictures come about without being constructed by anyone: reflections on water or on a smooth and shiny surface, and even echoes, if we may speak of auditory pictures, occur and are taken as images even though they are not fabricated. Many other pictures, however, are made by someone, by a painter, sculptor, designer, photographer, mimic, author, or someone drawing a sketch. The maker of a picture is a fourth to the three elements introduced earlier (the picture, the pictured, and the one who takes something as a picture). The maker of a picture is philosophically the least important of the four, even though he is the most important in regard to the industry of making pictures available. He is of least importance philosophically because he carries out his work within the possibilities established by the one who can see objects as pictures; he makes pictures only because things are already taken as pictures; picturing is a condition for his activity as a painter or designer. The painter may make a picture, but what makes his product into a picture is the fact that someone takes it as such. We have to look beyond the painter to understand pictures philosophically.

We must acknowledge, however, that the activity of constructing pictures occurs, in an extremely attenuated degree, even in the case of reflections and echoes, because someone has to put us or the object in the correct position to let the image take place. We who see the image may also be the ones who take the position, but our activity of taking the colored shapes as an image must be distinguished from our activity of getting into the right position to do so. (It may be objected that taking the right position to see the reflection is only a movement in space, but what, after all, is making a picture beyond arranging colors and shapes in space?) The maker of a picture is at work, therefore, in all cases of picturing, even those that involve images that are not, strictly, fabricated by anyone.

Still another case of picturing is found in what we call imagination or fantasy. This is the most difficult to analyze philosophically, because in contrast to material pictures and reflections on surfaces, it is hard to say whether anything is being "taken as" a picture in imagination; there is clearly no painted canvas or cut stone, there is no pattern of shapes on a surface, and yet in some sense we do picture things in our mind's eye. Just as we can use language in internal speech, we can imagine what things look like even while we do not see them, and both internal speech and imagination, as abilities, are parasitic on our speaking with others and our experience of things and pictures. Because imagination is an internalized transformation of perceiving and picturing, we will be able to get at it more effectively after we have explored in greater detail the structures of perception and "external" picturing.

The distinctions we have made are illustrated in the several meanings the word *picture* has in ordinary English usage. As a noun, the word names representations generally, whether fabricated images or simple reflections, and the noun form of the passive participle, *the pictured*, names the thing that is represented in the image or reflection. The verb *to picture* is ambiguous; a prominent meaning is the activity of fabricating a representation: "The artist pictured Napoleon seated on his throne." It is often used to name representation in the imagination: "Picture him in the saddle"; "I can picture her enjoying the garden." It can also mean the picture's activity of representing something: "This tableau pictures the signing of the Declaration of Independence." The only relevant achievement that the verb *to picture* does not name is the philosophically most important one, the achievement of taking something as a picture, the activity carried out by someone who sees this object as a representation of something else. His activity permits the realization of all the senses of picturing that we have listed. We tend to overlook this activity because our attention is pulled by the things and the relationships it permits to occur. When we see a picture, we are first drawn to the object depicted, that is, we think about the object that is absent and only represented in the image. Second, if we become reflective in an aesthetic sense, we may be drawn to the picturing material itself and pay attention to its parts and the relationships among them. Third, we may compare the picture with the thing it depicts and think about the accuracy of the depiction. Fourth, we may examine the picture as an object made by someone and evaluate his skill in making it. But in all these explorations, which are the ones we are normally engaged in when we deal with pictures, we overlook the fact that a picture is what it is only because we take it as such. Our taking of it is overlooked, and so is the activity of picturing which our taking permits; we do not think of what makes the invisible difference between this colored paper and this colored paper as a picture. We take it for granted that this is a picture and think only about what it depicts, its composition, the fidelity of its depiction, or its condition as a product; we do not ask what grants it its being as a picture. To ask what lets it be a picture at all, and what it is for it to be a picture, is to raise a philosophical question. And of all the achievements and relationships involved in picturing, only this one—the one which is philosophically the most important—does not have a name in the ordinary English use of the word *picture*.

"Where" does picturing occur? In the object taken as a picture of something. "When" does it occur? It does not take any extent of time for something to become taken as a picture; an object does not become a picture gradually, but changes suddenly from being only a thing to being a picture. Even if we have only a fragment of the picture, like a piece of an ancient mosaic portrait, the part is taken to be part of a picture. If we gradually add other pieces to the fragment we already have, or if a painter adds new parts to the portrait he is painting, the new parts are parts of the picture as soon as they are introduced. The achievement of taking

this emergent whole as a picture is not itself emergent as the
pieces fall into place; the enactment of a picture is a sudden, not
a gradual, activity, and it lasts once it occurs. Similarly, it takes
time for our eyes to range over the picture and to move from
one part to another, but all this occurs within the object already
established as a picture. The transition from being a thing to
being a picture does not take time, but a picture lasts as a picture
once it is established as such, and changes can occur within it
as a picture.

In some cases the depiction itself can be a process; if a mimic
depicts Winston Churchill or W. C. Fields, he does so by making
gestures, saying special things, speaking in a certain way, and
changing his facial expression. All this takes time, but the time is
entirely within the setting established by the man's being taken
as a mimic, and the transition from being taken as a man to
being taken as a mimic does not take time; it happens all at
once. The gestures and words that follow one another are like
the further parts of the painting that the artist adds to what he
has done, except that the earlier parts of the mimic's depiction
depart when the new ones arrive, whereas the painting's earlier
sections remain as the new ones are added.

Once we have acquired the ability of taking things as pictures,
we can exercise it at any time with no effort; it is no less easy to
do when we are tired than when we are rested, no harder when
we are young than when we are old. It is a way of minding things
and not a way of getting something done. The ease, suddenness,
and ubiquity of taking things as pictures make us esteem this
achievement, as well as the other works of the mind, as more
subtle than the things done by the body.

Although taking things as pictures is ubiquitous in the sense
that there is no place and no time in which we could not take
something as a picture, it is not ubiquitous in the sense that we
can take any thing at all as a picture. I cannot take my desk, or
this wall, or this tree, or this cat, as pictures. I can exercise my
picturing capacity wherever and whenever I wish, but I cannot
exercise it upon anything I wish. If something is to be capable of
being taken as a picture, either it must have been constructed as
an image by someone (by a painter or by someone imitating the
sound of something else); or it must contain a natural reflection

of what is depicted (mirrored images and echoes); or it must
be a combination of reflection and construction: a reflection
made permanent and detached from the object that generates it
(photographs and recordings). The two active elements I must
acknowledge in these three possibilities are the person who constructs a picture and the object that generates a reflection of
itself. I need their cooperation to carry out my achievement of
taking something as a picture; without the intervention of at least
one of these two, I cannot exercise this ability, because I would
have nothing before me subject to being taken as a picture. However, although I need the cooperation of such alien centers of
force, what I achieve when I take something as a picture is done
by me and not by them. By my activity I provide the setting for
the construction or reflection of images.

2

Pictures that are constructed by someone can be enjoyed in
the complete absence of the object they depict. A painting or
an imitation of someone's voice can be enjoyed when the object
painted or the person imitated are very far away, when they no
longer exist at all, and even if they never existed. Reflections,
whether visual images or echoes, are perceived in much closer
proximity to what is reflected in them. It is in fact rather common to perceive the original and the image together: the bridge
and its reflection in the water, the shout and its echo. There is
some differentiation between the original and the reflection, because we have to change the focus of our attention as we look
first at the bridge and marginally see the image, then focus on
the image and marginally see the bridge; and as we hear the
shout from this direction and the echo from that, and hear the
shout first and then the echo as the shout recedes from the center of our temporally stretched hearing. This divergence of image
from original in the case of reflections does not, however, disrupt
the unity of our perception; I do not have two perceptions, one
of the original and one of the reflection, but a single "paired"
perception of the original with its reflection, or the image with
its original.

Natural reflections differ in three ways from pictures constructed by someone. (1) As we have just noted, a greater degree of separation is possible in the case of constructed pictures. True, we can sometimes have reflections when we cannot see the original at all (a mirror allows us to see around a corner), and sometimes we can have a constructed picture in the same perceptual field in which we have the thing depicted. However, since a constructed picture is a product, it can be possessed in the sheer absence of what it depicts, while the reflection needs the original nearby in order to be continuously generated by it. Proximity is normal in the case of reflected images, and a "paired" perception of the original-with-reflection is almost always possible.

(2) To achieve the kind of picturing that occurs in natural, proximate reflections is a condition for achieving the picturing in constructed images. This relationship is analogous to how we come to take things as capable of being perceived by other people. Even if we are all alone, we experience things—trees and rivers—as capable of being perceived by others; however, this sense in things is established for us by the achievement of experiencing things in the actual company of other people, who see the same objects we see but see them from other angles. We appreciate the thing as also perceived by others who are there with us. This proximate shared perception is a condition for our solitary perception of the tree and the river as still capable of being perceived from another viewpoint by someone else while we perceive it from the spot that is the "here" for us.[1] Just as paired perception establishes a sense of other minds, a sense that belongs to objects even when no one else is actually with us, so the kind of pairing that occurs in proximate imaging, and especially in natural reflections, establishes the sense of original-and-picture that works even when we have only the picture and no possibility of bringing the original to it. Proximate natural reflections, mirror images and echoes, involve us in a more primitive activity of taking something as a picture than the activity we are engaged in when we deal with pictures that are constructed by someone.

(3) Because a reflection is generated by its original, we can find out what is happening in the original by watching the reflection. The reflection goes on while the original goes on; a reflection is a process continuously sustained by the goings-on in the original. A

constructed picture, however, catches and maintains (or repeats) only one profile of the original. It may catch something very revealing of the original, but it does not report what is going on in the original while we see the picture. The elimination of a continuous report is related to the separability of the constructed picture from what it depicts.[2]

A live television or radio program works like a reflection, for despite the complexity of the intervening apparatus, the images have ultimately to be given off by the original being imaged. The technical apparatus is not different in principle from the light rays between the bridge and its reflection in the water. The technology allows the reflection to be presented very far away from the original, but it does not destroy the contemporaneity of the two, and it still allows us to see what is going on in the original while we watch the image. However, a film or a recording is different: a temporal disruption is added to the spatial separation, and we lose the direct "informational" element. If I watch a film of what somebody did yesterday, I do not learn from it what he is doing now. Technological development in communication has expanded the ways in which reflections can be transmitted, and has further diversified the means by which reflections can be made available for repeated viewings and hearings. This development has led some people to prefer the preserved image to the imaged event; at ceremonies like important speeches or weddings, for example, which can be perceived only once, some members of the party put all their attention into taking pictures or recording what is said, and do not "see and hear" what is going on (they often make it difficult for others to see and hear as well). Then they have a photograph of the event instead of a memory of it, and look at the picture instead of having seen the thing. The power to perceive is given over to a machine, which is asked to "make" the perceptions for us, and to allow us to have them again and again. None of this technological development could have happened, however, if we were not the kind of beings that can take things as pictures, and if being did not allow things to be pictured as well as perceived.

Pictures can exist for vision and for hearing, but they cannot exist for taste and smell. We cannot, when tasting or smelling something, take it as an image of something else tasted or smelled; smells or tastes may suggest other odors or flavors by association, but they cannot be taken as pictures of them. There are two reasons for this. First, in these two cases, the perception involves an extremely strong impact on our sensibility. To look for pictures in tastes and smells would be like attempting to take something as a picture when the colors were so bright that they pained our eyes; or like trying to take a sound as an echo when it was so loud that our ears hurt. The force of the impression is so great that we simply undergo what happens to us; we do not have the distance to interpret what is presented as a representation of something else. Secondly, in tasting and in smelling we do not have the spatial diversification that permits the paired, divergent perception of an original with its image. The visual field allows us to see the reflection near the object reflected, and, in hearing, the sound comes from this direction and the echo from another; but tasting and smelling are concentrated and there is hardly any spatial differentiation within their actual field. There is no space to allow the divergence between an original and its image, and without this rudimentary form of reflected imaging, there cannot be the more evolved form of constructed pictures. Tasting and smelling do not have the latitude to permit picturing. The sense of touch is somewhere between vision and hearing on the one hand and smell and taste on the other. There is a strong impact in touch, but there is some spatial differentiation within the tactile field: I can touch an object with my right hand while I touch what is supposed to be its image with the left. I can, for example, take a piece of shaped stone as the tactile picture of someone's face. However, we rarely identify individual things with the sense of touch, and in touch the impression on our sensibility is very strong, so it is most unusual for pictures to occur to this sense.

3

Gertrude Stein makes the following distinction between an exciting scene we are involved in and an exciting scene we see in the theater, where it is depicted and not "really' lived through:

> If you are taking part in an actual violent scene, and you talk and
> they or he or she talk and it goes on and it gets more exciting

and finally then it happens, whatever it is that does happen then when it happens then at the moment of happening is it a relief from the excitement or is it a completion of the excitement. In the real thing it is a completion of the excitement, in the theatre it is a relief from the excitement, and in that difference the difference between completion and relief is the difference between emotion concerning a thing seen on the stage and the emotion concerning a real presentation that is really something happening.[3]

A real scene leads up to completion and climax, while a depicted scene leads up to relief. The relief is not caused by our reassuring knowledge that the actors do not truly hate one another, that Sir Ralph Richardson is not angry with Marlon Brando, that there is no real threat or danger. There is relief instead of climax because we are watching an angry man depicted, not an angry man. We have a kind of distance to the angry man depicted that is different from the kind of distance we might have even if we were totally uninvolved and unthreatened while we watched a real angry man. It is also different from the distance we would have if we watched someone only pretend to be angry and knew he was pretending; pretension is a maneuver in a real scene, it is not a depiction. The depiction allows us to be involved with the angry man, but with him as represented, and this insertion of the difference between the picture and the depicted permits us to experience the angry man in the special kind of tranquillity that Gertrude Stein calls *relief* and Aristotle calls *catharsis*. The distance in depiction is established by a new way of taking the angry man (as depicted), as well as by a new way of taking the human being who is carrying on before us (as depicting). It is not established by a further feature, like harmlessness, that characterizes the anger we see. Stein goes on to say that our own actual experiences gradually take on the tone of relief rather than climax as we go over them in memory:

As you go over the detail that leads to culmination of any scene in real life, you find that each time you cannot get completion, but you can get relief and so already your memory of any exciting scene in which you have taken part turns it into the thing seen or heard not the thing felt. You have as I say as the result relief rather than culmination. Relief from excitement, rather than the climax of excitement.[4]

Again, this sense of relief comes not from the comforting knowledge that the ordeal is over—it is not established by the temporal
difference as such—but from having the same ordeal in a new
way of presentation. The temporal difference is only a condition
for the new way of taking what we have experienced.

The terms *climax* and *relief* introduce an aspect of picturing
that we have neglected in our analysis so far. We have described
picturing as if it were free of concern. There are times when
pictures are merely objects of idle curiosity for us, and times
when they are taken as aesthetic objects, in which our interest in
the compositional relations of shape and color predominates in
importance over the interest we have in what is depicted; but it is
more normal for pictures to provoke the affective and personal
response that we make to the bodily presence of what is depicted.
It is good and it is important for us to have things present in
pictures. If the object depicted is a gratifying object, its pictorial
presence calls for the affective response the object itself would
summon: therefore we keep pictures of absent persons and places
that we love or admire.[5] The picture sustains an attitude toward
the object, and it does so more effectively than, say, the name
of the person or place would be capable of doing. It is only
because we are the kind of being that can enjoy things in their
presence and also intend them in their absence—because we
appreciate presences and absences as well as things—that we can
take something as a picture of what is absent. Having the object
only in a picture for a period of time may also enhance the
bodily presence of the object when it is regained. The distance
we have acquired in the meantime, while we had the thing only
as a picture, makes the contrasting direct presence of the object
more vivid. And no matter how articulated and intellectual our
response to desirable things may become, they still are desirable
things and it is good for us to possess them; when they themselves
cannot be possessed, there is still the presence in pictures to
serve, for the time being, in their place. If we have to do with
a distressing object, the pictorial presence serves especially to
bring the thing into relief. Picturing helps us rehearse the scene
and to acquire more tranquillity toward it. Simply naming the
object and working it out in words—if this, *per impossibile*, were
possible without some element of picturing, remembering, and

imagination—would not master the thing. But again, the pictorial distance does not make the bad object any less bad. The pleasure or the pain the object itself would give is reflected in the pictorial availability of good and bad things.

A special analysis of picturing is possible in the case of mimicry and acting, and it will help us understand the peculiarities of imagination in contrast to picturing. In mimicry and in acting, a human being serves as the vehicle that is taken as an image: the spectators take his actions as depictions, and he also takes himself as depicting. No matter how profoundly he can become lost in his role, the actor shares with the spectators the interpretation of what he is doing as a portrayal, not as a solid, real action. But the actor needs the support of spectators if he is to take himself as acting. He can take himself as depicting someone else only if he also appreciates himself as being taken in this role by an audience. If he tries to continue "acting" while he is alone, a change in the way he takes himself occurs: either (a) he slips into a simple practice of the mechanics of his performance (he says the words and makes the gestures something like an athlete practicing strokes; they are actions of his own, not those of, say, Richard III); or (b) he takes himself as still portraying Richard III, but he does so by remembering or anticipating the audience before whom he performs, and before whom he takes himself to be depicting someone (he could not depict Richard III to himself alone, without this marginal sense of an audience); or (c) he can shift from taking himself as portraying Richard III to beginning to imitate Richard III. That is, he begins to act like a king, and no longer depicts a king. He can begin to behave like a child who is playing at being someone he wishes to become. This activity is more serious than portrayal; we try the character on for size. The solitary thespian who has slipped into being a visionary would know that he is not Richard III or a king, but he would behave as if he were: he would "imagine" himself to be Richard III or a king. Any spectators he might also imagine would not be like the audience he remembers or anticipates when he still takes himself as portraying Richard III, for such an audience would be anticipated or remembered as taking him to depict Richard III; the spectators in our present case would be imagined as seeing him being a king, not as depicting a king. They are not imagined as seeing him imagining himself to be a king; they are imagined as involved in the scene he imagines. There is a difference between the formal structures of presencing in depiction and imagination.

Children often try on such characters in their overt behavior, while adults do it less in external actions but often "in imagination." Whether young or old, we modulate ourselves into new ways of behaving by imagining ourselves to be different from the way we are. This imitation of a new style, this rehearsal of what it would be like, makes it possible for us to become different; without it we would be locked into one pattern of behavior. Except in the most urgent circumstances, we do not decide upon a change in our way of life without imagining ourselves into it first and trying to "figure out" what we are going to do. Many of the actions we essay never become realized, but there are some that become more and more plausible as they are imaginatively repeated, and we gradually find ourselves, for better or for worse, living the way we once imagined ourselves to be. A child may lose himself rather completely in the imaginative role he is playing because his sense of self is not yet firmly established. An adult has a more solid sense of himself and is more clearly aware that he is imagining.[6] He has a more distinct awareness that he is there imagining and that he is also there imagined, as someone behaving, say, as an airplane pilot or as the mayor: and yet both of these agents, the imaginer and the imagined, are realized to be one and the same. In imagination there is a displacement, what has been called a *Versetzung*, of the self.[7] There are not two selves, but one self duplicated. What we generally call imagination, the activity we carry on while we daydream, is an internalized version of the imitative, imaginative overt behavior in which, for example, an actor begins to take on the character of a king. It is not a case of his depicting himself as a king, because in depiction we do not imagine "ourselves" being a king. We merely take ourselves as a picture of the king.

Imagination, therefore, must be distinguished from mimicry and portrayal. But imagination is more commonly confused with another form of picturing. It is often thought that in imagination we internally do something like what we do when we take a colored canvas as a picture. What distinguishes imagination, according to this view, is not a displacement of the self, but a phantasm which we see with the mind's eye and take as a picture of something absent. Taking something as a picture is used as a model to clarify what happens when we imagine, and in the place of the colored canvas the strange entity called the phantasm is postulated.

This explanation fails to take into account the displacement of the self into imaginer and imagined. When we take something as a picture, we do not distinguish ourselves into two selves (for example, into the perceiver and the one who pictures); we remain undifferentiated, and the duplication takes place in the object, which is not just an object but also a picture. If we try to use picturing as a model to explain imagination, we are forced to overlook the duplication of the self that occurs in imagining. Furthermore, because this explanation does not recognize the self as both imagining and imagined, it tends to neglect the lively activity of the imagined self. It makes imagination too passive and contemplative, and does not do justice to the self behaving in imagination: taking revenge on someone, being reconciled with someone, playing tennis, giving a speech as mayor of Chicago. In imagining ourselves doing such things, we do not simply watch pictures go by; we are engaged in the action we imagine. Finally, the status of the phantasm—Ryle's "paperless picture"—is almost impossible to describe.[8] What kind of ersatz picture can it possibly be? It is true that there are image-scraps in imagining, but they are attached to the imagined self as parts of his behavior. I cannot imagine myself playing tennis without some sense of motion in the arms and legs, some sense of a ball coming and being hit back, some sense of the sound made when the racket hits the ball: but all these are part of the sense of myself playing tennis. They are not pictures of someone playing tennis, nor are they pictures of myself playing tennis. They do not carry imagination, imagination carries them. Also, they are evanescent, discontinuous, ragged, and most arbitrary; they can change very much and still allow me to enjoy the same imagination, because the imagination is the experience of myself doing something, not a perception of these image-scraps.

Gilbert Ryle has argued against postulating a phantasm when we describe imagination. Picturing in fantasy is not, he says, like looking at photographs or listening to recordings. Instead,

A person picturing his nursery is, in a certain way, like that person seeing his nursery, but the similarity does not consist in his really looking at a real likeness of his nursery, but in his really seeming to see his nursery itself, when he is not really seeing it. He is not being a spectator of a resemblance of his nursery, but he is resembling a spectator of his nursery.[9]

A person who is imagining or visually remembering something "seems to see" the object, he "resembles a spectator" of it. Ryle's description is accurate but incomplete. If someone "seems to see" and "resembles a spectator," the questions arise, To whom does he seem to see? and To whom does he resemble a spectator? There has to be a dative for this seeming and this resembling. The answer, of course, is that he himself is the one to whom he seems to be seeing, and he himself is the one to whom the resemblance with being a spectator appears; when we are caught up in reverie, and remember or imagine, say, ourselves playing tennis, no one else sees us seeming to play tennis (others only see us with a faraway look in our eyes); we ourselves experience ourselves as seeming to play tennis. This is the displacement, the *Versetzung* of the self that occurs in imagination. Ryle implies this differentiation of the self but he does not assert it. The differentiation is also implied in his remark about "people fancying themselves witnessing things and events that they are not witnessing," in his observation that "there is only a child fancying that she sees her doll smiling," and in his statement that "what I imagine is myself seeing, hearing, doing and noticing things."[10]

There are two extremes in regard to the imaginative displacement of the self. At one extreme there is the totally undisplaced awareness that we have when we are captivated by what is going on around us. We are taken up by things and events about us and do not withdraw at all from them. At the other extreme there is the deep separation from our surroundings that occurs when we drop into daydreaming or reverie; until we come to again, we are not where we are but, as someone else might say of us, we are "somewhere else." We are reliving an experience, imagining something, or anticipating an event. From being an undifferentiated self captivated by the succession of things around us, we have become displaced into the imagining and imagined self, and we do lose touch with the people and things that are there around us now. However, between these two extremes there are

innumerable degrees of possible displacements, and they go on
all the time as we live through the day.[11] Even when we are concerned with things, we imaginatively slip into alternative ways
of doing whatever we are doing, bits of recollection come and
go, the continuity of our involvement is interrupted by displacements weaving in and out. Even our inventiveness in appreciating
a real situation depends on the quick and nimble detachments
we exercise while we are engaged in it. No perceiving self is, for
any length of time, deprived of the plastic contrasts that are provided by the imagining and imagined self. Perception goes on in
constant and labile comparison with imagination.

There is also structural variety in the setting we imagine ourselves occupying. If I imagine myself playing tennis, I can imagine
myself going through the motion of hitting the ball coming at
me, but then I can watch myself "from the outside" as I hit the
ball, or as the ball lands near the tape on the other side of the
court. I do not have to stay in my own skin when I imagine myself
doing something; I can be in the tennis-world imaginatively, then
I can see myself doing something in that world. Finally, besides
imagining ourselves engaged in an event, and besides imagining ourselves watching ourselves engaged in an action, we can
also imagine a scene in which we are not involved at all. We can
picture a landscape, a waterfall, people chopping wood, animals
running about, all entirely in the third person. We are there as
spectators of the scene imagined, but spectators who cannot be
perceived or affected by any of the persons and things engaged in
the event. This is the kind of impervious viewing that is adopted
in the writing and reading of elementary forms of fiction; we
survey from the outside a world of which we are not a part.[12]
Even in this case, however, there is a displacement of the self; I
who sit in my chair imagine myself seeing the waterfall and the
people working near it.

There is almost always some emotional concern in imagination, and its place in the displaced self can vary. I may calmly
imagine myself being angry at someone, but often enough the
passion in the imagined world straddles the imagining and imagined self and pervades both. Feelings tend to break the network
of representations that puts them into relief; they flood through
and become real and present. In times of sorrow, for example,
the memory of earlier happiness may be bitter because what we

enjoyed has been lost, but the memory can also be consoling as it asserts itself more fully, as it insists that the happiness did exist and still survives in remembrance, and as it breaks, for a while at least, the distress we now have.

4

Because we can distinguish between a picture and the object it depicts, we tend to think of the picture as referring away from itself to its original; if I have a picture of Janet, we tend to suppose the picture points away from itself to Janet when I look at it. But such an understanding would assimilate pictures to ordinary signs, which do indicate something different from themselves. The general's flag on his limousine indicates that the general is in the car; but the general is in no way in his flag. We move away from the flag when we think of the general. But in picturing we do not move away from the image; what is depicted is presented, as an individual, in the picture itself. The peculiarity of pictorial presencing and representation is that pictures do not merely refer to something, but make that something present. I see Janet in her picture, I do not, in the picture, see a sign of Janet. Because this is so we can speak of an object depicted in a picture even if there is no original actually existing apart from the image. I have a painting of a copper kettle, and it remains a picture of a copper kettle even though there may never have been a real kettle of which this is a copy. I can still refer to "the" kettle depicted in my painting, and when I do so I need not refer to a kettle in some storage cabinet; I mean the one in the painting.

When we recognize a thing in a picture, moreover, we do not merely identify the thing. In pictures we see the thing doing something: there are children playing, a man dying, people crossing a stream; even when something is depicted at rest, there is still *life*, for the object continues at least to show one of its sides. In a picture there is a presencing or a manifestation of the object, whether in an action or in a quiet disclosure of features. In the picture the object makes an appeal to whatever in us responds to what is presenced. In some extreme cases, the power of picturing can cause some viewers to lose the sense of the detachment of the image from the original; they may believe that actions performed on the image affect what is imaged in it. An idol becomes the actual presence of a demon or a deity, a voodoo doll can be a way of influencing the human being it depicts.[13] Even persons can become embodiments of spirits; masks and costumes reinforce this confusion of a pictorial with a direct presence, and the identification that occurs in such a ritualistic extreme of imaging must be distinguished from both imagination and theatrical portrayal. The other participants in the ritual identification are not spectators who take the central figure to be depicting someone or something different from himself; they react to him as to that someone or something else. The imaged distance and relief which are found in the theater are both forsaken. And the central figure himself also loses any imaginative or imitative distance and relief.

We can consider such ritual identification as the loss of a distinction, because we have become accustomed to a clear difference between the perceived and the depicted, but at a time when the two were not so explicitly differentiated, all depictions may well have been disturbingly like the actual presence of what they depict. At that time the distinction between image and imaged could not have been lost because it had not yet been achieved. When pictures were not as common as they are nowadays, their very scarcity may have made them appear to be a more unusual presencing of an object than the bodily presence of the thing itself.

The use and the theology of icons in Eastern Christian churches provide an interesting contrast to the ritual identifications found in primitive religions. When icons were introduced, there was a distinct understanding that a picture differs from the thing it depicts; but there was also an insistence that, because of the nature of the thing depicted in sacred images, the icons could participate in the presencing or the epiphany of what they display.[14]

Many more pictorial structures remain to be discussed. How do pictures become transformed into hieroglyphs, ideograms, and rebuses, and what changes in the mode of presencing occur when ideograms give way to alphabetical writing? What are the kinds and combinations of presencings that allow such transformations to take place? How do pictures differ from maps, diagrams, and graphs?[15] How do dreams differ from reverie? How are pictures different from symbols? Many symbols are also pictures, but they symbolize something different from what they picture. A statue of a blindfolded figure holding a balance depicts a woman but symbolizes justice. In such complex cases of imaging, language has to intervene and tropes like metaphor and metonymy enter into the explanation of what is being expressed; but simple picturing is also necessary as an ingredient and as a foil for such images complicated by language. About each of the pictorial structures surveyed in this paragraph, there is something essential to be said, and the network of presences, absences, and displacements appropriate to each case must be philosophically unraveled.

5

Picturing must be related to naming in order to be philosophically clarified. An object becomes a nameable object when we appreciate the object as the same in its presence and in its absence. That is, we must become aware of the object as capable of being present and as capable of being absent, and as remaining itself in both conditions. What we name when we name an object is the object as the same in presence and in absence: it is through the play of presence and absence that the object becomes nameable. That is why we can name the object when it is present and also when it is absent.[16]

An implication of this is that when the object is present to us, and is nameable in its presence, we have become aware of its presence. We are not just aware of the Lincoln Memorial, we are aware of it *as* present. Moreover we are aware of *its* presence; we are not just aware of an empty, general form of presence, but of the "Lincoln Memorial presence."[17]

What happens in picturing is that the "Lincoln Memorial presence" gets achieved without the Lincoln Memorial, but on the occasion of some vehicle—appropriately colored paper, or the water in the Reflecting Pool—which allows us to enact the presence. Only because we have become the kind of being that uses

names, only because we have come to distinguish between a thing
and the presence of the thing, can we take something as a picture
of that thing: then we achieve the presence of the thing without
having the thing itself there.

While we remain in the prephilosophical attitude, and if we
have evolved to the point of naming, we have inserted a distinction between a thing and the presence of the thing. This difference is what lets us name the object. But until we do philosophy,
this difference does its work anonymously; we are not yet aware
that naming is brought about by this distinction. We also do not
yet know that this distinction is what permits picturing. Part of
the reason why we are not aware of this while we have not yet
made the philosophical turn is that we are simply captivated by
the good and the bad in things themselves, and hence overlook
the presences and absences through which the things, good and
bad, are disclosed. Also, we do not talk or think systematically
about presences and absences, even though we are familiar with
them. We tend to take presences and absences as further features of the thing, and often interpret them as the object's being
"here" or "there," or "going on now" or "all finished"; that is, we
take them as spatial or temporal attributes. But presence and absence are not features of things, they are modes of presentation
and require an appropriate articulation.

In philosophical reflection we name presences and absences
directly. We do not first introduce them when we begin philosophy, for they were already distinguished from things in prephilosophical experience, where they remained anonymous and
overlooked. We name them in philosophy and are able to describe how they move about and are interlaced to permit the
various achievements of disclosure that we execute in our prephilosophical experience. In the case of picturing we are able to
say that the "Lincoln Memorial presence" is what we peel off the
Lincoln Memorial and achieve in pictures of that thing. When we
take something as a picture we enact this presence without the
Lincoln Memorial: the important element in picturing is that we
carry out this activity of executing the presence of a thing without the thing itself. Only because we exercise this activity can we
then look for pictorial similarities between the picture and what
it depicts.

Moreover, the achievement of taking something as a picture is not merely a psychological exercise. Things do present and absent themselves; things must be distinguished from their presence, and their presence must be distinguished from them (because they remain themselves even when they are absent). The presences of things can be achieved without the things themselves, provided a proper dative of manifestation is available. By letting things be pictured, we allow them to exercise their manifestation. This is not a change in their makeup, for instance in their chemical or biological features, but it is an exercise in their being and truthfulness.

A *thing* must be distinguished from its *being*. A thing is what is contrasted against its picture, against its name, against this or that view of it, against its being remembered or imagined or dreamt. The thing is what is "real" against its various ways of being presented. But *being* includes the modes of presentation; it encompasses presence and absence as well as what is presented and absented. Hence, pictures and names and remembrances and profiles "are," even though they are not things.[18] In the prephilosophical attitude we rush right by pictures and the other kinds of presentation and fasten on things; the pictures and the other kinds of presentation are dismissed as "unreal," and truly they are unreal in contrast to things. They are not themselves things. Even in our prephilosophical stance we have to acknowledge that pictures and the other kinds of presentation in some sense "are," but because our language and interest are so much under the sway of things, we cannot get our terms right. We tend to place the kinds of presentation "in the mind" and call them psychological or subjective, in contrast to things, which are the only objectivities we allow. This consignment to the mind-bin is rather easy for remembrances, imaginations, dreams, names, and propositions, and even perceptual aspects and views (which turn into sense impressions when so consigned), but it is less easy for pictures, which even to the unreflective seem somehow to be "out there" next to things. For this reason, pictures provide a good access to the question of being and manifestation.

It is only when we acknowledge that *being* ranges more widely than *thing* that we can do justice to the various kinds of presentation. Only then can we avoid the contradictions that inevitably

follow from our attempt to speak about presences and absences
with terms and syntax appropriate to things. In fact, only then
can we begin to speak consistently and coherently about what
it is for something to "be" a thing: the thing that we have in
our prephilosophical experience and discourse is presenced precisely in contrast to the pictures, images, remembrances, and
views which we have of it, and which we dismiss as not the real
thing. The thing has one sense of reality by being contrasted
to its picture (not a picture of my car, but my car itself); it has
another sense of being real in contrast to being named in its absence; and still another by being contrasted to its remembrance
or anticipation or imagination or dream. All these senses are woven together and the thing is at the intersection of all such plays
of presence and absence, which are overlooked by our concern
with the thing, but function in allowing the thing to be presented
and absented to us.

In exploring the being of pictures, we have described how
presence and absence, sameness and otherness, and rest and motion are at work between pictures and what is pictured. However,
there is a dimension that underlies even these structures. For
these couples to be at work in pictures and the pictured, it is
necessary for pictures and the pictured to hold together: there
must first occur "picture-and-pictured." Only upon this condition can we say one and the same car is in the garage and in
the photograph, that the garaged car is present and yet not bodily there in the picture, that our minds can move from one to
the other in various ways and continue to find the same persist-
ing in both. Furthermore, the picture and the pictured are not
just added to each other; they hold together in such a way that
they would not be picture and pictured apart from each other.
That is, picture-and-pictured, although involving two elements,
must be enacted as one. The togetherness of picture and pictured is prior to the work of presence and absence, sameness
and otherness, rest and motion. Thinking about pictures leads
us, therefore, not only to the question of presencing and being,
but also to the most original divergence and togetherness that
permit presencing and being to occur.[19]

2
Quotation

Quotation is not merely repetition, even though it involves repeating what someone else has said. Quotation is repeating something as having been stated by another. The difference is one of presentational or intentional form. There may be no difference in the words being repeated, but they are repeated differently: it is as though we no longer saw an object directly but now only in a mirror.

To quote is to say something as said by someone else. Why are not all the statements I say simply my own? Apparently just saying them does not make them my own: I can be saying them as another's. My voice is not exclusively possessive. In contrast, however, a dog cannot quote another dog. A dog's barks are inevitably and inescapably its own, even though they may sound like the barks of another dog. What is it in human speech that makes it possible for me to use my voice to say what another has said, and to say it as said by the other? This strange duplication in one stream of sound is intimately related to having a mind. The activity of minding involves many duplications such as this. To explain what thinking is involves not just describing the activity of the brain, but also analyzing patterns of presentation such as quotation.

1

When we speak, we speak about something: Karen makes statements about her car, John makes statements about Karen, about her car, and about what she is doing. What happens when John quotes Karen? It is tempting to say that John then makes a statement about the words Karen uttered or the thoughts she had or her activity of speaking; that is, that when he quotes Karen, John simply speaks about Karen and what she does. It is tempting to say that John, when he states, "Karen said the car's battery is low," has made her words or her thoughts or her activity the direct and exclusive topic of his statement. But to understand quotation this way would flatten the statement quoted into being a thing, one more thing alongside the cars, trees, people, and their features which we encounter. It would also reduce the activity of quoting into being an ordinary case of stating, no different in principle from statements about rivers and trucks.

What then does happen when John quotes Karen? John continues to talk about the car, just as Karen did, but he talks about the car as talked about by Karen. We can let a thing become manifest and articulated simply by ourselves, or we can let it become manifest and articulated as by someone else, and we can specify who that someone else is. Whenever anything becomes articulated and shown to thought, it is in principle publicly displayed not only for the immediate registrar but for others as well. And the point is that we are dealing with a thing displayed when we quote, we are not dealing with something simply in someone else's brain or simply with the sounds made by another. John deals with the car when he quotes Karen. It is even misleading to say he deals with Karen's words which refer him to the car: this would put all the weight on his relationship to Karen and make the relationship to the car secondary and dispensable. It would be one of those pictures that hold us captive and confuse the presentational relationships. First and foremost John is related to the car when he quotes what Karen says.

But he is related to the car as it is displayed by Karen, and presentationally Karen does get in the way. If John merely repeated what Karen said, instead of quoting her, he would more immediately be related to the car: "The battery is low." In such mere repetition, John would still be under the sway of Karen's speech; the car would be appearing to him as Karen articulated it, but he would not differentiate between how the car is and how Karen says it is. To be taken over by someone else's opinion is not just to transfer something from another's brain to one's own: it is to behave toward something, toward the object spoken about, in a certain way; it is to assume a manifestation, but to assume it naively, not distinguishing what is cognitively mine from what is another's. When we repeat, we assume the thing manifested as such and such, but we discard its having been so manifested by someone else. We leave out a dimension that bears on what is being manifested.

It is not incorrect to say that we can take over someone else's thoughts or that we can take over what is in someone else's mind, but if we say this we must remember that thoughts and the mind are never just what is *in* someone. Thoughts are a manifestation, and the mind is the ability to manifest, to identify and to differentiate. When we take over thoughts and what is in the mind, we take over the objects as manifested, as differentiated and identified; we do not just take over "signs" or "concepts," things that only give us hints of objects. The radical publicity and the being-with-things of thoughts and of the mind must not be overlooked. We must overcome the persistent myth of concepts separated from things, and the study of quotation can help us to do so.

Nelson Goodman observes that when we quote, whether verbatim or in paraphrase, our words are used to do two different things: they are used both to refer to and to contain what we quote.[1] When John says, "Karen said, 'The battery is low,'" or when he says, "Karen said the battery is running down," John's sentence includes a phrase ("The battery is low," or "the battery is running down") which serves to name Karen's statement and also serves to contain it. This curious conjunction of being able to name and contain makes up quotation. If John's statement merely referred to what Karen said ("Karen said *this*," or "Karen said something strange," or "Karen said the statement made up of the following words and letters"), John would not be quoting; and if his sentence merely contained what Karen said, he would be repeating what she said but, again, not quoting her. In order to quote, John's statement must both name and contain another statement.

But as John Searle has said, what we refer to when we speak about someone else's belief is a representation.[2] We do not name an ordinary thing; we present or represent a representation. And we cannot present a representation without also presenting what it represents. It is a representation only by virtue of what it represents. Since we are presenting the representation and are aware of it as such, we do not merely repeat the representation: that would be simply to say again what the other has said. Instead, we know we are presenting the thing as it has been represented by someone else: to present the representation or to present the thing as represented are one and the same procedure, the procedure of quotation. It is not the case that presenting a representation is to present *only* the mind of another; the mind of another is itself the manifestation of something in the world.

Quotation therefore is the extraordinary procedure of using a phrase to refer to someone else's statement, and so to take a distance to that statement and to see it as accomplished "over there," by someone else, to see it as a statement outside the statement I make now. But quotation is also using the same phrase at the same time not only to name but to present again what the named represents, i.e., to contain what is named. It is quite remarkable that we should be able to do this. Our philosophical analysis of quotation should not consist in raising or "answering" false problems about it, such as asking how we can get outside our own minds and into the mind of another, or asking what sort of magic mirror must exist in a representation, so that its target can be presented again in a quotation. Philosophical analysis is to exhibit the structure of quoting. Its task is to point out the various dimensions of quotation, to keep us from eliminating important aspects of it, and to help us recognize the domain of presentation or intentionality, the domain in which such differences as those among thing, representation, presentation of representation, and repetition can occur.

But how can intentionality or presentationality be like this? How is it possible that we can name and contain a representation? How and why can we quote? It does appear that it could

not be otherwise. It is not possible that something should be statable by someone but not, in principle, quotable by another. The
necessity is not brought about simply by the development of the
brain, even though a certain brain development may be required
as a condition for our ability to quote; the presentational structure must be seen as a structure of its own, in its own domain. We
enter into presentational possibilities, they do not happen simply because of something that has happened *to* us. Manifestation
and quotability are possibilities of being; being is determined by
such possibilities. The necessity and possibility of quotation are
also not merely the result of linguistic development, not merely
the result of how a particular language has evolved grammatically. It is not just because there are subordinate clauses that we
can quote. The difference between statement and quotation, although reflected in language, is a presentational difference that
finds expression in language. It is there in how we can cognitively
behave toward things and toward one another.

2

The fact that we use language in articulating the presence of
things helps explain how quotation occurs. In our normal experience and speech, while we perceive the object we talk about,
we can *register* the object as featured so and so; we distinguish
the object and its feature, and we register the object's being so
featured. The distinction is also an identification, the object is
articulated. We use words to help us do this. S names the object,
p names the feature, and a grammatical particle or form, such
as the word *is* or some significant placement of terms in the sentence, expresses the togetherness of S and p, which is presented
to us as we perceive and register the thing. Words and their grammar help us *report* the same state of affairs when we are no longer
in the perceptual presence of the object talked about. In such
reporting we remain concerned with the object as featured, even
though the object is not immediately there before us.[3]

When we quote, we take advantage of the words used to register and report; we repeat them or their equivalents, but we repeat
them differently: we use a device (such as "She said *that* S is p")

to highlight them as being said by another. But their mention now is also a use, because they do remain verbal articulations and they cannot help executing their reportorial articulation, even though in quotation marks. The car's battery does get articulated as being low when John quotes Karen as saying it is low. This verbal articulation lets us range very far from things and still remain cognitively with them. Reporting allows us to articulate things we know while they are absent from us, and quotation lets us articulate them as they are articulated by others.

I can thus be related to things either on my own cognitive authority or refractedly, through the authority of another speaker. When I quote someone, I have the quoted state of affairs as proposed by someone else; but in principle it is always possible for me to go on to possess the state of affairs by myself without an intermediary, to register the situation on my own. This is *disquotation*.[4] When, after having quoted, I thus see for myself, I do not just register the situation; I register it as confirming or disconfirming what someone else has said. The situation is there for me in a modally different way. The space opened up by quotation is therefore triangular: I at point *A* can be related to the situation at point *B* either directly along the line *AB*, or through another speaker at point *C*, via lines *AC* and *CB*. The immediacy of my own cognitive possession of a situation becomes itself a qualified immediacy because I now know that I can be cognitively related to it not only by myself but also through another. *By myself* takes on a deeper hue. The flexibility introduced by quotation can fail to be appreciated by two kinds of people or two characters of mind: by the gullible person who always just takes over, repetitionally, as his own and as being the case, anything the others say; and by the obstinate person who is so saturated with his own point of view that the statements of others are seen either as little more than echoes of what he says, or else as rather foolish fancies that he never really entertains as opinions.

Our basic and spontaneous way of registering and reporting is to do so with belief. Belief is not added to disclosures; disclosures are originally belief-acts. But quotation permits a wide range of doxic modifications. I may quote believingly ("Why are you moving so slowly?" "Because Andy said the road is slippery here") but the intrusion of another speaker as the one being quoted inevitably introduces a hiatus between my voice and the statement mentioned, between what I think and what I say, since I am now engaged in displaying the mind of another (and, simultaneously, displaying what the other minds). Even when I quote believingly, I do not speak simply in my own voice but let the voice of another carry the weight of articulation. I exercise a refracted belief and I take some distance to the responsibility for the truth of what is said. Furthermore, once I allow another's mind into my own voice, I can quote neutrally, not taking a doxic position regarding what I quote, or I can quote disbelievingly. And a wide range of possibilities exists between belief and neutrality, between neutrality and disbelief: I can quote doubtfully, assuredly, with probability or with certainty, suspiciously or mockingly. Such doxic variations are made possible by the distinction between my own statement and what I quote. Furthermore, while what I quote may be stated in one doxic modality (I may quote suspiciously), my own statement initiating the quotation ("She said . . .") comes across with its own belief, its own doxic form, which may well be different from the modality belonging to the quoted statement.

The differences in doxic modality can get inside and cut through the quotation itself. I have a double access to whatever I am talking about when I quote: my own access, and the access I have through the person I quote. Therefore (1) I can exploit this difference and say, "About the high school Latin teacher: Helen says he is confused." In this case I use my own access (and that of my interlocutor) to establish a reference, but I use the cognitive authority of the one I quote for the articulation of the object referred to. I establish the existence of the teacher on my own, apart from any quotational warrant, but I appeal to Helen for something said about the teacher. (2) At the other extreme, I can obtain both the reference and the articulation on the authority of the person quoted: "Helen says that there is a high school Latin teacher and that he is confused." Here my own authority recedes into the background; everything, even the reference, is taken from Helen. (3) But both the quotations we have examined are somewhat artificial. Normally we do not explicitly either split or fuse our quotational references and articulations. Normally we just say, "Helen says the high school Latin teacher is confused."

When we speak this way we incline really toward the first of the cases we have just discussed, to the establishment of reference on our own authority. I and my interlocutor are exploiting our own access to, our own handle on, the object of reference. We are assuming there is a high school Latin teacher and we look to Helen to tell us he is confused. The use of the definite description ("the high school Latin teacher") implies we believe there is such a target of identification. However, we place this target as to be "hit" by the person we quote, and we normally assume that the person we quote also has access to the object, under the description we use to target it. If Helen heard us talking she would agree, "Yes, the high school Latin teacher is confused, as I said he was."

But this structure can be made more complex when my interlocutor and I establish a target of reference under a name or a description that is unknown to the person we quote. Suppose that Paul does not know that the man working in the post office is Max. I might say, "Paul says that Max is rude." Here I am taking advantage of the fact that I and my interlocutor know who Max is, so I establish a reference to him under an aspect familiar to us, but then I present Max as he is presented by Paul: as being rude. Paul could not say that Max is rude; he would say only that the clerk is rude. But if my interlocutor and I know that Max is the clerk, it would be silly for me to say, "Paul says the post office clerk is rude." I would not be identifying him appropriately in my speech situation; indeed my interlocutor might not even know that Max works in the post office. I have to establish a reference in terms of the audience I am addressing, not in terms of some disembodied or unsituated speech. I refer to the target in terms clear to us but opaque to Paul, the person I quote.

And the structure exemplified in the case of Max does not occur only rarely. It is not a quirk in quotation. It happens whenever people who are in the know speak about, or quote, the opinions of those who are not. It is how we can present the opinions of those to whom the thing discussed only partially or only accidentally appears: "He said the heart attack was indigestion" (we doctors know it is a heart attack, but he says it is indigestion); "He said the heart attack (his 'indigestion') came on slowly at first but then became severe." The startling thing here is not simply that a thing can appear to someone as other than it is; nor that we can quote the one to whom it so appears; but that we can register precisely the thing's appearing other than it is (or the thing's being other than it appears) when we quote the person, even though that person does not realize the thing's otherness. The object as we refer to it is concealed to the speaker we quote, and we the quoters are aware of the concealment; and yet the same object is manifest under another aspect to the one we quote, and it is the presence of this other aspect (". . . is rude") that makes up what we quote him as stating. This is an extraordinary exercise in display and verification.

This same structure takes place in deception, when those in the know may want, for example, to make Paul perceive the clerk as rude but not to know it is Max who is the rude clerk; or to make someone think something indicates where and when the invasion will occur, but not to think that the sign has been deliberately planted by someone ("They think our decoy indicates the attack will start tomorrow"). All such relationships are based on the triangular structure of quotation, on the fact that I can be related to situation B either directly or through C, through the person whom I quote. They are based, not just on grammatical or semantic structures in language, but on the structure of intentionality and on the presentational possibilities of things.

The presentational orders become greatly amplified when we introduce theatrical depiction, particularly in the case of disguises and revelations among characters within a play. In examining the phenomenology of such situations, we must keep in mind not only the relationship of the characters one to another, but also the cognitive or disclosive relationship of the characters to the audience. A character in *Der Rosenkavalier* could, for example, say, "The Marschallin says she loves the young man Oktavian," but a member of the audience could not really say, "The Marschallin says she loves a mezzo-soprano," or "The Marschallin says she loves Christa Ludwig." The audience is not in the know in the same way a doctor is in the know regarding his patient and his patient's symptoms. But a character in the opera could say, after Oktavian has dressed as the maid, "Baron Ochs says Oktavian is stunning." We enjoy watching such depictions because they give us the opportunity to pull off complex distinctions and identifications, both on our own and as multiply refracted through others.

Any conversational use of language, even the conversations of mentally ill speakers, assumes considerable referential continuity.[5] But referential contact is not simpleminded; it is not just what I sustain in regard to an object in my own stream of words. It is established among interlocutors and it is sustained even when other voices, the voices of absent speakers, are introduced into the discussion through quotation. My referential continuity is also yours, when we speak together, and it is that of the other partners in our discussion as well as of those who merely listen and look on. The speeches of others who are quoted but who are not now themselves speaking are woven into our referential continuity: sometimes as authoritative statements, sometimes as things to be merely entertained, sometimes as positions to be destroyed, sometimes just as dicta to be noted. The thing to be studied when we study quotation is not a single mind, nor is it a single sentence that happens to have a quotation inside itself; it is rather the complex pattern of discussion, argument, and discourse with its plasticity, its capacity to include so many different voices, so many different assertions, even those of speakers who are not with us while we speak. The whole is the conversational setting, not the relationship of a single mind or a single sentence to an object.

This is the conversation that Socrates turns to in his second sailing (*Phaedo* 99C–100A): "It seems to me that I had to flee to what is said and look for the truth of things in that." Socrates turned from things to things as stated (and, we might add, to things as presenced in all the ways they can be presented and intended), just as one might, to save one's sight and to see better, turn from looking at the sun to looking at the sun reflected in water. Dimensions of things show up in the medium of what is said that do not show up when the things are looked at directly.

Many of the quotational phenomena we have discussed have been treated in recent decades under the rubric of referential transparency and referential opacity. Our phenomenological approach, however, introduces the domain of presentation or intentionality and does not treat transparency and opaqueness exclusively in terms of logical and linguistic structures. The logical and linguistic structures reflect and express presentational possibilities, such as the possibility of presenting something as it is being presented by someone else, or the possibility of speaking about things as being spoken about by someone else. Quine says, "If we are limning the true and ultimate structure of reality, the canonical scheme for us is the austere scheme that knows no quotation but direct quotation and no propositional attitudes but only the physical constitution and behavior of organisms."[6] Quine thus eliminates the quotable representation of things, or things as represented; the "direct quotation" he allows is merely the repetition of the words stated by others, and this in turn "we can even dissolve . . . altogether, into spelling, when we please."[7] Speakers dissolve into organisms, thinking into brains, language into sounds. The basis for Quine's reductionism is his rejection of propositions as mental entities; with propositions gone, there seems to be nothing for propositional attitudes to be about, hence there are no propositional attitudes. However, his understanding of propositions is inadequate; we need not posit propositions as mental or intentional entities, but we can legitimately acknowledge that we not only talk about things but speak about them as spoken about by others or by ourselves. This modification, this quotational ascent, is all that is needed to permit quotation and subsequently to permit various doxic attitudes and the presence of mind. The "true and ultimate structure of reality" contains the things we talk about, but it also contains their being talked about and presented and represented in a multitude of ways.

3

Although we cannot reduce quotation to the repetition of words or sounds, there are cases in which the point of quoting is not to convey another's proposition—the way things seem to him or the way he says they are—but to convey primarily the words stated or the sounds made: but always as words stated or sounds made by another. There are cases of quotation in which the propositional dimension recedes and the sentential, the verbal, or the phonemic, increases in prominence. In cases like these, paraphrase is not possible; we must convey the exact words or the exact phonemes.

Vulgar words or swear words fall into this category: "*What* did he say?" "He said *X*." "Outrageous." So do other offensive words: "What did he say when he described your clothes?" "Rags. He said 'rags.' " Such a quotation is almost propositional, but it really tips into the verbal; it is not the concept or the proposition but the word, with its emotional overtones, that is conveyed in the quote. At the other emotional and aesthetic extreme, a beautiful phonemic line, an elegant word or phrase, a well-turned sentence can be quoted as such: attention is drawn to them as sounds, words, and sentences, and the one who spoke them is given credit for saying them: "Tom once said, 'Take two totals and total the two.' Only *he* could have said that." The quoter repeats them as having been achieved by another, and he quotes them or embeds them in his own speech. Such quotation is different from giving an example of a sound, word, or sentence; if I show how the German *ch* or the Polish *cz* is pronounced, or if I give the Greek word for "battleship," I do not quote a German or a Pole or a Greek. But if I show what Hans said when he got angry, I do quote him as having uttered *that* then, even though I may not use my quote propositionally; I may not display a state of affairs or a view of things through him, but I still quote and do not mimic Hans.

We run into an interesting marginal case when I show how Hans pronounces his *th* in English: "Here's how he says it: 'zees' for 'these,' or 'zeeater' for 'theater.' Yesterday for example Hans said, 'Zees people vent to ze zeeater.' " When I do this I mimic and no longer quote, even though I embed the vocalization of another in my own discourse. And with the case of mimicry we reach three duplicative possibilities: (1) propositional quotation, as studied above in sections 1 and 2; (2) linguistic quotation, i.e., phonemic, verbal, or sentential citation; (3) mimicry of sound.

When I mimic Hans I do not quote him, even though it may appear that I do so ("Listen to this. Yesterday Hans said, 'Zees people vent.' "). I imitate him, reproduce his material achievement, much as I might imitate his limp or his gestures. My voice is made to resemble his. I do present another as other to me, but it is his physical behavior that I represent, not the words he

accomplishes. In contrast, if I say, "Tom said, 'Total the two,' "
and if I wish to emphasize the phonemic pattern and not the play
of meanings, I do pick up a phonemic pattern that can be detached from Tom, even though it bears his stamp and few other
people would have said anything like that. I do not mimic Tom,
I quote him, even though the point of the quote is phonemic
and sentential—the alliteration of *t*'s and the balance of *o*'s and
the chiasms—and not propositional. My voice does not resemble
Tom's and I need not make it resemble his (whereas in mimicry
I must make my voice resemble another's); precisely in my own
voice I am able to say phonemically what he said.

Why is it that I can quote Tom phonemically, verbally, and sen-
tentially? Why does such linguistic citation not become mimicry?
The reason is that speech involves a *selection* of sounds and patterns on the part of the one who speaks. The phonemes, words,
and grammar have been chosen by the speaker. The choices
are selections made within the possibilities that our language
gives us. When someone speaks, the penumbra of the alternative phonemes and words and grammatical moves, of those he
could have chosen but in fact did not, always surrounds what
he does say, and these unchosen options are appreciated, with
greater or less explicitness, by the one who listens to him speak.
The unsaid cushions what is said. The speaker's speech is thus
shot through with choice, and the speaker's ability to choose—
his linguistic and intellectual character—asserts itself in what he
says. But linguistic mannerisms, such as saying "zees" for "these,"
are not the deposit of choice. Hans does not choose "zees" as
opposed to "these." Linguistic mannerisms are simply a bodily
insistence, like a twitch or a snore.

Now a quotation is an imitation of choices, not an imitation
of behavior; mimicry is the imitation of behavior. I can quote
Tom even though my voice is very different from his because
in quotation I repeat the selections he made within the linguistic matrix. But Hans does not linguistically choose "zees" over
"these"; he cannot help talking this way, hence mimicry usually
involves some ridicule. I display how his materiality intrudes on
his speech and I do not submit my speech to his choices. But in
quotation I let someone's choices occur again: the similarity of
the choice is more important than the similarity of the sound.

The element of choice makes quotation more spiritual, more independent of the actual physical sound, than mimicry could be.

But in quotation I do not simply make the same choices Tom made (that would be mere repetition, the submission of my mind to Tom's). I make the choices as having been made by Tom. I imitate his selections. What is it to imitate a choice? It is to make a selection, actually to choose this phoneme, word, or structure, but to make it clear that it is not my choice but someone else's. How can we make a choice precisely as the choice of someone else? We do so by inserting in what we say some sort of signal that what follows is not ours, that the next few choices have already been made by someone else and are here only being repeated. The cutting edge of our present choosing is allowed to rest momentarily while some cuts already made in our language, cuts made by someone else, are made again.

It would be wrong, however, to see linguistic choices as done for their own sake, to see language as a matrix just for structure and patterns. If linguistic choices were made simply for their own sake, language would be music. The selections made in language, yielding executed phonemes, words, and sentences, are made in view of a display of things that are not language: of trees and houses, anger and revenge, molecules and clocks. Unless we are just dabbling in language, which we can do only provisionally, we must be aware of more than language when we make linguistic selections. We must be aware of what we display with the words we choose.

And when we quote, our normal form of quotation is not just linguistic but propositional. We normally quote not just to display word-choices but to display something that is exhibited through word-choices. This can be illustrated by an analogy with the game of chess. Merely *linguistic* quotation would be analogous to imitating, on a board of my own and for an interlocutor of my own, the chess moves of another person playing at another board. I imitate the choices he makes within the options that the chessboard and the game of chess (analogously, the language) make possible for him. *Mimicry* would be imitating his grunts and wheezes or the way he moves his hand when he moves a piece. But *propositional* quotation would have an analogue if I were able to imitate his chess moves in order somehow to show my interlocutor how the quoted player opines that this or that thing is featured in the world. I would thus display not just someone's game within the world of the chessboard, but something in the world as such, as presented by the one I quote.[8]

The choices men make in the world are never repeatable: if I choose to attend this concert or to buy that car, to help this person or to defraud that one, my choice is made within a definite situation and it rearranges the world in such a way that the occasion for that choice will not occur again. But language, the matrix within which we choose phonemes, words, and sentences, is more stable; the structural options remain the same for a long time, so I can repeat the same linguistic selections many times over. Language is something like the world of chess and the chessboard; it is an island of relative stability over against the ever-changing scene the world presents to us, and it allows us to bring a stronger sense of identity to things and experiences. It allows consolidations that experience without language could not provide.

In the world of language I can make exactly the same choice over and over again; I can state exactly the same sentence, word, or letter. And someone else can make the very same choices too. In the world of language we are not as radically riveted to a situation—to my situation here and now—as we are in the world in which we live. When I make a linguistic choice by saying something, I appreciate that I or someone else can make the same choice again later. That other person may be under the domination of my mind when he makes the same choice: he may repeat what I said without realizing that he is saying it because I said it. This is the kind of domination of one mind over others that Machiavelli considers a more powerful type of rule than the rule of worldly princes over their subjects.[9] But the other person may later make the same choice as I did and be aware that it was my choice: here he gets out from under my domination by the very act of attributing the choice, the statement, to me. He exploits the linguistic dimension of repeatability, he brings that dimension to mind, he tags his "choice" as not really being his but only echoing someone else's; he quotes another speaker. We cannot do this in regard to political or moral choices, but we can do it in regard to language because of the kind of world the world of language is.

But the world of language is not the last world, and choices in it are almost always made with a view toward a display of what the world itself is like; this display will often invite other choices, nonlinguistic choices, in the world itself. So in imitating someone else's linguistic choices I also display how the world seemed to him, how the world might seem to me and to you, and how the world might invite me and you to act.

4

The world of language is seductive. Whereas the real world imposes a dreadful finality on our choices in life, language seems ever-forgiving. People who live in words can always go back to what they said and say it again and even revise or reverse it, but people who act must live with the consequences of what they have chosen. In action there is no doing again. The ideality of linguistic formulations gives us a more concentrated power of identification with which to cope with the world, but it also tempts us to escape from the world of real choices and to live in the pure identities it provides, in the elegant, regular, and always repeatable patterns that can be made with words. But since words are meant to display things, words themselves draw us out of the isolation of mere language. The semantics of language pulls us into the nonlinguistic. However, there is a way for us to get rid of this semantic element, to cut loose from the world of choices and situations, to enter into a pure and regular world, a world of patterns that do not display anything beyond themselves; we do this when we enter into music. Music is like a language that can rest entirely in itself.

And in music there can be citation, even though not all musical repetition is citation. If someone asks, "What was he humming?" and I say, "He was humming this: [whistle some notes]," I do not quote the hummer; I simply present the piece of music, another token of the same type. I "say" it myself. If a performer plays a potpourri of tunes, he also does not quote them; he "states" them. But if one piece of music is being executed, and it picks up or quotes a melody from another, or even picks up a whole melody that exists and is known as a separate melody, if the quoted melody clearly remains as a subordinate part embedded in the piece being played and does not take over on its own, the melody can be recognized as "spoken by another." In this way, for example "Ein' feste Burg ist unser Gott" is quoted in the *Reformation Symphony* and the Dies Irae in the *Symphonie Fantastique.* On the other hand, the popular song "Stranger in Paradise" cannot be said to quote Borodin's *Polovtsian Dances.* The song does not embed the other piece in itself. Furthermore, a composition based, say, on a folk song does not quote that song but rather absorbs it, unless the folk song is asserted as another song by and in the new composition.

In musical quotation one *speaker* does not quote another speaker because the music is not used propositionally to display something about how things are to someone; the music displays only itself. It is not a substrate for proposition, as language is, unless the music is part of a song. But musical citation is not just mimicry because music involves choices; the sounds must be each selected in a musical piece, just as phonemes are selected in saying a word, and in musical quotation we imitate the choices as they have been made in another setting, in another composition. Our quotational choosing is presented as one step removed from the original choices as they were made elsewhere. The quotation is not a mere continuation of the melody we are playing but the interruption of another melody into it for a limited period. Musical mimicry would really stop emphasizing music as such: it would become one performer imitating another (Victor Borge imitating Rubinstein, for example). Mimicry again descends into the materiality of the performance and withdraws from the formal pattern and its choices.

When we turn from musical quotation to citation in the visual arts, two critical questions arise: What works as a name or a reference in a painting? and What works as a quotation? If a painter wishes to mention another painting inside his own, he does not write the name or the description of that other painting; that would not be a pictorial reference. Instead he depicts it in a special way. He puts it into his painting as a picture that some

of his depicted characters—whether actually there in the painting or only possibly there—might look at. For example an artist
may paint a view of the Phillips Gallery and include Renoir's *The
Boating Party* on the wall as a pictorially mentioned or named
painting, a nominalized painting. The purest form of a merely
mentioned painting would be a few dabs of paint, just enough to
suggest that it is *The Boating Party* that is there for the "viewer"
who is inside the larger picture. The few brush strokes would
be analogous to a name or a definite description of the painting being referred to. Thus the artist who painted the view of
the Phillips Gallery would, by his bits of color, have mentioned,
pictorially, *The Boating Party* to me, the spectator looking at his
painting, and he would have mentioned it to me as a painting
that someone inside *A View of the Phillips Gallery* could look at
and pictorially articulate; and he would also have mentioned it
as a painting that Renoir has originally stated.

Pictorial quotation, on the other hand, would involve making
the cited painting a more active part of the new, stated painting.
An excellent example of this is Matisse's *Nasturtiums and "The
Dance."* Matisse painted a group of human figures dancing in a
ring and called the painting *The Dance.* For a while he kept this
painting in his studio. He placed it behind a stand on which there
was a pot of nasturtiums, their tendrils curling down around the
legs of the stand. Matisse found this arrangement interesting and
painted a new picture with *The Dance* cutting across the back and
the nasturtiums in the foreground, hence *Nasturtiums and "The
Dance."* The background is not simply the ring of figures, it is
the painting of these figures, and that painting is now part of
another painting. But it is compositionally more active in the
larger painting than *The Boating Party* would be in our imagined
painting of the Phillips Gallery. *The Dance* is quoted by Matisse
for his interlocutor, the living viewer of *Nasturtiums and "The
Dance"*; *The Boating Party* would be just mentioned to the viewer
as a picture that someone else—someone "inside" the depicted
Phillips Gallery—might be looking at. This would be like my
referring to "The statement Helen made yesterday," which she
made to another listener in another context.[10]

Pictorial quotation helps us see that propositional quotation
too must be a living, articulated part of the discourse in which it

is embedded. It is *not* the case—as the treatment of referential opacity might make us think—that our speech goes on smoothly in its relation to the world and that it suffers intermittent truth-value gaps only when quotations occur, when it stops disclosing the world and just talks about other minds or other speakers or other speeches. All our discourse, even what we say when we quote, discloses the way things are or might be, and it does so in being articulated. While speech is articulated, the world and things in it are articulated. Some of the disclosures and articulations are achieved by us as being done or as having been done by others, but these too are woven into manifestations that you, I, and they carry on. We always go back and forth between what is and what is said to be. The only time a gap occurs, the only time a manifestation is folded up and made truly opaque is when it is nominalized: when we only refer to it and do not articulate it and what it displays ("What she said," "The statement he made"). But even that is represented as a disclosure and articulation that have been achieved somewhere and sometime else and are not now unfolded in our conversation.

Finally, allusion is different, as a presentational form, from simple repetition, quotation, reference, and mimicry. Allusion is characterized by being fragmentary, partial, and casual. It is something like repetition because it picks up a passage or a tone or a style that belongs somewhere else: in the line, "To summon the spectre of a Rose," T. S. Eliot alludes both to a passage by Sir Thomas Browne and to the ballet, *Le spectre de la rose*; Debussy in his Prelude, *La terrasse des audiences du clair de lune*, alludes to the song *Au clair de la lune*; Manet in *Le déjeuner sur l'herbe* alludes to Raimondi's *The Judgment of Paris*.[11] However, allusion is not simple repetition because the audience is supposed to recognize the source as other to the new context. Allusion is also not quotation, because it mentions just a fragment of what is alluded to, or it assimilates merely a dimension of the original statement—the prosody, some figures, some chords or a tonal structure, a rhythm, a rhyming scheme, a prominent word—and does not reproduce the whole original statement itself. Allusion is something like a reference, but it is a reference that is merely hinted at, not one that is explicitly made, not one that breaks definitively with the course of things being said now. Allusion

echoes and absorbs, it does not point away. Strangely, allusion
has much in common with mimicry, but it is mimicry not of the
materiality but of the form of something else. Allusion brings
something from another context into the context of our present
statement, but it does not break away from our present context
as distinctly as do the other forms we have examined.

5

Quotation in philosophy can only be carried on in language,
so it is different from musical and pictorial citation. Philosophical quotation is also, obviously, different from mimicry and from
merely linguistic citation. The issue for us is to discuss how philosophical quotation differs from propositional quotation.

Speakers who quote propositionally, whether in direct or in
indirect quotation, are engaged in conversation and in what we
might call the enterprise of verification. They are concerned with
what is and in this concern they often show what is said to be.
They want to find out what is the case. But we who enter into the
philosophical enterprise turn our attention to the verificational
conversation itself. We therefore are not simply engaged in the
conversation; we take an unusual distance toward it and try to
state its formal, presentational structure, that which establishes
it as conversation. Husserl has used the term *bracketing* to name
what we do to what we wish to study when we become philosophical; such bracketing can be seen as an analogue to the quoting
we execute when we converse. When we quote someone in our
normal course of conversation, we take a kind of distance to what
that person says and to how things seem to him; we can use that
distance as an analogue for the different kind of distance we
assume when we adopt the philosophical stance.

In this essay, for example, we have given instances of speaking and quoting: we have used the speeches of Karen and John
and Paul and we have presented John, for example, as quoting
what Karen said. But when we as philosophers did this, we did
not quote John again from still another conversational position;
we ourselves were bracketing what John said (including his citation of Karen) and we also bracketed Karen's statement. What

happens when we act this way? What occurs when we display the conversation itself, along with the conversants and what is stated and disclosed by them? What kind of quotation is the bracketing done by philosophy?

It may be tempting for us to think that the move into philosophy makes us to be in the know in a more radical sense than doctors are in the know in regard to their patients, or than my interlocutor and I are in the know in regard to Paul, who does not know Max as the post office clerk. We might think that philosophers are a sort of superconversants in the human conversation, those who know the true being of things, the things themselves, while others know only appearances. We might suppose, for example, that philosophers know that everything is really atoms in the void, while other people think there are animals, colors, and sounds; or that philosophers know that perception is really the excitation of sense organs and the brain, while others think we can really perceive tastes and surfaces. If we were to think this way, philosophical quotation, bracketing, would indeed be an extreme form of ordinary quotation, one in which the philosopher would never quote believingly: the way the world seems to everyone would have to be quoted with doxic rejection, with disbelief. All opinions of what is manifest would have to be dismissed. Only the philosopher would have a handle on the way things really are; only he could succeed in the verification enterprise. His big voice would drown out the others in the human conversation.

Such an understanding of philosophy is at work in the philosophical and scientific enterprise initiated by Descartes. The Cartesian scientist is a competitor with the other conversationalists; he is supposed to do what all men do when they converse about the way things are, but he is supposed to do it better. As a Cartesian thinker I am supposed to "detach my mind from my senses"[12]—that is, to disbelieve the way things appear to everybody—and I am to speak about things only insofar as they do not appear, only insofar as they are the hidden causes of what does appear, the causes known just to the mind and quite definitely not given to the "senses": ". . . I distinguish the wax from its external forms"; ". . . it is now manifest to me that even bodies are not properly speaking known by the senses or by the faculty of imagination, but by the understanding only, and . . . they are not known from the fact that they are seen or touched, but only because they are understood."[13] The manifest is disqualified. There is thus a kind of extreme and total opaqueness of reference between the ordinary speech used to articulate the manifest image of the world and the speech of Cartesian science and philosophy. For the thinker there is a definitive truth-value gap—a truth-value abyss—regarding the way things appear and the way they are said to be. The scientist or philosopher may have to entertain the views enjoyed and the statements made by others, but he can never assimilate them as his own, despite what Descartes calls "a certain lassitude" that always inclines him to do so.[14]

The Cartesian enterprise is established by a shift in the way we are to understand intentionality and in the way we are to be able to quote everything said and presented in the prephilosophic attitude. This shift is more basic to the Cartesian enterprise than are the more obvious arguments Descartes gives to persuade others to follow his lead, arguments such as his appeals to the occasional fallibility of the senses, to the difficulty of providing secure criteria for the difference between dreaming and being awake, to the impetuosity of our wills. These arguments are introduced by Descartes only to make us adopt the new frame of mind, and after they have served their purpose he, at the end of the *Meditations*, effectively withdraws them.[15] Descartes proposes his new point of view as a way of improving on the verificational enterprise of the human race, a way of getting the enterprise on a better track than it had been on before, a way of avoiding the deceptions and errors toward which we are inclined by our nature.

But Descartes forces quotation into a destructive excess. Philosophical bracketing is not a rejection of ordinary experience; philosophy is not the loudest voice in the human conversation. Instead of competing with other voices and almost attempting to replace them, the philosopher simply turns toward the human conversation and the voices in it, and he considers it for what it is in itself. In doing this the philosopher also speaks about the things that are discussed in the human conversation, and he speaks about them as being discussed in the human conversation. He does not just talk about the concepts or ideas people have of things; he talks about the things themselves as they are the targets of the human conversation. He thus quotes what others say about the things, or quotes the things as stated by others; his interest remains with things and in this respect his philosophical quotation, his bracketing, is analogous to John's still being concerned with the car when he quotes Karen about the car.

But there is an important difference between the philosopher's citation of what others say and John's citation of what Karen says. John, like anyone else who quotes within the human conversation, may take a distance to Karen's statement as he repeats it, but this neutralized attitude rests on an engaged, doxic acceptance of many other things: of Karen herself, of Karen as speaking, of John himself as the root speaker in this situation, of the world as the general setting for the speech. When John says, "Karen said the battery is low," he may have distanced himself from the battery's being low, but he is doxically engaged in "Karen saying" and in the peripherals that cushion his own saying of his entire statement (his own voice, his being there, his audience, the world). The somewhat distanced "battery's being low" is highlighted as cited against a massive context of uncited, shadowy, and merely accepted elements. This context of the uncited must remain there and remain dark if John is to remain a member of the human conversation. His being and remaining a part of the conversation is defined by the presence of the unexamined context.

Now, in philosophical quotation, the entire conversation and everything in it, including its peripherals and also what it is about, gets citationally highlighted. The context itself becomes illuminated and seen as context, as being dark to those who are speaking within it. Even the philosopher's own person as also being, under another aspect, a member of the conversation—he is also Spiro, friend of John and Karen, the one who sold Karen the battery—is highlighted or bracketed. And rather than drowning out the human conversation, the philosophical voice is quite thoroughly subjected to it, because the access that philosophy has to things is in the way they are presented and represented in ordinary experience and in the arts and sciences. Philosophy describes the ways in which a thing can be perceived, articulated, registered, reported, forgotten, and remembered; how it can be quoted by John as articulated by Karen; how it can be clearly or confusedly experienced, mistaken for something else, and identified and differentiated by those who experience and talk about it. In doing all this philosophy targets its things by citing them as they are presented and absented in the human conversation. Philosophy does not circumvent the conversation in getting at things, but neither does it slip simply into being one of the conversationalists, the one who lords it over everybody else. And what philosophy actually does from its special standpoint, what it does to what it brackets, is to carry out the kind of distinction-making that we have carried out in this essay.

In propositional quotation I do not merely mention and use the quoted statement; I also mention the speaker who makes the statement, and I mention him as the one who holds the opinion, the one to whom the position is attached. The speaker's authority is invoked. But while I remain one of the participants in the conversation, I quote the speaker as a kind of alternative to myself; I myself become somewhat defined by not being the speaker quoted. The philosophical voice is never in competition with speakers in this way, because as philosophical it does not hold opinions that are in conflict with other opinions in the conversation. It mentions speakers but brings them out simply as speakers; it shows how having an opinion, being quotable, makes them up as speakers and shows how they can become disregarded if their opinion loses weight, how they can become prominent if their statements become repeated by others, how they can even remain hidden and yet influential if their statements are repeated by others as the way things unquestionably are. Philosophy examines the conversationalists formally as identifiers of the things, facts, features, and goods that are identified through the multiple forms of presentation and intention. It brackets not only what the speakers say but the speakers as well.

What a quoted speaker says is presented by the engaged conversationalists as what we and our interlocutors should either verify or disconfirm or take into account. The quoted statement might become a disquoted report if we come to accept it and assert it on our own. But in philosophical quotation the philosophers never enter into the conversation in the same way as propositional quoters do. The quoted remains quoted and is analyzed as such, and so are the reported as reported, the registered as registered, the disquoted as disquoted. Verification or falsification is accomplished by the conversationalists, not by the philosophers; the philosophers' function is to show what verification and the other elements and forms of the conversation are. The philosophers' statements are thus not an alternative to the statements made by the conversationalists, and the philosophers do not surface as yet more antagonists in the debate; what the philosophers say passes through the conversation without causing the sort of effect that the claims of the participants bring about. What the philosophers have to say seems in a curious way obvious and noncontroversial to those who have to settle which of the competing claims in the discussion are true and which are false, and the philosophical distance engenders a kind of nonchalance that contrasts sharply with the urgency of the engaged human concerns. Error, confusion, loss, and vice are as interesting to philosophical analysis as are truth, clarity, possession, and virtue; indeed the latter could not be philosophically defined except as distinguished from the former.

And finally the philosophical citation of the prephilosophical is not a wholly new and alien element added to the prephilosophical. It is a completion of the kind of thinking, the distancing, that occurs in the quotations we carry on in our ordinary and our scientific exchanges.

II

3
Making Distinctions

Chaucer's Wife of Bath says, "But conseilling is nat comandement." Samuel Johnson told Boswell about a headmaster who "was very severe, and wrong-headedly severe. He used to beat us unmercifully; and he did not distinguish between ignorance and negligence; for he would beat a boy equally for not knowing a thing, as for neglecting to know it."[1] And finally there is a friend of mine, whom we shall call Jack, who is attended by a very careful physician. Jack was told by someone that he could obtain a stress electrocardiogram at a good price for a limited time only at a local clinic. It involved running on a treadmill at different speeds and having the activity of the heart measured as the speeds were increased. Jack took the test and brought the results to the physician, who looked at them and said, "Well, I will put this in your file; but we do distinguish between medical data and medical care."

1

Distinctions are not made anywhere and anytime, nor are they made in no place and at no time; they are made in a situation in which they are called for. Distinctions push against an obscurity that needs the distinction in question. In the story about Jack and the doctor, the obscurity against which the distinction is made is included as part of the story; in the quotation from Chaucer the obscurity that provides the setting for the distinction is not mentioned—although you would find it if you were to read the Wife of Bath's tale—but it is easy for us to imagine a setting in which the distinction between counseling and commandment ought to be made. When we entertain a distinction, such as "Counseling is not commandment," "Ignorance is not negligence," or "Medical data is not medical care," we always experience or imagine an obscurity against which the distinction arises. When we think philosophically about executing distinctions, we must pay attention to the obscurity that lets the distinction occur.

In order to achieve and recognize a distinction, it is sufficient if we imagine the setting in which the distinction is to be made. An imaginary setting is sufficient to register a real distinction. Sometimes, of course, distinctions are made in situations that are not imagined but lived. Jack, for example, was actually doing certain things; he had taken the test and was giving the results to the doctor. He was not imagining that all this was going on, and the distinction was made in force for him in his lived context. But you, the reader, only imagine this scene; you do not even know who Jack was or who the doctor was, you do not live through what Jack lived through, and yet you can register the same distinction that was registered for him. You could in fact register this same distinction even if my story were not true but only fictional; and you could register this same distinction even if I were to have thought up another story in which it could have been presented. What is a distinction, that it can be appreciated both in actual experience and in imagination?

At first blush we might think that the imaginative registration of a distinction is merely secondary, derived, and parasitic on the registration of distinctions in real life; but distinctions could not be appreciated in real life if they could not be achieved in imagination. The distinction between medical data and medical care struck Jack with such force because he could imagine as well as perceive the setting in which it had to be made. The distinction shed light on what Jack had lived through because it could also work for him in a situation he might only imagine. Jack may not

have adverted to this need for an imaginative foil when he appreciated the distinction, but without the foil the distinction could
not have occurred in the situation that was lived and not imagined. When we reflect philosophically on what occurred to Jack,
we must take the imaginative aspect into account even though
Jack did not.

When a distinction is made, it is made as holding everywhere
and always. It is made as having held before it was made, as
continuing to hold after it is made, and as holding even if no one
is making it. If we say that the distinction needs to be understood
against the obscurity that calls for it, are we not saying that the
distinction only holds when it is propped against its particular
setting? Are we not making the distinction relative to a situation,
at least an imagined one, and do we not claim that the difference
between medical data and medical care holds only because Jack
proceeded and spoke as though there were no such distinction?

When we as philosophers pay attention to the setting in which
a distinction is registered, we do not deny that the distinction
holds beyond that setting. We continue to agree with the Wife
of Bath, with Samuel Johnson, and with Jack and the doctor that
whenever there is counseling it is not commandment, whenever
there is ignorance it is not, as such, negligence, and whenever
there is medical data it is not, as such, medical care. Moreover,
even if we imagine our earth to be wiped out and there to be
no more people anywhere, it would still hold that counseling is
not commandment, that ignorance is not negligence, and that
medical data is not necessarily medical care. We must recognize
the great holding power of distinctions, the power that lets them
survive so many changes and disasters, so many contingencies;
but we must also observe that the Wife of Bath and her distinguishing colleagues can assert the distinction and recognize its
durability only because they can imagine these various settings,
even the setting of the earth's being wiped out, and through
such imaginings acknowledge that the distinction holds, come
what may.

A distinction, with its necessity, is displayed to the Wife of Bath,
and her attention is focused on the distinction. Imagination and
a setting marked by obscurity are needed to display the distinction, but they do not enter into what is distinguished, nor do

they make the distinction imaginary or local. Samuel Johnson
would not say that the distinction between ignorance and negligence is imaginary or that it holds only when he makes it; he
sees through the display of the distinction to the distinction itself
and recognizes it as permanent. But when we do philosophy we
pay attention to the display and must note the place of imagination and obscurity in it. In doing this we are different from
Samuel Johnson and the Wife of Bath; we neither absorb them
into ourselves nor do we simply adopt their stance, because we
think about them as recognizing distinctions. We let them be
agents of distinction, and we try to show how they are able to
reach a necessity that stretches beyond the setting in which they
think. It would be a confusion of the philosophical viewpoint
with prephilosophical experience and thought if we were to say
that the philosophical acknowledgment of imagination and of
the obscure context somehow localized the distinction itself or
made it less necessary or less universal.

Can we ever possess a distinction without the imagination's
intervention? We can possess one if verbally repeating the distinction without insight is to count as possession of it. Suppose I
am unfamiliar with legal matters and a lawyer says to me, "Torts
are not class action suits," and I happen to remember the phrase.
Later when someone is talking about torts I repeat the phrase
and my interlocutors find it a surprisingly apt remark. I may have
conveyed the distinction but I did not possess it; my failure to
possess it stems from my unfamiliarity with torts, class action suits,
and other legal matters, and this unfamiliarity means that I also
cannot imagine new settings for torts and class action suits, imaginative settings in which the necessity of the distinction would have
forced itself on me. It is not just unfamiliarity that makes me incapable of handling the distinction; it is also the unimaginability
that unfamiliarity breeds.

Of course, the unfamiliarity in such cases is not total; I would
have to have *some* sense of legal matters to know that the terms
torts and *class action suits* belong in the law and not in cooking
or card playing. But I am not familiar with torts or class action
suits as such, except as very vague things that I cannot really distinguish from one another and from other things in the genus
of legal matters. Vague acquaintance with something is precisely

the inability to move on from repeated perceptions to an imaginative projection. It is the inability to recognize something as the same again not only in further perceptions of it, but in imaginative sketches: sketches of settings that are different from those we have perceived, but that are capable of still presenting the same thing again. Imagination goes to work within the obscurity that provides the setting for the distinctions that are to be made.

2

How is making distinctions different from other activities of the mind? How, in particular, is it different from judging and defining? When we make a judgment we declare that this individual or group or type of thing has a certain feature or is an instance of a kind: "He is temperate"; "Young people are optimistic"; "Argon is an inert gas." We subsume a case under a predicate. The achievement of judging is to unify, so judging is not the same as making a distinction, but judgment does presume that some distinctions have been made. Only because the predicate has been distinguished from other kinds or features is it definite enough for us to say explicitly that this or that is a case of the predicate. This reliance of judgments on distinctions comes out neatly in sentences that both place an instance under a category and, at the same time, display a distinction: "He could practice abstinence, but not temperance"; "We had talk enough, but no conversation"; "I have found you an argument; but I am not obliged to find you an understanding."[2] Behind such judgments, and also showing through them, are the distinctions "Abstinence is not temperance," "Talk is not conversation," "Argument is not understanding." And if the judgments were simple, devoid of the contrasting element—"He could abstain," "We talked," "You have the argument"—the distinction would still be behind them but would no longer show through.

Of course every category we possess can be distinguished from an indefinite number of other categories. Abstinence is not only different from temperance, but also from deprivation, gluttony, desire, selfishness, and an infinity of other things. We might on a given occasion explicitly engage one of these distinctions—

"Abstinence is not temperance"—but if we do not specify a distinction, we do not necessarily engage all the distinctions a term can enter into. The context will almost always pull one or two distinctions to the fore and emphasize certain contrasts even if they are not expressed; the point of almost any assertion is not only to state something but to distinguish it from something near it which might have been anticipated and with which it might have been confused. Certain distinctions are activated, perhaps silently, and these distinctions are always within a genus set by the context of discourse. The genus can shrink or swell depending on the precision of the speaker. For a careless speaker, words have relatively little exclusionary force, whereas a careful and intelligent speaker engages many distinctions in what he says.

But is it true that predicates or categories must rest on distinctions that stand behind, sometimes show through, and are activated by predications? Are predicates not simply built up through familiarity and repeated experience? Do we not see one brown thing, then another, and gradually develop by generalization the idea of brown? This appears to be an entirely positive process; does *brown* or any other term need negation and contrast to be what it is?

There is a level of experience and speech which admits of some generality, but in which the distinct exclusion of one kind from another has not yet set in. This is associative experience and speech, the sort used by children, by people strongly moved by emotion, or by careless speakers or agents, and since reason involves definite exclusions, this level of awareness and behavior is prerational. A child, for example, may be able to apply a term like *dog* or *white* to several individuals, but it is most unlikely that he would volunteer a phrase like, "But a dog is not a horse." The point of such a statement would be lost on a child. The child's "predications" are really active involvements with things; he uses the word *dog* to call the animal or to further an action, not to assert something about it. He is not engaged in the relatively detached activity of making statements about dogs, and only when we enter into such activity would a rather theoretical remark like "Dogs are not horses" be appropriate. The distinction is achieved in a contemplative act. It is a simple recognition of how things are and how they have to be.[3] Even if it is uttered in an intensely active situation, the making of the distinction is a detached acknowledgment of necessity, not a further step in the course of action. It may register a necessity that we in our activity must pay attention to—"Embezzlement is not borrowing," "Medical data is not medical care"—but it is not a move in the action. It has its detached, objective authority precisely because it steps out of the action and makes a distinction that is in the nature of things.

If a distinction is made in the midst of an exciting scene, it is an attempt to bring the presence of mind to an emotionally charged situation. The distinction may be made in a brief phrase or it may be elaborated in a long argument, but the point is to make someone see that there are two things where he presumes there to be only one. Presence of mind is to see two where many can feel only one. Letting a distinction assert itself can be a troubling process, and it can, if the issues are personal, take a very long time. And not everyone is capable of letting the distinction emerge, or of sustaining it once it has come forward. Our concern in this essay is not to make a distinction in such a situation, but to discuss what it is for a distinction to emerge and to be kept alive, and to discuss what one has to do to let the distinction come about.

Furthermore, the achievement of a distinction is no guarantee that the distinction will be sustained. It is possible for the distinction to wobble, perhaps for an extended length of time, and finally to slip away, with the generic obscurity returning. Even if the distinction is authentically achieved, it is not easy to let it work its way into behavior, and there may be periods in which the required presence of mind fluctuates. The ability to formulate the distinction in words is no assurance that the grasp of its two elements as two and as necessarily exclusive is there. However, if we do manage to get even the slightest hold on the distinction, or if it is allowed to get the slightest hold on us, it can serve as an orientation during the period of turbulence and indicate the direction toward which we should be moving. Remarks like, "She didn't hate you; she loved him," or "He's not angry because you did it; he's angry because it happened," may not dissipate our distress at the moment they are stated, but they make a difference in the long run.

Finally, if we have achieved a distinction and then lose it, we do not fall back into the condition we were in before we first made the distinction; the distinction we once made stays around to haunt us, but only as a shade of its former self. There is the memory of something we can and ought to remember. We anticipate recovering the distinction, we do not anticipate making it for the first time.

An emotional scene provides a good setting in which to examine the ability to make distinctions because we can notice how a distinction comes and goes in such a scene, and how it changes what is going on. But a distinction can also be conspicuously absent in carelessness, and in what we call by the harsh names of dullness or stupidity. Stupidity is not ignorance; it is an ignorance that cannot be overcome. It is the rather permanent inability to let appropriate distinctions occur. Someone may, for example, be unable to distinguish another person as a friend and as an official, and may be disappointed because he does not get political favors from him. The failure to distinguish may be caused by some passion, like ambition or vanity, and then there is at least in principle the hope that the distinction might be made to break through; but the failure can also come from dullness, from the constitutional inability to cut one into two, and then there is no hope of differentiation. All one can do is dismiss that particular issue and approach the person through other ways, ways in which no corresponding discriminations have to be made.

The kind of verbal activity that can be found in children, in emotionally tense speakers, and in the careless or the dull, is a prejudgmental use of language, and it is prejudgmental because distinctions of kinds have not been made by such speakers and agents. We cannot place something under a category until the category is sufficiently determined. Making distinctions therefore comes "between" vagueness and distinct judging; it is the emergence of reason and thinking. But how are distinctions related to definitions? Distinctions may be prior to judgments, but are they also prior to definitions?

Before we can define something, like courage for example, we must have made some distinctions as initial demarcations of the topic; we must have registered that courage is not rashness, that courage is not greed, that courage is not hostility. We must have registered such distinctions as being necessary. These negations are not just coincidental facts; they belong to courage in itself, and some of them must come between the casual acquaintance we have with courage and the ability we may acquire to define what it is. The definition itself is a positive process, for we select the specific difference, within the genus, that determines what the object is; but the selection of the difference is possible only because the difference has been distinguished from its possible alternatives. The definition does not make the distinction, it presumes it.

But are there not exceptions to this? Are there not cases in which it is the definition that permits us to see the necessity of a distinction? For example, a literary theorist has distinguished between the bardic voice and the prophetic voice in poetry.[4] To express this distinction, one might say, "A bard is not a prophet," or "To be a bard is not to be a prophet." Someone familiar in a general way with these terms might ask why this distinction is necessary. Why could not prophets, as prophets, also be bards? The response consists in definitions: a bard is one who stands within a community and speaks its past; a prophet is one who takes a distance from his community, criticizes its past and present, and urges new behavior in the future. These definitional refinements are not mere stipulations; they bring out a sense that is vague but latent in the ordinary use of the terms. And once these definitions are made, we see that a bardic voice is necessarily not a prophetic voice. The distinction seems to rest on the definitions, not on its own evidence.

However, the definitions themselves depend on other distinctions, such as "Inside is not outside," "Criticism is not repetition," and "The future is not the past." One or other of these may in turn be explained by further definitions, but not all of them can be. We come finally to distinctions and exclusions that cannot be clarified by definitions of their terms, but must be seen as holding necessarily by the strength of the terms. Any attempt to define *inside* and *outside*, for example, would involve a surreptitious use of the distinction between inner and outer. Distinctions are the pegs from which definitions hang. To know that inside is necessarily not outside is more elementary than to know the definition of anything that involves being inside or outside.

It may even be hard on occasion to say whether a particular distinction can or cannot be clarified, without circularity, by definitions. When we try, for example, to get behind "Ignorance is not negligence," we find ourselves using terms that are very much like those in the distinction we are trying to explain. However, this uncertainty does not matter. There will be some cases in which definitions clearly establish the distinction, and there will be other cases in which the distinctions are clearly terminal, but there will be many cases in which it is hard to tell which has precedence. It is not the case that our language and our world are vividly divided into the terminal and the derivative; often enough we may not be able to get clear about a particular instance.

It might appear that the function of philosophy is to isolate those terminal, irreducible distinctions that can be identified, to explore the meaning of their terms, and to show how other definitions and distinctions stem from them. Philosophy, in this charting of being, would explore such fundamental categories as inner and outer, chance and necessity, before and after, and the like. Such a clarification is worth doing, but philosophy's more important role is to talk about distinctions as distinctions, about their terms as terms of distinctions, and about what permits distinctions to occur (the place of imagination, the role of the obscure matrix, the moment that calls for distinction). The study of the forms of manifestation at work in distinctions is more significant philosophically than the project of drawing up a catalogue of the basic items that show up in the distinctions. Because philosophy's more urgent concern is with the formal structure of presentation, it can tolerate uncertainty about whether a particular distinction, like that between ignorance and negligence, is terminal or not. In fact we come to see, philosophically, that some uncertainty about the terminal character of particular distinctions is unavoidable.

3

Can we isolate the formal, syncategorematic element involved in making distinctions? In predication we can differentiate the formal structure "_____ is . . . ." from the material or core content; what is the corresponding frame in distinctions? On a superficial level, it is something like "_____ $\neq$ . . . ." What sort of operation is symbolized by "$\neq$"? Clearly, it is an activity of separating or excluding two terms. But that is not all; in order that the terms be excludable, they must first be brought together, so there is also the activity of bringing together, along with the annulment of their being together. Making a distinction is the activity of articulating two terms and registering them as separate, as two, as not one; but all this involves the two terms' having been brought together. Otherwise they could not have been excluded from one another.

Would it then be correct to say that $\equiv$ precedes $\neq$, that the fusion of two as one precedes the distinction? It would not be correct to say so, because the unification symbolized by "$\equiv$" and illustrated by a statement like "But patriotism is loyalty," is itself realized in contrast to the possible exclusion expressed by "$\neq$." The nondistinction does not come before the distinction. It is not as though we first get used to being able to hold two things as one for a certain period, say between the ages of two and four, and then acquire the power of negating their union. Instead, the ability to hold two as one comes along with the ability to hold two together as distinguished: holding two together as one is holding them precisely as not distinguishable. The possibility of their being distinguished, and the denial of this possibility, is part of holding them as one. Before the possibility of distinction arises, we live simply in assimilation and do not see the one as one. The activity "$\equiv$" is correlated to the activity "$\neq$." Neither comes before the other.

Then what does come before the two of them? We can isolate a more basic activity that precedes, categorially, $\equiv$ and $\neq$. It is the gesture of bringing out two or bringing two together to decide whether they are two or one. The activities "$\equiv$" and "$\neq$" are closures, and the more basic activity is what they close. It is the raising of the issue, "One or two?" in a concrete case. It is like the solicitation of affirmation or denial. Let us call this more basic activity the *urge* to distinguish or to identify, and let us symbolize this categoriality by X. Urgence, in this sense, precedes both $\equiv$ and $\neq$, but it is not to be distinguished from them as they are to be distinguished from one another. Identification and distinction are determined by each not being the other, whereas the urgence we speak of enters into either identification or distinction. It is like the tension that gets resolved by one or the other.

In fact, it is rather loose talk to say that identification and distinction are distinguished from one another, because distinction takes place inside one of these terms, inside $\neq$. What occurs in $\neq$ cannot be applied to the difference between $\equiv$ and $\neq$. All we can do in our philosophical analysis is make further refinements and contrasts that will bring out what is special about the difference between $\equiv$ and $\neq$, refinements that will show how each of these is different from the urgency X that precedes both. Distinctions and identifications do not apply to themselves, reflexively, in the same way they apply to things we normally distinguish, like ignorance and negligence, counseling and commandment, or medical data and medical care. This should not be a cause for panic but should simply prompt us to recognize the special character of philosophical discourse, vocabulary, and syntax.

Still another way of isolating X is the following. When we make a distinction, like "Kindness is not fondness,"[5] our attention is focused on the terms distinguished, on kindness and fondness, and we have to make a reflective turn to focus on the distinction, $\neq$, that lets these terms come forward as distinct. Now when we speak about $\equiv$ and $\neq$ as categorial forms, we are again caught in a kind of naivety analogous to that which prevailed when we were busy with kindness and fondness. Again we have to make a special reflective turn to that which permits $\equiv$ and $\neq$ to come forward as options "differentiated" from one another. What do we turn to? We turn to that which comes "before" and "between" $\equiv$ and $\neq$, to the urgence X, to the raising of the issue whether $\equiv$ or $\neq$ holds between A and B, between kindness and fondness.

But now that we have gotten at this urgency X, what can be said about it? The urgency occurs within the generic obscurity that calls for a distinction, and it takes place with the help of the imagination. The urgence occurs when we become dissatisfied with the generic and feel that some sort of distinction (or identification) needs to be made. It is the state of tipping into thought. A person who is dull does not sense this urgency, even when someone else tries to provoke it in him. A person who is dull fails not primarily in being unable to appreciate a completed distinction; he fails primarily in not sensing that there is an issue for distinction. He lives quite contentedly in the generic obscurity even though words pulling beyond the obscurity float around him. What can be exasperating in such a person is not his inability to grasp a distinction, but his failure to see the need for one.

The urgence toward distinction involves the imagination and it occurs not as a clash of abstract ideas but concretely. It involves a split between two concrete things presented to us. It can involve a perception against which an imagination is contrasted, or it can involve an imagination against which another imagination is contrasted. To return to one of our first examples, while Jack was engaged in collecting and presenting medical information, the possibility of engaging in medical care occurs to him in a concrete form (because of what the doctor said to him), and this imagined projection resists being assimilated into what he has been doing. It would be to do something else. Here we have a contrast between perception and imagination. If you, the reader, merely read the story about Jack and imagine him collecting data, your appreciation of the distinction is based just on imagination, with one imaginative projection played off against another. In either case the conceptual distinction is rooted in a concrete and preconceptual, urgent sensing of a difference. Without this imaginative power the abstract distinction would not register for us; it would be a distinction without a difference. Hence we often say that someone who is dull lacks imagination, the capacity for engendering and sensing concrete differences.

Of course the concrete cases are perceived and imagined as cases of a certain kind, but the category under which they fall does not come into prominence until we seal the distinction into an abstract formula. Sometimes we are given the distinction not in an abstract formula, like "Ignorance is not negligence," but in a story or legend or parable or illustration. The story may hold the truth for us in an urgent, concrete form; we know a distinction of general import is at work in the story and preserved in it, but it may not be possible to state abstractly what the terms of the distinction are. Often what is at issue is more richly possessed in the concrete recital rather than in the abstract statement; and always the abstract statement needs to be nourished by cases if it is to be more than an idle, merely linguistic distinction. An abstract formula like "Counseling is not commandment" has force and urgency because it is played off against the concrete case we perceive or imagine with the formula, the concrete case in which the obscurity that calls for the distinction is preserved.

When we do rest with the concrete recital, we still realize that it holds a distinction (or an identification) that goes beyond the particulars of this instance; it urges beyond itself and wants a distinction (or identification). The story of Cinderella, for example, tends toward some such distinction as "To be held in disdain by small-minded people is not to be worthless," or perhaps "Excellence now unrecognized is not excellence forever unrecognized." The story has import because it urges us toward such knowledge. Then there is Aesop's fable of the dog who had a piece of meat in his mouth, saw his own reflection in the water, tried to get the other piece of meat, and lost the one he had; this fable tends toward an obvious identification such as, "To covet can be to lose what you have," and it plays also on a more subtle, almost ominous distinction of appearances, something like "Your own image is not someone else." The stories are obviously better than my clumsy abstractions, and stories often seem profound because they urge a distinction but do not make it obvious what the distinction is. What, for example, could express the distinctions and identifications at work in von Hofmannsthal's *Die Frau ohne Schatten*, Poe's *The Purloined Letter*, and Shakespeare's *The Tempest*? But even if the concrete is in such cases better than the abstract, the concrete is good only because it urges toward the abstract.

4

There are two important ways in which distinctions can go wrong: (1) we may fail to make a distinction that we ought to make; and (2) we may make a distinction that does not really exist. In the first we underdistinguish, in the second we overdistinguish.

(1) It is quite legitimate to distinguish kindness from fondness, but we can easily imagine someone who cannot appreciate kindness from another person unless it is also fondness; whether

it be because of a romantic understanding of human relationships, or because of emotional involvement and tension, or simply because of a lack of experience in what is possible and in
what can be expected from people. Because of the failure to distinguish, the kindness exercised may not be recognized as kindness but may be deciphered into condescension or flattery or
insinuation. And not only the recipient but even the one who
performs the kindness may be confused and distressed in what
he is trying to do if he cannot make the required distinction.

Because the appropriate division of kinds is not made, an instance of one of the kinds is not allowed to be itself. It is not just
the abstract distinction that fails to occur; because the distinction
fails, a concrete situation is misinterpreted. Kindness and fondness are confused or "poured together," and since in the concrete
occurrence there is no fondness, it is assumed that there could
not be kindness, so that which is going on becomes interpreted
as something else. The failure of an abstract distinction has a dis-
orienting and dissolving effect on a particular occurrence: we do
not accept the plain sense of what is before us, and try to read it as
something other that it might be. "It *could not* be kindness, even
though it looks like kindness, so it must be something else." And
it must be something dissimulative, because the apparent sense
has to be dismissed.

One species (kindness) can therefore fail to be distinguished
from another species (fondness). One species is confused with
and hence conceals another. But the structure of such confusion
is even more complex. The confusion reaches into the genus
from which both species arise. Suppose that something like benevolence is the genus for kindness and fondness; a person who
confuses kindness and fondness also confuses benevolence with
fondness, and hence assumes that if there is to be benevolence
there must also be fondness. He does not see that benevolence
can also "be," as kindness, even if there is no fondness. The
making of a distinction preserves the genus. If the distinction is
not made, the genus of benevolence is deciphered as something
else, such as clever self-seeking, and benevolence is not allowed
to be itself. The failure to make an appropriate distinction again
forces us to reject an obvious presence and to interpret it as a
disguise. The manifest becomes something that conceals.

This play between the failure to make a distinction and the refusal to accept something obvious can make it exasperating for someone who has to explain to someone else what is going on; if a person cannot get the distinctions between, say, kindness and fondness, loyalty and obsequiousness, diligence and compulsion; or if he cannot appreciate distinctions like those made by John Henry Newman when he writes, "But attachment is not trust, nor is to obey the same as to look up to, and to rely upon";[6] it will be practically impossible for him to understand the plain sense of what is going on around him. He will instead tend to fall back on a few favorite decipherments of behavior, explaining things in terms of concealed greed or self-interest, sublimated desires, or clever moves to obtain influence. One is driven into reductionism when one is not cultivated to possess an array of distinctions rich enough to let things be what they are. In contrast, making the decisive distinction has an illuminating and liberating effect because it lets the concrete occurrence stand forth for what it is. We understand it not in terms of a decipherment, but on its own terms.

The bias of education and general opinion now is clearly toward explanation by decipherment rather than explanation by distinction. Astronomy, physics, genetics, economics, psychology, and sociology have inclined us to interpret what we directly experience in terms of things we do not directly encounter, like nuclear particles, fields, genes, unconscious desires, and concealed laws of money, exchange, labor, and demand. Because such hidden things are taken as the truth of what appears, the distinctions that structure the world of direct appearance are taken to be merely conventional or ideological. We tend to feel, consequently, that there is little value in making and clarifying manifest distinctions, and equally little value in teaching others such distinctions and in helping them to make distinctions themselves; it seems better to teach them "the true theory" that tells what is behind the things that appear. This preference for the hidden is a bias; it overlooks the fact that the things described or constructed in science are dependent on distinctions and identifications made in the world in which we live. But it is not a harmless bias, because someone "educated" to neglect distinctions like those between teaching and indoctrination, liberty and license, politics and advertising, or production and action, will not be able to live and act rationally. In public affairs he will be as disoriented as the person who, in private matters, cannot see the difference between kindness and fondness. Our present uncertainty about what should be taught in the humanities stems from the belief that making basic distinctions in the world we inhabit is not a form of knowledge and understanding.[7]

(2) If we limit ourselves to repeating standard distinctions, it might appear that there are a precise number of distinctions and "trees" of distinctions, going from the generic down to specific kinds. The world appears to break down, in Porphyrian fashion, into definite series of genera and species. But once we move into less familiar distinctions, like those between trust and attachment, kindness and fondness, "that which is most important and that which is most talked about," and medical data and medical care, we realize that distinctions are not so definitely ordered. There are, it is true, many distinctions that any intelligent and educated person should know, but it is equally important that such a person should be able to go and do likewise, to make further distinctions on his own. It would be impossible to collect beforehand enough categories and trees of categories to cover any contingency; the thoughtful observer must be able himself to make the incisive distinction that fits and clarifies what is occurring before him, and such a distinction may not be capable of being ordered into a systematic plan.

But just as it is possible for us to fail to make an appropriate distinction, is it not possible for us to go too far and, like Taylor in *The Looking Glass War*, engage in "emphasizing a distinction which did not exist"?[8] What would it be like to do this? We are not talking about a distinction that is valid but just happens not to be relevant to a case before us; nor are we talking about a distinction between nonsense terms; we are talking about an apparent division of kinds which is not truly a division of kinds. How can something look like a distinction, and even be taken as a distinction by many people, and yet not really be one? To clarify this possibility is more significant for the problem of truth and falsity than is the treatment of less fundamental untruth, such as that which occurs in lies or in simply false statements or in ignorance.

It is hard to imagine an example of an unreal distinction, because the distinction must be plausible if we are to take it seriously; but how can it be plausible if we know it is unreal? Perhaps it would be best to take a controversial instance. Many writers have written about a virtue which they call authenticity.[9] I do not think that such a virtue, as described by these writers, exists. I think authenticity is a philosophical construct, that it can only be understood as the historical result of the development of certain philosophical ideas, and that the term *authenticity* does not name a moral phenomenon. I invite you, the reader, to entertain my position. Then we will both imagine someone who thinks authenticity is real, and we will imagine him trying to distinguish authenticity from other things. This will provide us with a convincing example to work with in describing what happens when one "makes" a distinction that does not exist.

There are some acceptable distinctions one can make regarding authenticity. One can say "Authenticity is not stubbornness," or "Authenticity is not selfishness." However, the legitimacy of such distinctions is derived from genera stacked above authenticity: authenticity is taken to be a virtue in the generic area of seriousness and honesty, and it is really this genus that is being contrasted with stubbornness. Likewise, something like *benevolence* is a genus above authenticity, and is the genus which we contrast with selfishness. The insubstantiality of authenticity becomes manifest when we try to make distinctions that are more specific to this putative virtue. For example, Plato describes a kind of moral dissimulation in book 2 of the *Republic*: a man is depicted who in fact does bad things, but who achieves a reputation for being good (359B–362C). The contrast is between his actions, which are bad, and his reputation, which is good; this is a legitimate moral issue. Now in the issue of authenticity we are supposed to be able to perform good actions, and yet not actually be good. This is the vice, the "bad faith," that authenticity is opposed to. The contrast is not between our reputation and our actions, but between our actions and something that, in principle, never shows up as an action. Now someone who thinks *authenticity* names a moral phenomenon must, at some time, be able to make the distinction, "Authenticity is not the moral honesty discussed in the *Republic*." But if I am right in my suspicion of authenticity, we can show that authenticity is not to be distinguished from the honesty Plato deals with; authenticity is a confused extension of that honesty, brought about by subsequent historical interpretations.

Another phenomenon that authenticity, if it were real, ought to be distinguished from is self-understanding, the ability to appreciate that we are, for example, jealous or envious or generous or modest when we act in certain ways. Still another "kind" that authenticity ought to be distinguished from are the theological virtues of faith, hope, and charity, as they were described by medieval Christian theologians. My contention is that when someone tries, as he must try, to distinguish authenticity from moral honesty, from self-understanding, from a secularized version of the theological virtues, and from other kinds of virtues as well, authenticity cannot stand up in the distinction; it becomes absorbed into things it should be distinguishable from. As we clarify what we mean by these various kinds, authenticity is seen gradually to dissolve into them. A sort of layered sedimentation and overlap of ideas has made us think there was a new moral phenomenon to be named, but it was only an illusion created by the ideational medium through which our actions are seen; and the illusion is disclosed as an illusion when we show that the putative species, authenticity, is dissolvable without remainder into other species from which, if it were real, it should be distinguished. A true kind resists such absorption; its distinctions hold up.

A similar dissolution could be carried out for terms like *creativity* and *relevance*, as they are commonly used, and for other words without substance, words which seem to name but do not. The unreality of such words is more clearly recognized in their inability to be distinguished than in the ambiguity and uncertainty we experience when we try to apply them to anything.[10] The point of our discussion is, of course, not to prove the claim that *authenticity* is an insubstantial term, but to illustrate what happens when we make a distinction that does not exist. The distinction does not exist because one or both of the terms of the distinction do not exist, even though many people may think that they are real. And correlatively, and perhaps on a deeper level, one or both of the terms of the distinction do not exist because the distinction itself "is" not, as we shall now demonstrate.[11]

5

Unreal distinctions can be clarified by an examination of acceptable or true distinctions. It might appear that after we have made a distinction that seems to be decisive, there still remains the task of showing somehow that the terms of the distinction do exist. It might be thought that the distinction may be "only dialectical" or "only a matter of words," and that we must bring further evidence to show that it has something one might call "existential import." A suspicion of this sort betrays a misunderstanding of how words are related to being. There is an ontological force to distinctions as such. When we make distinctions we are not just determining language in isolation from being. In determining language we are also articulating being, not as two activities that only happen to be conjoined, but as a single activity that has two aspects which may, on special occasions, be separated from one another, but which normally are what they are only by being together. Determining language and articulating being is a hendiadys. Consequently a distinction does not normally have to be followed by a proof that its terms exist.

If we start off with the strong conviction that there is a special domain of language, meaning, dialectics, or the conceptual, and that this domain subsists quite independently of what is real, it seems like the most obvious thing in the world to say that distinctions first occur in the mental domain and then must be given some sort of ontological confirmation to be admitted as true. But this is letting our convictions dictate what the phenomena ought to be. If we instead look at how distinctions actually occur, we find that they are practically always immersed in both language and being. When we distinguish between ignorance and negligence, the bard and the prophet, kindness and fondness, or medical data and medical care, we do not feel compelled to go on to show that the terms of such distinctions are real. There is a kind of obvious reality to the disjuncted terms, and their reality seems somehow warranted by the possibility of distinguishing them. Even when we want to argue about the legitimacy of a particular distinction, or about the reality of one of its terms, we appeal ultimately to other distinctions, and the very achievement of these distinctions seems to make manifest the reality of what is distinguished. Can we clarify how distinctions are able to warrant the reality of the terms distinguished?

Before we enter into distinctions, we are immersed in simple familiarity with a particular type of thing. But when we have to distinguish that kind of thing from other kinds, what we were familiar with emerges as necessarily excluding something, something that was also around in our experience. Our vague, familiar experience is a matrix that permits an exclusion to occur, and each of the terms distinguished becomes manifest as real precisely because it is, necessarily, not something else. The simple familiarity that precedes a distinction does not provide this sense of being real; only a distinction between things establishes it. The distinction provides each term with a sense of definiteness and with a sense of otherness: the thing is itself, and it is not this other; it is other than this other thing. This presence of sameness and otherness occurs on the basis of a distinction. The definiteness and exclusion are not first recognized as attributes of the things we are familiar with; they are not first recognized in the things and then subsequently related to other things and expressed in a distinction. The being distinguished is the registration, the disclosure of sameness and otherness, and it is the emergence of each term as some thing.

Of course familiarity has to come before the distinction, and it contributes to the sense of reality of both terms. If we distinguished terms we were totally unacquainted with, the distinction would not in fact take place. We need familiarity with kindness and with fondness before the distinction between them can occur. But the distinction is not just a yoking of two completed beings; until the terms have entered into distinctions, they are in a kind of mist in which the difference between the real and the apparent has not taken effect. Something has to exclude something, and to exclude something specific in its genus, if it is to be real. It has to be able not just to be presented, but to be presented as distinguished, and it is so presented in a distinction. And all this is not just a matter of language, for what we are familiar with as kindness, for example, cannot be said to be until it emerges as distinguished from something else.

When we say a distinction is a "true" distinction, we mean that it is genuinely a distinction, we do not mean that it is a correct distinction, one that can match something outside itself. Truth as being genuine is different from truth as being correct. Gold can be said to be true gold, and love can be said to be true love, in the sense that they are what they seem to be. But a judgment can be said to be a true judgment in the sense that it can be brought up against something outside itself, a state of affairs, which the judgment must match in order to be true. We go outside the judgment to determine its truth of correctness; the truth of correctness implies an external standard by which whatever is true is determined as true. But in the truth of genuineness we do not go outside the thing to measure its truth; we simply determine the thing as being truly what it seems to be. Any "going outside" in the case of genuineness is merely going to illusions or to false appearances to deny that the thing is any such falsehood or counterfeit.

Now when we think that a distinction has somehow to be brought to things to be certified as true, we are supposing that distinctions are like judgments and that they have to be made to correspond to states of affairs to be qualified as true. But there is no way to possess any objective correlate for a distinction except in the distinction itself. There is no way to verify a distinction except by making it. There is nothing beyond a distinction for it to correspond to. Distinctions are not like judgments. Hence the truth of a distinction is truth in the sense of being genuine, not in the sense of being correct. There can be false distinctions, but they are false in the way "false gold" or "fool's gold" or "false love" are false, not in the way a false opinion is wrong. A false judgment can be a genuine judgment even though it is false, but false distinctions just are not distinctions. They seem to be distinctions but they are not. And the genuine thinking that must occur in true distinctions is a more fundamental kind of thinking than what we do when we make judgments, entertain opinions, and try to determine whether what we or others say is correct or not. Distinctions are prior to judgments and to definitions.

There will probably always be a lingering feeling that distinctions can somehow be only conceptual and that they stand in need of being brought to the things themselves in some sort of verification. But what does "going to see the things themselves" signify in the case of distinctions? When we go to experience, we still have to engage our imagination in order to make the true distinction. The same true distinction can be made whether we are in the middle of the experience of things or in an imaginative dwelling with them; in either case the imagination is needed as an element in letting the distinction come forward. And if we only carry over someone else's words when we pretend to distinguish but do not really understand what we say, we do not have a genuine distinction at all; it is not the case that we have a genuine distinction that is false because it does not match a state of affairs. There is no way of getting around distinctions to have the things distinguished, apart from making the distinction itself.

6

In discussing distinctions we have not so far said much about the persons who make the distinctions, the datives to whom the distinctions appear. We have proceeded as if the agent of distinctions were more or less an uninvolved spectator, someone who clearly possessed his own self and, as a kind of supplement, managed to make or failed to make appropriate distinctions. But the articulation of the self is a factor in the making of distinctions. We become capable of making distinctions in things because of distinctions that take place in regard to our selves; and we can accept those distinctions that give the sense of the self only because distinctions generally can occur in and for us.

We begin everything by assimilation; not only the absorption of new kinds of objects, which are first brought in for us associatively as like the things we are already familiar with, but also the development of our own styles of behavior and the determination of who and what we are. We achieve self-identification, and correlatively self-differentiation from others, at all stages of life, early and late. For example, if someone falls into a state of emotional distress and, in a rather sustained way, loses his nerve, one way of being helped is to associate with someone else: to be with and to act with someone whose patterns of behavior he can assimilate. Sometimes people pick up mannerisms in such association, but more profoundly they pick up a more confident or more relaxed or more optimistic pattern of behavior. They handle issues imitatively at first, then gradually handle them more and more on their own. They do not become duplicates of those they imitate, but threads and patterns of what they imitate do become woven into their own way of doing things: "We cannot be taught self-esteem; we absorb it. Similarly, conscious learning plays no part in the acquisition of defense mechanisms; rather the response of people outside of us—not just events—shapes our modes of adaptation. A great violinist's style owes as much to his incorporation of dedicated and gifted teachers as it does to his own innate talents and idiosyncrasies or to his rote learning of notes and scales."[12] We can only identify with others by being around them and by acting with them. Assimilation happens, it is not deliberate; it is like getting warm. We can put ourselves in a position where it may happen, but we cannot choose the assimilation itself. We have to let it occur. And sooner or later conflicts must arise, as the associative and imitative pull is stronger, along one direction or another, than we are able to absorb or than we want to absorb. Amid the assimilation, the urge to distinguish asserts itself, and this urgence is concerned not with objects we deal with but with our own selves.

This assimilation and distinction is always going on. In the very early years of life it occurs in a massive way in regard to fundamental issues: eating, laughing and crying, smiling, becoming angry, undergoing loss and recovery, movement, babbling and initial speech, and the like. The patterns we pick up then underlie all subsequent assimilations and are preceded by practically no prior assimilated behavior. But then of course distinctions have to be made in this associative matrix, and they are the early adjustments we make as we come to know "I am not you" and "We are not that" and "Mine is not thine." The child does not formulate these distinctions, he knows them in their urgent form. Even when we state them now, we realize that the verbal formulation is as nothing compared to the concrete difference that underlies the abstract distinction; and yet the concrete difference has its force precisely because it urges toward distinction. As we grow older, all the identities the self achieves through the stages of life are simply the other side of differentiations it accomplishes within assimilations it has been undergoing.[13]

Not all assimilation is profound. There are light touches of style and gesture that we get from acquaintances, from the way people generally do things, and from prominent figures. And when we are said to assimilate the behavior of others, we do not merely imitate but also react on our own to a tone and pattern they set, and then we see how they react to our reaction. In this give and take we internalize other people.[14] But the time always comes when we have to differentiate ourselves from what we assimilate; what we differentiate as ourselves contains, in turn, what we differentiated earlier in other assimilative matrices, and the style of earlier distinctions persists in modifying the tone of those we are making now.

We must have made some of these self-differentiations in order to "be there" at all to make distinctions about things other than ourselves. The distinction-making process establishes us as makers of distinctions. But we can never eliminate the obscure matrix that stands at our back: it can be hard for some to distinguish themselves even from rather superficial assimilations like those of style of dress or passing mannerisms, but it is impossible to unravel completely the matting at the base of what we are; those "parts" are not distinguishable. And it must be noted that the very power to let distinctions and identifications come about, in ourselves and in things we encounter, is not picked up as a pattern from others. It is ours by nature; it lets us pick up patterns and differentiate within them, it is not one of the patterns we absorb.

A central role in bringing about the self-differentiations that are possible and necessary for us is played by the imagination. As Husserl and others have stressed, the imagination is not a power of examining internal images; it is a possibility of displacement, of *Versetzung*, which helps actualize the self.[15] In imagination we become distinguished into an imagined self and an imagining self; we imagine ourselves doing something, even if the activity is something so contemplative as perceiving a scene of some sort. We appreciate ourselves (as imagined) at some distance to ourselves (as imagining), and "the self" is that which is the same in both dimensions, the imagining and the imagined. The same structural displacement occurs in memory, except that repetition instead of projection dominates. We continually mix memory and desire, of course, as recollection blends with imagination, but the same displacement remains through both. This displacement of the self is itself a distinction and an achievement; there are early stages in life in which the distinction "Fantasy is not reality" has not yet come about for us, and there may be periods, like the times of dreams and of emotional illness, in which the distinction is overcome.

Because of its projective character, imagination is especially significant for differentiating the self from patterns it has imitatively assimilated. While we are in one condition and while we carry on one behavior, we can imagine ourselves in another. This occurs in simple daydreams, but it also occurs when we are trying to determine "a way out," a way of being and acting that resolves something painful and confusing. Such confusions occur only in the concrete, and only the imagination of a concrete possibility can resolve them: and such an imagination is precisely what we have called the urgence of a distinction. If for example we are in the vicious double bind in which fondness is enjoined but made impossible, and if we are accused—or accuse ourselves—of cruelty or of indifference, the only resolution is to have the power to imagine a behavior, always in the concrete, which we could call something like kindness or concern, something distinguished from cruelty and from indifference, without yet being fondness, and to perform this behavior. We might be able to formulate the distinction in words, "Kindness is not fondness," or "Concern is not fondness," but the formulation is not very important; what is important is the imaginative urgence that breaks the bind and releases the difference; without the concrete imagination the verbal distinction is hollow. Because the concrete circumstances and the concrete possibilities of action are so complex, we might be able to imagine and execute an action which fits under no standard category: not fondness, but something between kindness and concern with perhaps a touch of a reprimand—but certainly not cruelty and not indifference. We need to be insightful, prudent, and virtuous to be able to imagine what we can and ought to do in the complexities of actual situations that call for action, and if we succeed it will be obvious to anyone who appreciates what is going on that what we did was the right thing to do, whether or not the right term can be found to name what we did.

The imaginative projection of an action works not only in private, personal relationships but also in how we solve problems and how we change things and institutions. We may imagine a new development in livestock or in plants and proceed to breed it, we may realize that a public institution should be adjusted along certain lines to respond better to its present situation, or we may figure out how to handle a sudden change in the things we deal with ("The ship is sinking; what shall we do?"). If we think at all in such circumstances, if we do not just respond automatically, we engage our imagination, and it must be an imagination in touch with the things as they actually exist.[16] We carry out an imaginative projection in which the thing we are dealing with can remain itself in a new condition. Some people fail in such challenges because they are too inflexible and have no imagination; they can do things only the way they have always been done, and circumstances may now make such performance impossible. Because of a failure to distinguish, the thing is destroyed. Other people fail because their imaginations run wild; anyone can imagine different ways of doing things, but it takes insight to imagine the different ways that will preserve the identity of what is at issue. It is a matter of making the strategic distinction that preserves the genus by letting it continue to be under the form of one of its species, when its existence under the form of the other species is threatened.[17]

7

The uses of imagination that we have just surveyed deal with the projection of behavior and with bringing about changes. There is another use of imagination that deals with things that we cannot change, things in regard to which a projection of possible new behavior makes no sense. We can use the imagination to bring out identities and distinctions that belong to what Husserl calls the *eidos* or the pure essence of things. Husserl calls this usage *free variation*.[18] In it we do not limit ourselves to what we have actually experienced or even to what we can possibly experience; we are to imagine all sorts of changes that can occur only in fantasy, and we are to see whether these imaginative projections do or do not leave intact the kind of thing we are dealing with. If our imaginative variation causes the thing to shatter—when we try to project a material body without the possibility of exercising or undergoing causation, for example—we know we have removed an element that belongs to the *eidos* of the thing; if not, we have removed something that is not eidetically necessary. Our imaginative variation is supposed to yield eidetic intuitions.

Imaginative variation and eidetic intuition are related to making distinctions. They make up a process that is far more complex and mysterious than Husserl's rather summary descriptions of it would suggest. It is a process, furthermore, that is carried on by all writers when they perform what we call *thought experiments* in order to bring out what one would call *conceptual necessities* if one were more or less nominalistic in taste, or *essential necessities* if one were a realist. What eidetic intuitions do is to bring out distinctions in all their necessity, and to bring out, consequently, the identities that are the other side of distinctions.

To get a sense of how imaginative variation and eidetic intuition work, we may examine Yves Simon's analysis of authority.[19] Simon asks whether authority can "be" if there are no people who have to be ruled for their own good, such as the vicious and the deficient. He says authority is often equated with substitutional authority, and it is said that if everyone were mature and decent, authority could be dispensed with. Simon then imagines a society made up of mature and virtuous people, and shows that there would still be a need for authority to determine how that society should act when it acts as a whole. He develops the notion of the common good, the relationship of means to end, the necessity that there will be difference of opinion regarding the means, and the necessity that there will be some strain between the common good and private goods even in a society made up of ideally perfect people.

In pursuing his argument, Simon shows that the generic matrix, authority, is confused with one of its species, substitutional authority, and hence is not allowed to be itself. His resolution is to show that *substitutional* authority is only one species of authority and that it is not equivalent to the whole; and he does this by making the distinction between substitutional and what he calls *essential* authority, the kind or species that would be around even in a society of ideally perfect people. Simon makes this distinction by imagining something that can never, empirically, be found, a society of perfectly intelligent and virtuous people. And although his topic, authority, is related to human action, his use of imagination is not a projection of possible action. It is purely disclosive and contemplative, not practical. He wants to bring out the borders, the definition, of a concept or a nature. We cannot *do* anything about the fact that there are essential and substitutional forms of authority, that authority "is" under both these species. It is important for us to know this distinction so that we can live in the real world, avoid confusion, and escape all the binds that confusion brings; but nothing we can do will change the truth that authority can be both substitutional and essential. To think that we can change the nature of authority because we can imagine a society of ideally perfect human beings would be to confuse the practical with the theoretical use of imagination. The theoretical imagination is restrained only by conceivability, whereas the practical imagination has to be restrained by many contingencies.

The two uses of imagination also differ in that the theoretical must reach an explicit verbal formulation of the distinction, whereas the practical can rest in the concrete urgence. In action the important thing is to determine what ought to be done, and finding the right words to describe exactly what we are doing, when it is possible at all, is more an adornment than a necessity. But in theoretical distinctions the formulation is everything. Until we find the words to state the distinctions, we have not achieved what we are after; an inkling of a distinction is not enough.

Husserl describes imaginative variation as though we simply let our imaginations wander freely, but it is much more a directed exercise than that. We sense a confusion within a particular genus, and we want to lance it; we sense the obscurity as obscurity and want to dispel it. The genus is sensed as obscure and as ripe for a distinction, it begins to come forward as a genus or an origin, when it seems to be pushed and pulled in two directions at once: it is somehow both affirmed and rejected.[20] Authority, for example, is said to belong only when there are imperfect persons, but then it does not seem right to constrict it in this way. It does

not matter where this pushing and pulling comes from: from
conflicting opinions, from opinions of others and our own experience, from different experiences we have had, from musing on
what we have perceived. When we sense this urgence we put our
imagination to work (the random wandering of the imagination
does not generate the urgence). We try to imagine what would
happen if the genus were equated with this particular form, if
authority were only substitutional: we make the equation explicit
and try to determine what would then be excluded as impossible. We find that some things get excluded that we know must
belong to the genus, for example that common action for the
common good would be excluded; and we see that this remainder has to be collected into another species of authority, another
species from which what we now call substitutional authority is
to be distinguished.

We have to appeal to the imagination, not to perception, in
this process because we try to project something that cannot
exist: authority as being *only* substitutional. We must have the
insight that this cannot be, that authority must also be able to
be what Simon calls "essential," and that therefore we must be
able to say "Substitutional authority is not essential authority"
and "Authority is not necessarily substitutional authority" (or, in
the other cases, "Ignorance is not negligence," and "Counseling
is not commandment"). Only imagination can bring this play of
negations to light, because it is the power to project beyond what
we have experienced, and also the power to remain with concrete
cases, with the lived obscurity of something that calls for a distinction. This imaginative dimension operates on the margin when
we make distinctions in the midst of lived experiences, when for
example Jack realizes, while dealing with his physician, that medical data is not medical care. Jack realizes that this distinction
is not just a matter of fact that he has not attended to, but a
distinction that he could not imagine being otherwise.

The imagination gives us flexibility in both acting and thinking. We are not locked into what we have been and what we have
experienced, but are able to test borders and in some cases move
beyond them. In other cases, however, our projection rebounds
and we find that what we, confusedly, might have thought to be
possible is in fact impossible: authority, for example, cannot be

equated with substitutional authority, and it cannot be eliminated from human affairs. To exercise our imagination in such free variation, we must have achieved the distinction between ourselves as imagining and ourselves as imagined. The flexibility we need to disclose eidetic necessities and to bring essentials to light depends on a flexibility and distance that we must have in regard to ourselves. The imagination displaces the self into the conversationalists that carry on the discourse of the soul with itself that Plato calls *thinking* (*Theaetetus* 189E–190A, *Sophist* 263E–264A).[21]

We have used Yves Simon's remarks about authority as a concrete example of making distinctions, but other examples can be found everywhere in philosophical writing. Saul Kripke imagines a situation in which the things we call *cats* are really demons; Peter Strawson tries to imagine a world without space and without material bodies but with reidentifiable particulars; Gilbert Ryle imagines a doll actually smiling at a little girl, and imagines imagination as the internal viewing of picture-phantasms; Richard Rorty imagines "the possibility that the trees and the bats and the butterflies and the stars all have their various untranslatable languages in which they are busily expressing their beliefs and desires to one another"; Hannah Arendt imagines a society in which there can be no forgiveness; Plato imagines a community in which no one knows who his parents and relatives are; Aristotle imagines tools that accomplish their work by themselves.[22] Such things are imagined to show that they are really unimaginable and impossible, that they involve the confusion of a genus with one of its species, and hence the confusion of one species with another; and they are imagined in order to bring out the crucial distinction that dissipates the confusion. The imagination is used to disclose how things have to be.[23]

When we make the distinction that prevents the assimilation of a genus into only one of its species, we set up the opposition between the two species ("Essential authority is not substitutional authority"). The two opposite, distinguished species then serve as the parameters for cases that fall between them. Most of the cases we experience will be intermediate and will involve elements from both extremes; hence the determination of the two species in their pure opposition will seem to be a move into an abstract unreality. But the empirical instance could not be recognized in its intermediate and ambiguous state if the pure extremes were not articulated and if the distinction between them were not made.

8

The process of making distinctions is discussed by Aristotle in a polemic against some thinkers, presumably Plato and the Platonists, who thought that the division of kinds was able to prove, somehow, the definitions of things (*Prior Analytics* 1.31). Aristotle concedes that the process of division can help us formulate a definition; it helps us organize the various attributes of a thing and it helps us be sure that we have not omitted any features (*Posterior Analytics* 2.13.96b25–97a6). But, he insists, a division of kinds is not a syllogism, not a coming-together of several assertions that establish a conclusion: "But still [division] is not a syllogism, but if it makes us know, it does so through another way" (*Posterior Analytics* 2.5.91b32–34). The point of Aristotle's remarks is that a distinction does not serve to prove anything beyond itself, but there is another implication to what he says: if a distinction of kinds is not a syllogism, the distinction itself is not the conclusion of a syllogism; that is, the distinction cannot be established by statements beyond itself. A distinction is immediate and shows its necessity on its face; it is not proved by any assertion apart from itself.

Aristotle also speaks about a form of immediate knowing in *Metaphysics* 9.10, where he describes knowledge that does not involve the composition of subject and attribute. Such knowing, he says, is more like touching something, and the objects it knows or touches are also incomposite (*asuntheta*, 1051b17–25). Commentators disagree as to what these incomposites can be, but it is possible to interpret them as the terms that emerge when a distinction is made. Each term in a distinction is taken simply, even though it may be found, when we examine it further, to be composed. At the point of distinction, *inside* is seen to be simple in its opposition to *outside*, for example, and *bard* is seen as simple in contrast to *prophet*. Aristotle brings us to focus on one of the terms, like *inside* or *bard*, he observes that this "grasp" of a simple term is uncomposed, and he says that the thing grasped is uncomposed too. But he neglects to bring out the process of distinguishing that lets each term come forward in its simplicity.[24] Aristotle adds that this sort of "touching" knowledge involves a special notion of truth and falsity (1051b22–23). Unlike predications, which must conform to things if they are to be true, the grasp of simples either occurs or it does not occur; there is no way for it to fail to conform to something. In the formulations we have used earlier in this essay, a distinction is true not by matching a pair of terms beyond itself, but by being a genuine distinction. *Truth* in the case of distinctions is like the truth of "true gold" or "true friendship," not like that of a true statement; it is truth in the sense of being genuine, not truth in the sense of correspondence. Aristotle also says that ignorance in regard to such simple things is not total blindness; it is not the total deprivation of the power to think (1052a3). In our formulation, this would mean that a failure to achieve a distinction and to identify one of its terms is not total unfamiliarity with the thing we want to "touch," but the vague, associative awareness that does not succeed in achieving a contrastive insight. If we interpret Aristotle's remarks on the grasp of simple things this way, as related to the making of distinctions, we can avoid making him postulate a mysterious, unstructured, atomic intuition at the basis of our knowledge.

Plato's most extensive treatment of division occurs in the *Sophist*. He rehearses the process of dividing when he tries to show what an angler is, then he uses the process in trying to pin down the nature of the sophist. Plato's procedure looks like a simple cascade of divisions: we begin with a very "high" distinction, like "man with an art" versus "man without an art" (*technitēs* versus *atechnos*, 219A). The distinction, presumably, comes out of the genus *man*, although Plato does not make this explicit. The first distinction then gives way to succeeding distinctions, as one of the terms distinguished becomes, in its turn, a generic matrix for another division of kinds: the art possessed by a man, for example, becomes the genus for the distinction into productive and acquisitive arts. Distinctions occur within what other distinctions have brought forward.

However, this procedure is not merely the unrolling of one distinction after another, because the process begins with a target.

We begin by looking for, and looking at, the angler. When we establish "man with an art" as a very remote matrix, we select this matrix because it is clear to us that the angler stands inside it. We have a genus, but we also have a "this" within the genus. The genus is a genus only because it stands behind and surrounds the target we are after. And then it does what every genus ought to do, if it is true to its etymological sense of giving birth: it gives rise to distinctions within itself, distinctions which narrow the space around the target until no further narrowing is necessary; that is, until the target has been effectively distinguished from that which is its proper and specific other. When we have come to that critical distinction, we know what the target is. We have defined it.

Plato's example of the angler does not work in the same way as the examples we have been using in this essay to illustrate the process of making distinctions. The angler is already identified or targeted as a kind. The Stranger and Theaetetus in the *Sophist* are not talking about something obscure which is immediately confronting them when they speak about the angler; they begin with a kind of thing that they merely talk about in its absence, not with something that is intruding on them, puzzling them, and concealing from them what kind of thing it is. They know they want to define the angler, and their problem is to go from the remote genus to the definite kind that they wish to determine. But in the examples we have been using, we begin with an obscure issue that needs to be identified in its kind. We begin with something that vexes because it is obscure and because its kind is undetermined; we begin with something we can merely indicate as "this." It is true that in our examples a genus arises behind the "this," but the target itself is not determined in its kind. We begin, for example, with "medical activity" in general for what Jack is doing, but we do not, at the start, have anything like "the angler" to name specifically what Jack does. "Medical data" and "medical care" have to emerge as the final kinds appropriate to what Jack is doing; it would be as though the Stranger and Theaetetus were watching someone fish and one of them were to say, "Angling is not spearing," or, working on an issue higher up the scale, "Catching something is certainly different from having to make something." There is a target in the examples we have been using in this essay, but the target is something we can only indicate; we cannot yet classify it.

Furthermore, we have emphasized the strategic role of a single crucial distinction rather than the orderly arrangement of a series of distinctions. We have tried to describe the dawning of a distinction, the event that occurs over and over again in Plato's descending sequence as the Stranger leads Theaetetus to glimpse one distinction after another until the target is reached. Plato is concerned with the ordering and we have been concerned with the event that yields items to be ordered. There is something academic about Plato's procedure; it is the thoughtful arrangement of things discussed in their absence, when they do not urge themselves on us. It is as though one wanted to make arrangements to handle obscurities in advance. But if we look to the perplexing situations in which a distinction urgently needs to be made, we find we need the single critical division that resolves the issue ("Kindness is not fondness"), not the cascade of divisions that discloses more relationships than we at the moment want. The cascade of divisions does however remind us that any distinction is nested inside many other distinctions, and that any one resolution of an issue can give way to perplexity on another level.

Plato does get inside the event of a distinction when he introduces the theme of the greatest or highest kinds: being, sameness and otherness, and rest and motion (254C–255C). Things are distinguishable from other things because sameness and otherness are at work in them; a thing is what it is by being other than some specific other things. Being, sameness and otherness, and rest and motion are not the greatest kinds in the sense of being the supreme matrices, the highest genera, out of which all distinctions descend; they work immediately in everything because any thing can be distinguished from other things, and any thing "is" by being so distinguishable. And when Plato examines rest and motion, he discusses them not in terms of sheer matter, but in terms of the rests and motions of knowing and being known, the work of the mind, the work which occurs most vividly in the division of kinds (248D–249C).

We also find in Husserl an interesting use of the process of making distinctions. In his earliest published work, *The Philosophy of Arithmetic,* Husserl mentions that there are simple concepts that cannot be defined: "One can define only that which is logically composite. Once we run up against the final, elementary concepts, all defining comes to an end. No one can define concepts like quality, intensity, place, time, and the like."[25] What are we to do if we want to clarify such concepts? "One can only show the concrete phenomena from which they are abstracted, and make clear the form of this process of abstraction." All this is a simple appeal to intuition. But Husserl goes on to add something else we might do: "When it appears necessary, one can sharply delimit (*umgrenzen*) the related concepts and so avoid confusing them with concepts that are akin to them." This final possibility of working out distinctions seems like an afterthought to the more central activity of showing the phenomena from which a concept is abstracted, but it is not a harmless supplement. It is the other side of clarifying what is presented. Husserl does not introduce this theme of distinctions with much fanfare, and he probably always thought of it as somewhat secondary, but it always tags along as part of the philosophical enterprise that he proposes. In *Ideas 1*, for instance, when he formulates his "principle of all principles," he asserts that he will just accept what is presented directly in intuitions, but he then adds, "but only within the limits (*Schranken*) in which it presents itself."[26] He frequently says that part of his philosophical task is to eliminate equivocations and to distinguish overlapping concepts: in *Ideas 1* §66 he says he will fix the meanings of the words he uses by bringing them to the things they are supposed to name, but also by canceling out ambiguities that are attached to such words, that is, by making distinctions; and in *Formal and Transcendental Logic* he often mentions that he must avoid equivocations and the confusions brought about by "associational overlappings."[27] In fact *Formal and Transcendental Logic*, Husserl's most elegant work, is really a book of distinctions, distinctions made in an almost musical dependence on one another. In Husserl's writings, making philosophical distinctions is not something extra added to the phenomenon to be analyzed, but an intrinsic element in the process of bringing the phenomenon forward; how, for example, can the transcendental ego be made plain except by being distinguished from the psychological self? The distinction does not follow an identification, it helps achieve it.

Philosophy itself, no matter by whom it is carried on, is established as an enterprise only when a crucial distinction is made, a distinction that has been variously named as the difference between the psychological and the transcendental ego, or that between *Seiendes* and *Sein*, or that between being and being as being. So long as this distinction does not function, philosophy remains confused with psychology or myth or natural science or ideology.

If philosophy thinks about differentiation and distinction, and if it is itself established by a special kind of distinction, it must be supplemented by a further kind of thinking that takes up the oneness and the dyadic divergence that permit distinctions to occur.[28] Distinctions exemplify sameness and otherness and rest and motion, so the thinking that tries to get inside, under, and beyond distinctions must qualify the normal inclusions and exclusions that occur in our speech, and it must cautiously slip toward its topic rather than try to approach it frontally.

4
Explaining

The theme of this essay is the difference between the simple and the complex in speech and in disclosure. I claim that the task of philosophy is not to get at the simple but to illuminate the simple and the complex in their relation to one another, and thus to bring out what it is to be simple and what it is to be complex.

1

There is a difference between simply naming something and articulating it in some way. It is one thing just to say "illness," and another to say "Illness is a burden," "An illness is not as bad as a moral collapse," or some of the many other things we say when we speak about illnesses. The name just presents the thing all at once, the articulation brings out something definite in or about it.

Furthermore, names are a part of articulations, whereas articulations do not seem to be part of names: *Illness* is part of "Illness is a burden," but *Illness is a burden* does not seem to be part of "illness." Names therefore seem more elementary than predications, relations, and other forms of assertion. It might also seem

93

that what is named is more elementary than what is achieved in articulation: that, for example, illness as a simple thing is more elementary than illness's being a burden.

Since this seems to be the case, we might be tempted to look for the most elementary names of all, and to look for the most elementary nameable things. We might be tempted to try to find atomic names and atomic things. If we could find such names and things, we could, it seems, get a kind of control over all the articulations that can be made with and upon them. We would have some sort of key to something.

But this expectation is misguided. It presupposes that names and the nameable have a priority in being over articulations and the articulated, and that we can get to what is prior just as we can get to the bricks out of which a house is made. But in fact names and articulations are equally primary. There are names only because there are articulations, and there are articulations only because there are names. Furthermore, there are simple nameables only because there are articulated patterns, and there are articulated wholes only because there are things that can be simply named. The things that *are* move back and forth between being simple and being articulated; being is not to be identified just with the simple. The philosophical task is not to show how articulations can be melted down into names and the named; the philosophical task is not to get down to some sort of element or base: the philosophical task is to think both names and articulations in their reciprocities; the philosophical task is to think them in their distinctions from one another, because they *are* only in these distinctions.

If there is a difference between names and articulations, there is another difference between asserting something and explaining what we have asserted. Correlatively, there is a similar difference between what is stated (a state of affairs) and what explains a state of affairs (its causes).

In the case of assertions and explanations, we deal entirely with articulations. We go from one statement to another, from one state of affairs to another. We go from a fact to its explanation. There is no temptation to melt the articulation down into its elementary names and their elementary nameable things. But there is another kind of reduction we may be tempted to make.

We may be inclined to want to reduce all statements into two kinds of ultimate, atomic propositions: (1) to statements that are atomic because they merely register or report an immediately experienced simple fact; and (2) to statements that are atomic because they are self-evident and true by virtue of the terms used in them. We will call the first group *protocol statements* and the second group *self-evident statements*. Protocol and self-evident statements together seem to be the rock-bottom basis for argumentation, just as simple names seem to be the rock-bottom basis for assertions.

And once again, over on the side of things as opposed to the side of argumentation, we might be inclined to reduce all states of affairs to two kinds of ultimate, atomic arrangements: (1) to simple factual arrangements, and (2) to essential relationships that hold, necessarily, among various kinds and features of things.

We might then be inclined to think that the task of philosophy is to find out which statements are protocol statements and which are self-evident; or at least that philosophy should provide a technique or a criterion for identifying such statements. It seems that if it could do this, philosophy would provide us with a way of controlling argumentation and making it work well. Philosophy would also provide us, it might seem, with a more secure access to what is real: to the plain facts presented in protocol statements and to the ultimate, essential relationships disclosed by self-evident statements, the relationships that provide the unquestionable context for particular facts and individual experiences.

But once again, the task of philosophy is not to work its way to such ultimate building blocks, but to think assertion and explanation in their reciprocities: to think both what is the case and the reasons why things are as they are; and to think these two in their distinction from one another, since both facts and causes *are*, as such, only by being distinguished from one another. The philosophical task is to clarify a fact as a fact, a cause as cause, and an assertion as such, an explanation as such. This philosophical task can be accomplished only by positioning a fact against its causes and the causes against what they explain; and by positioning an assertion against its explanation and the explanation against what it explains.

We have distinguished the following elements:

1. atomic names and basic statements;
2. atomic objects (nameables) and basic states of affairs.

Within the level of articulations, we have distinguished:

3. protocol statements and explanations (at the extreme, self-evident explanations);
4. plain, protocol facts and causal states of affairs (at the extreme, self-evident or essential causes).

And we claim that philosophy should not be drawn off into the artificial abstraction of atomic names and atomic statements, or atomic objects and atomic states of affairs; that philosophy also should not be drawn off into the artificial abstraction of protocol statements and self-evident statements, or simple facts and ultimate explanations. Instead, philosophy is to recover and clarify the concrete activity of thinking and disclosing, an activity in which names, assertions, and explanations, as well as things, states of affairs, and causes, all play a part, and in which no one of these could subsist without the others.

2

In order to be as concrete as possible, let us work with the larger whole. Instead of beginning with the relationship between names and assertions, let us work with argumentation or discourse and examine first the difference between assertion and explanation.

In the simplest type of speech, one statement of fact just follows another in a continuous display, the speaker leading and the interlocutor following or joining in: "He got very angry then." "And what did she do?" "She left the room. He went to the telephone and called his office." It may be necessary to repeat a statement if the speaker wants to emphasize something or if he has not been heard correctly, but such repetition is not an explanation of what he wanted to say; it is just a pause in the concatenating display.

But sometimes it is necessary to explain. What was said arrests the conversation in a new way. We no longer simply concatenate, and the speech does not simply pause to repeat; what was said becomes not just said again, but said as a target. Instead of moving on to say more about yesterday's meeting, the conversation becomes riveted on something that was said about yesterday's meeting: the "that" becomes an occasion for a "why?" This "that" is not left behind as we go on to others: it becomes what we ask about, what we delve into, what we are called upon to explain. One statement, one fact, becomes highlighted, identified as questionable, arresting as an issue.

When such an arrest occurs, there are two different ways in which the target can be explained. In one, the truth of an articulation is established by saying something other than what was said in the questionable statements: "Why did she get angry at that moment?" "For several days before, she had felt offended by what they were doing; this was the last straw." This outburst of anger is explained by all those other irritations. But in the second way of explaining, a fact is explained by bringing out more fully what the fact itself is, so that the questionability of the fact evaporates. This is not merely to repeat the fact, but to bring out more clearly what it is: "Why did she get angry when she was being mocked?" "Well, she was being humiliated, and before her friends and family. People get angry when that happens. That's what anger is. Don't you see that?"

This second form of explanation, bringing out more fully what the thing is, is an appeal to self-evidencing. It does not explain through an other but through the same. However it *is* an explanation; something more has to be said, even though the more is not other. It does not just repeat what was said before; rather it turns what was said before—"She got angry when Steve mocked her"—into a theme to be dwelt upon and thus explained.

When we explain something by giving a cause that is other to the fact to be explained, it is obvious that we are doing more than we did when we stated the fact. The otherness makes the more to be palpable. When we explain by appealing to self-evidences, however, it might appear that we are not explaining, not doing anything more, but only repeating what had been said. Indeed, in silly answers this may be the case ("Why did the Redskins play fewer games in 1969 than they did this year?" "Because the season was shorter then"). But not all "redundant" answers are trivial;

there are times when it is necessary to bring out more fully what is there before us, to bring it out in its own necessities and on its own terms in such a way that those who do not comprehend may be helped to comprehend.

Such clarification is more situated, more rhetorical, more tailored to an audience than is the explanation through a cause other than what is explained, a cause which is more independent of the circumstances of the speech ("The plant has turned toward the left because the source of light lies in that direction"). However, the appeal to an external cause, although it seems more objective, is really derivative; it presupposes the explanations in which what is going on is displayed on its own terms for what it is in itself. And although situated, such a clarification through self-evidencing is still objective. It brings out what the thing or the fact truly is, not merely how it happens to seem to someone.

The point is that things and facts very often have to be brought out for what they are in themselves. It is not the case that the only causes we are ignorant of are the hidden causes, those not already visible in what is being questioned. When we look for a cause that is other to what we want to explain, we usually know that we are ignorant and that we should inquire. But often the very thing before us is not present in the way it should be; it may be only vaguely presented and its internal, axiomatic necessities, those that should show up on its face, may be obscured. Such ignorance is often called a failure in the conceptual understanding of what is going on; often it issues in the vague, inauthentic use of words that are merely associated with the phenomenon and do not name or register it. How we can *not* know what is plain to see is a perplexing philosophical issue.

And so sometimes a question that we ask is a call, not for more other information, but for a clearer view of what is already there. Such questions into self-evidences can be of two kinds. In some cases they are real calls for help. The questioner does not understand what is going on and needs a clarification. His inability to understand may be formulated as a request for an external cause of what is happening, but in fact there is no external explanation for what he wants. There is only a more vivid and precise display of the occurrence. In other cases the questioner is not at a loss, but simply contemplates questioningly. He does not ask the reason why humiliated people become angry, but contemplates and hence questions anger as the response to insult. He is involved in a different kind of questioning: not a helpless kind, but one well in control. Knowing what anger is, he sets out as both questioner and respondent to bring out what it is ever more completely. He probes the axioms of anger.

But let us stay for a while with the case of the questioner who needs help to understand what is going on. Even here there are two ways in which the questioner can be answered.

In one case the respondent will know that anyone who understood what is going on would not ask a question like that. The questioner shows that he thinks there are two distinct things here—the insult *and* the anger—whereas there really is only one: insult/anger go together as one, not as a two whose being together needs a cause. The intelligibility and the unity of the reply come out of the necessities of the thing itself. The questioner is ignorant of the unity in what to him seems like two things, and the respondent's task is to bring this unity out.[1]

In another case, the source of the fact is not the thing itself but some agreement or convention made by someone. The fact itself is the kind of thing that comes to be by agreement. "Why did he stop running after he crossed home plate?" "That's what the rules are. There is nowhere else to go after you have crossed home plate." This response clarifies what is going on, and it does so by appealing to a kind of external cause, one that informs the procedure and makes it to be what it is (a crossing of home plate); but the fact is what it is not simply in and by itself (as anger, the roots and branches of a tree, the future, and heat all are), but because someone said it should be so.

This gives us two kinds of self-evidences: those that bring out the essence of a thing; and those that stipulate what a thing will be. The first kind lies in the nature of the things, the second lies in convention. Each, furthermore, has its own sort of ignorance. If I do not know why the football game has been stopped and the Raiders have been penalized fifteen yards, someone can simply tell me what the rules are and why they are being applied now. My informant may go on to explain why these rules make sense in the full context of the game, but ultimately he will have informed me that the rules have been decided in a certain way and that this is now happening as it is because of those rules. This activity is one of those rules in action, one of those conventions being applied.

But if I say I do not know why people who have been insulted feel resentment, or why we anticipate the future and remember and forget what is past, it makes no sense for my informant to appeal to a decision made by someone to explain why these things are so. I do not need an informant; I need someone to clarify things for me. I do not, furthermore, need someone to clarify just the meanings of words, because no one clarifies "merely" the meaning of words; one clarifies the things that are meant by the words. In this case one would clarify insult and resentment; or the future, the past, memory, and anticipation; or law and reason; or religion and politics; or whatever is especially questionable at the moment. Someone has to show me that these things just are and have to be the way they are and that we could not imagine them otherwise.

Conventions, rules, and decisions are somehow "inside" the activities that illustrate them: the Raiders' losing fifteen yards *is* the penalty for clipping. And yet the conventions, rules, and decisions have their original being somehow "outside" their illustrations and applications: their origin is the agreement that establishes them as rules. But the order of insult–resentment and the order of time do not originate anywhere else apart from this exchange and that remembering. The same ordering may occur in other instances, but it does not have an origin or a cause apart from its being in its instances. It was never chosen to be as it is; it does not exist by virtue of having been decided. Therefore there is nothing "else" or "other" to appeal to in explaining these forms and relationships. They are to be explained only by being more fully brought out.

Furthermore, we are not upset with someone who does not know why the game has been interrupted or why, say, this man is speaking for such a long time in the Senate ("He's carrying on a filibuster, which means . . . "). It is quite normal for people not to know such things: to see the bodily manifestation of the rule but not to know the rule itself. It does not diminish their humanity not to know this sort of thing. And the remedy is straightforward. It is simply to tell them what the rule is, and perhaps to tell why it was formulated as it was. But we do get upset with someone who says or shows he does not know the ordering of the natural kinds and necessary forms that are common and prominent in the life we live. He should know these things just by having grown up. And we are exasperated in searching for a remedy. If he does not know these things already, what can we appeal to in making them clear to him? There is nothing other to them that explains why they are as they are.

Sometimes stories are told that seem to try to explain why things are as they are. Such stories are legends, myths, and fables. We can, for example, imagine someone reciting a legend along these lines:

> Human beings at one time were so constituted that each lived entirely in the present, with no future and no past. Some were stronger than others, and the stronger asserted themselves by destroying the weaker when they came in contact with them. The weaker were simply annihilated, the stronger went on as though nothing had happened. The gods were distressed at this injustice, so they changed men into time-filled beings, in order to make them more equal to one another. At any moment a man would have lived through only part of his life and would have to wait for the rest. This change made men more subdued; no matter how strong an individual might be at a particular time, he could not tell how he would compare with others in the future and so was careful to make friends with others even while being the stronger, so that he would not have to fear others if he became weak. Furthermore, besides concealing the future from man the gods allowed him to remember his past, so that he would strive to be a friend to himself, since he had to live in the present with his past self. Thus time was given by the gods as a way of generating justice and friendship among human beings.

A story like this seems to try to explain a natural ordering—in this case, the form of time—as though it were the outcome of a decision. It seems to try to treat a natural kind as though it were a convention. But in fact such a story only appears to be an explanation through something other than what it strives to explain; in fact it has a much more contemplative purpose. It makes us think about time. We know that the events did not occur as the story says they did, but we still like to hear stories such as this. We like them precisely because we know they are not true, because we realize that they are telling us something distinct from what they explicitly state. We know the story is false; we also know that any other story like it would be false; and therefore we come to appreciate that the things being discussed just are in their relationships: nothing has made them to be the way they are, and nothing could explain them except the shape or form that they have themselves. By the recognized falsity of the story, we are thrown back on the things themselves, on time or wrath, forgiveness or generosity, war or death, in their internal ordering. The stories help us sense the self-evidencing, as such, of the things themselves.

3

Let us look back at the various forms of explanation we have discussed. We have distinguished:

1. Explanations through an other, through a cause that is external to that which is to be explained: "This car was crushed by that explosion."
2. Explanations through a decision, rule, or convention: "He left the plate and stopped batting because he had three strikes, and when you have three strikes, you're out." Such explanations work through an other, through an agreement distinct from what is going on here and now, but this cause is both external and internal to the fact being explained, since the rule, although formulated by others at another time, constitutes the fact and makes it to be what it is.
3. Explanations through the same as what is to be explained, not through an other; explanations done by clarifying the internal ordering of the explicandum itself: "Insult provokes resentment; that is the way it is." This kind can be subdivided:
   a. clarifications made for someone who does not grasp the internal ordering of the thing;
   b. clarifications made out of contemplative enjoyment of the ordering itself.

4. Explanations through legend, myth, fable, and stories, which seem to go outside the thing in explaining it and seem to appeal to a decision or convention that establishes the thing as it is, but which really amount to a contemplative enjoyment of the thing itself as an issue or as a perplexity.

The third kind of explanation, the most elusive and problematic of the four, suffers from neglect in our current cultural and philosophical climate. This sort of explanation presumes that something like *natural kinds* exist, that there is something like an internal ordering or a definition or form in things, something that makes a thing to be and to show up as it is. This sort of explanation works within what was once called the formal cause. But the ruling opinion in our time resists acknowledging a form or nature in things, and for at least three reasons.

First, the explanations that have been so successful in the natural sciences, in biology, chemistry, and physics, make us inclined to explain things in terms of the elements and forces that make them up. The "definition" of an animal or a plant or even a human mental activity, such as perception or recognition, would generally be held to designate only an apparent unity and ordering, only an epiphenomenon. The "truth" of the thing in question, we are inclined to say, is the sum of "its" gravitational, subatomic, electromagnetic, neurological, and other elements and forces. Natural kinds seem to be dissolved into the stuff or particles of which they are made.

Second, we generally turn to evolutionary and historicist explanations for the current appearance of things. We tend to see the forms of living things as the outcome of evolutionary pressures, opportunities, and accidents; we tend to see human forms as the provisional outcome of the historical process; and we may see everything as the current state of an evolving universe. Once again, natural kinds dissolve, this time into temporary organizations that are to be explained by what went before them, as well as by what they are made of, but not in terms of what they themselves are.

Third, another reason why we are inclined to dismiss natural kinds is that they would impede the control we think we can and should have over nature and its processes. Natural kinds and essential necessities would get in the way of the enterprise of mastering nature. If things are thought to be reducible to their elements, and if they are considered to be the outcome of the evolutionary process, we feel free to rearrange their elements in some other way. Our arrangment would be no less natural than the one that has evolved apart from our intervention, by chance, and the new arrangement will probably prove to be more useful for our purposes than the one that nature gave us. And in our enterprise of mastering nature, we hope to be able to control not only the things outside us but even our own organisms and our neurological and mental life. We hope to do this by discovering the appropriate elements that make them up and the formulas that govern their combination.

The analysis we have presented in this essay runs, of course, counter to this prevailing opinion. We recognize a form in things. And we do not limit forms merely to organic and animal species; indeed, the plant and animal species may be the weakest examples of natural kinds, since they are relatively modest variations on the forms of *Plant* or *Animal* as such. But there are more definitive natural kinds and formal orderings to be found in such things as time, the future and the past, imagination, pictures, numbers, political society, poetry, choices, generosity, greed, and other things that can be named as one. It is true that what is named as one may in some cases turn out not to be one; it may turn out to be an accidental or coincidental unity, not a substantial one. In such cases no axioms or self-evident essentials will surface in the thing. The attempt to clarify what the thing is in itself will result in showing that the thing is not "one" in itself: but this discovery too is an achievement, and it may be of considerable importance if the thing in question is a factor in some major public controversy or policy. But the fact that some things that seem to be one do fall apart into many and exhibit no axiomatic necessity when they are analyzed does not mean that there are no substantial unities at all. Indeed, the possibility of recognizing something as only seeming to be one implies that we can tell the difference between a merely apparent and a true substantial unity.

And besides natural kinds, there are also things that are one by convention, such as a home run, a penalty for clipping, or a presidential inauguration, and things that are one by virtue of having been made, such as my car, the Air and Space Museum, Park Avenue, and the Chesapeake Bay Bridge. Such things are not accidental conglomerates; they each are one and not many, but they are one by virtue of an anticipation (there has to have been an idea of each of them before it could come to be). But they do have their axioms and their internal necessities, and they do reward our investigation by presenting a form to our curiosity, even though the form was first apprehended in someone's design, not in a thing.

If we are dealing with a true form, with a nameable something that yields self-evidences upon analysis, we should be able to say things about it that are necessarily true. We should be able to clarify the thing in itself. But the best example of such clarification is not necessarily the production of a few essential statements, such as "Resentment is the response to insult," or "The past can be relived in memory." Rather, the best example will lie in an extended discourse in which the essentials of the thing are both shown and stated, an extended discourse in which the gist of the thing can be recognized. Someone who denies there is anything essential in things would have to assert that there is really no difference between a scatterbrained, loose, associative account of a topic, and an account in which the thing is effectively presented. He would have to say there is no difference between a speech in which the speaker never gets to the point and one in which the point is clearly made. No one can really deny that such differences exist.

4

We have discussed the relation between statements and explanations, between facts and causes. Let us now turn back to the contrast between names and articulations, and between the named and the articulated. In both these pairs, each member is what it is only as positioned against the other. The object named is named only to be articulated, and the articulated is there only to be absorbed back into what is named. The named is latently articulated, the explicitly articulated relapses into the sense of what is named.

If I name an object ("Pennsylvania Avenue") I bring it into focus as the first step in unpacking it. I unpack it by saying of it something simply factual, or something proper, or something essential: "Pennsylvania Avenue is being resurfaced"; "Pennsylvania Avenue is *the* national avenue"; "Pennsylvania Avenue is a thoroughfare." In such statements what the predicate expresses is not merely attached to the Avenue; the predicate expresses the Avenue in one of its ways of being and being manifested. The object is and is presented in its features. And a thing is named in preparation for its being registered or reported as being or being manifested in its features. Naming prepares for articulation.

But an articulation is not stated continuously. As a statement it is episodic. Once it has been made, what has been articulated settles back into the object as part of the object's sense, part of the object's recognized way of being able to be manifested. Once I have registered that Pennsylvania Avenue is being resurfaced, I behave towards the Avenue in an appropriate way. I may avoid it for a few days, then I may drive on it with the expectation that the surface will be smoother than it was the last time I was on it. I may also say certain things about it that are implied by its being resurfaced. I have a lasting conviction that it is being, or has been, resurfaced, but this conviction is not simply an attribute of my own psyche and my own nervous system. It is the way Pennsylvania Avenue "seems" to me, whether as bodily present, or as remembered, imagined, or talked about in its absence. All the articulations are folded back into what is named; they may either be restated again, or they may serve as unstated premises for other articulations that depend on them. They become part of its recognized sense.

Furthermore, it is not just the features of the object that become folded into what is named when the object is named; the internal causes of those features' belonging to the object are also folded into it. "John insulted Helen and she shouted angrily at him": from that point on Helen will have been the one who answered John in a flash of anger, but she also will have been an instance of the link between insult and resentment. She will have illustrated the form, the internal ordering of anger as such, and we will be able to contemplate anger by thinking about what she did (as, on a much larger scale, Homer contemplated wrath by thinking about what Achilles did). Not only protocol statements or simple facts become absorbed into Helen, but the self-evident forms that create the space for protocols and that clarify what the protocols are, become absorbed into her as well.

Whenever we name anything, we appreciate that what we name has all these dimensions latent within it. If the thing we name is familiar to us, its factual and essential sediments are also familiar: we can say a lot about the history of our old house, for example, or our old car. And we appreciate a difference between our car's having been repainted three years ago, and its being able to traverse distances; we appreciate the difference between the factual and the axiomatic. If the thing we name is new to us, we may understand its kind, with all the concomitant essentials, while not knowing much about its particular history and features ("Here's a parka that you've never seen before"), or we may not even know at all what the axioms of the thing are ("Look at this"; "What is it?"). But even if we do not know "what it is," we do anticipate being able to unpack it both for what it is and for what it happens to be. We expect it to have some "what" and some "thats." As nameable it promises articulations and explanations, unless of course it merely appears to come forward as one, unless it is just an accidental unity. The nameable always presents itself with the aura of facts and causes, the aura of statement and explanation.

If we do penetrate to the axioms of the thing—if we go beyond this poem and its features to the form of poetry as such—we come to relationships that present themselves as necessary. But these relationships can be possessed in two different ways. They can be recognized as self-evidencing; because of our thinking, we may appreciate that they could not be other than they are. We may have an insight into their necessity, we may enjoy what Husserl calls an *eidetic intuition*. Or we may hold them rather as strong opinions. We may sense vaguely that they are more than mere factual attributes of the thing, we may appreciate that somehow they are necessary, but we may not have thought about them long enough and well enough to grasp their necessity. In some cases we may be content to turn to the legend that explains them instead of to an analysis. There is nothing wrong with leaving many necessities in the form of opinion; we cannot push every issue to its final definition.[2] But the possibility of an axiomatic analysis is always there, and we always sense the difference between just moving on to more features of what we name, and moving into its necessities.

In our normal involvement with things, we move from the thing to its features and to its causes, then we move back to the thing again. We look through the forms of being nameable, being articulated, and being explained. But in our philosophical reflection we look at what we normally look through: we look at the forms of presentation through which we identify things. We examine, as we have in this essay, the form of being nameable, the form of being articulated, and the form of being explained. In turning our attention to this aspect, we do not leave the being of things; instead, we recover the larger context and the more concrete whole.[3]

5
Timing

The kinds of time we are now most familiar with are those that involve clocks and calendars. Both kinds involve motion, but clock time puts us in the direct presence of the motion in question while calendar time deals with motion that is absent from us.

1

Clock time involves two motions, one of which can be easily counted, such as the movement of one of the hands around the face of a watch or the movement of sand from one part of a timer to another. The repetition and regularity of such motions make them easy to number. They can be made to keep on repeating themselves, each can easily be taken as the same as any other, and we can easily tell that there have been "three" or "eight" of them. At one time the primary instance of clocking motions were the movements of the sun, moon, and stars, but the precision of our clocks has made these celestial motions recede into the background in our handling of time. Six A.M. or seven P.M., 600 hours or 1900 hours, are more prominent for us than sunrise and sunset; we say that the sun rises at 600 hours and sets at 1900, as though the rising and setting were placed against a process more fundamental than these solar events. But of course our clocks still run against the pattern of the sun, moon, and stars, and many of the standard sums we reckon with in clock time are defined by the less accurate but larger wholes, the days, months, and years, that the movements of the heavens provide.

Clock time requires that we hold two motions together, the motion that is easily numbered and the one we wish to measure. The motion of the hand on a watch is held together with the motion of a man running around a track or that of a car moving from one spot to another. We begin counting the measuring motion when the motion to be measured starts, and at the end of the measured motion we will have come to a sum of the motions by which we measure. We then equate the sum and the motion measured: the run was two minutes long, the drive was three minutes and a half.

In the ordinary activity of timing, we are concerned with the "how longs" of particular motions, so we take pains to count accurately. Or we may wish to devise a better clocking motion than those we already have. But in what we are doing now, in our philosophical reflection, we are concerned with time and timing as such, not with times measured or the means for measuring. We want to show how time and timing surface; we will therefore bring out many things that we simply look through, and do not look at, when we time motions. To some readers what we say may seem trivial, but that will indicate that the readers are looking for the wrong thing; most likely they will be looking for a better way of measuring time or a way of making sure that we have measured time correctly. Our concern is to become aware of what we already possess and what we take for granted, not to learn something entirely new.

But does clock time really need two motions, one held against another? Could we not consider the clock motion by itself? Could we not just watch the sand move in the hourglass or the hands

move on the timepiece? If we watch only that, we do not involve
the motion in time. It remains only motion. For the motion to be
involved in clock timing, it has to be placed against some other
motion, at least against some vague, undifferentiated process. If
we watched an hourglass perform and finally said, "Five turns
of the hourglass!" we would, most probably, not be concerned
only with the hourglass and its movements; we would be observing that "so much life" has gone by. Or we might surreptitiously
have changed the movement of the sand from being the clocking
motion to being the clocked motion; we might think that while
a whole afternoon has gone by—now clocked by the movement
of the sun—the sand has shifted back and forth five times. One
or the other of these contrasts would have to occur, either measuring the passage of something by means of the hourglass or
measuring the movement of the hourglass by means of another
motion, if we are to keep the sand's motion involved with clock
time. If we removed every contrast, if we stayed with the sand's
movement all by itself, the timing would disintegrate.

But suppose we do focus only on the single motion by itself. If
we count the repetitions of the motion, if we count the five turns
of the hourglass and so "measure" the sand pouring through the
glass, do we not somehow involve the motion with time? Not
really; when we say, "One," "Two," "Three," "Four," "Five turns,"
we have not measured; we have only counted. To reach a total
is not to measure. To reach a sum is not to make an equation,
which is what we do when we measure. In measuring we say one
whole is the same as another; in the case of timing we say, for
instance, that this run is equal to two revolutions of the hand on
the stopwatch. But simply totaling does not involve placing one
whole with another and calling them equal.[1]

So simply to count the sand passing through the timer is not
to be engaged in measuring motion. But perhaps we could find
some other motion that is attached to the motion of the sand,
one that would provide the differences needed for time. What
about my own process of watching the sand move, a watching
that is interrupted by my counting out the numbers? Is not the
motion represented schematically by:

"....One ....Two ....Three ....Four ....Five"

a motion different from the sand's falling? Perhaps this movement of mind could serve as another motion, positioned against
the sand's passage, to make up time.

There are two reasons why this will not do. First, the activity
of watching is not one of the processes that can measure, or be
measured by, the motion watched. Watching is like the spotlight
shining on the actor and the stage props; just as the spotlight's
illumination is not one of the objects presented on the stage, so
watching is not one of the motions equated when one movement
is measured by another. Both of the motions involved in clocking
must, so to speak, be on stage and spotlighted.

Second, saying "One," "Two," "Three," "Four," "Five" does not
cut up or count the watching. It counts parts of the motion of the
sand. We have not had three watchings when "Three" is said but
three turns of the hourglass; but we have had three rotations of
the clock's hand when we say "Three minutes" while we measure
the sprinter running. In addition, the saying of each number is
not continuous or fluid. It does not go along with the sand's
motion, as the clock's motion runs along with the man racing
on the track. Furthermore, each number marks an end; it is not
positioned against a process to be measured. When the number
is stated the motions are over.

Both watching and counting are presentational. They present
something other than themselves, and in the case of timing they
present two other processes—the man running and the stopwatch moving—as well as the time that occurs in between the
two. Of course someone else could time my watching; someone
else could observe and say, "He watched the ocean for fifteen
minutes." This would be like placing a spotlight on the stage and
using it and its illumination as props, while lighting the stage
with still another spotlight. But in such a case the new observer's
watching is not the process being measured. His watching is the
presentational process that lets something else—my watching—
be clocked.

Clock time requires therefore that two motions, the clocking
and the clocked, be held together. In our ordinary involvement
with time and in our practical concerns, we focus first on the
motion clocked—the water boiling, the man running—and take
the clock for granted. When our clock needs repair, or when we

want to build a better clock, we turn our attention to the clocking motions. But the togetherness of both motions is almost never regarded because there is really nothing we can do about it; their being together never stands in need of repair. We also tend to look through and not at ourselves as the ones who hold the two motions together and register an equation between them. Thus the use of clocks and the phenomenon of time occur in a setting that we congenitally overlook. We must invoke a special kind of recollection to become aware of this matrix.

2

Let us now turn away from the activity of holding two motions together in clock time, and let us concentrate on the single person watching the sand move in the hourglass, counting the turns of the glass. When he says, "Three" or "Four," he marks what has just finished, the complete passage of the sand from one side to the other. He gives a number to what is over. Calendar time is something like this. In a calendar we give a discrete number to the whole day or the hour and thus consider the day or the hour as a single completed thing. But calendar time is not enmeshed in the motions that time and are timed: in calendar time there is no "watching" process. We do not continuously observe the day or the hour and then number it at the end; we just have the number. There is also no positioning of one motion against another, nothing like the movement in the hourglass being placed against the movement of, say, the water boiling. There is no present motion, whether measuring, measured, or observing, in a calendar. A calendar works at a distance to and in the absence of what is counted in it. It reports its wholes as terminated, not as going on. Calendar time is to clock time as a final score is to a game.

Of course a calendar does not only look backward toward the completed hour or day; it also looks forward to a coming period. But even in such a prospect, it reports the day as a whole and each event as an episode, not as going on. It signals the start or the finish of each process, it does not go along with the process. Even my current use of this year's calendar, although contemporary with part of this year, is not a clocking of this year. It puts a distance between this year, or today, and me, even though I use it during this year or during this day. My using the calendar is not an observational counting of the day or the year, nor is my using it the motion against which the day or the year is measured. A calendar is the fruit of the distance from life that sheer numbers let us have. Instead of leaving us engaged, almost buffetted in motion, calendars put us on dry land where we can think about and arrange beginnings and ends. But this distanced relief, powerful and far-seeing as it may be, does not of itself accomplish anything, no more than looking at a road map, helpful as it might be in organizing a trip, will as such get us anywhere. The numbers in a calendar have to become again the numbers used to mark the active beginning and end of motions, such as the "Three" or the "Four" stated at the turn of the hourglass or the "Two o'clock" I note as I walk into my dentist's office. The numbers used in reporting have to become numbers used in registration.

And what was once, in my appointment calendar, a schedule to be done can become a record of what has been done. This occurs with no action being taken on the calendar itself, so distant is the calendar from immersion in motion; we just have to let time go by. There is, of course, a movement involved in using a calendar; we have to turn the pages, scan each page, and carry out the processes of anticipating or remembering, but these motions are not placed against the movements reported in the calendar. They are neither the fluid measure with which we number an ongoing motion, nor are they the process of watching and counting a motion going on before us. They are an encapsulated motion, one kept distant from the processes mentioned through the calendar.

We may note that a digital clock resembles a calendar in some ways and a normal clock in others. Strictly speaking, a digital clock does not present a continuous motion to be placed against another motion as a measure; it marks only an end or a beginning. It counts and does not measure. However it does not provide us with the possibility of surveying, as a calendar does. It gives only the last counted number, the number we would have uttered if we were placing a clock motion against the measured motion. Hence it involves us in the direct presence of the clocked motion, while a calendar does not. However it dries out the fluid measuring motion that a normal clock provides and gives only the discrete borders. The flip of a number in a digital clock is not like the sweep of a hand on the face of a watch.

The various motions we have distinguished in discussing clocks and calendars are:

1. the motion being clocked (running around a track);
2. the clocking motion (sand passing in an hourglass; hands rotating around the face of a watch);
3. the observer's activity, the action of the clocker (perceptually holding the two motions together and measuring one by the other);
4. watching and counting a single motion by itself;
5. using a calendar.

The first three motions are all aspects of one activity. In this activity, and in that described under the fourth heading, we are directly involved in the presence of the motion measured or counted. We register time. In the fifth case we work in the absence of the motions to which we refer; the motions, and the time they involve, are here reported and not registered.

3

Clock time and calendar time can be correlated with two temporal forms: that of *present, past, and future;* and that of *before and after.*

Present, past, and future are determined especially in terms of a clocking motion, the motion against which the measured motion is to be held. "The present" is the particular unit of the clocking motion that is going on. If I am using a sand timer, say a "three minute" timer, the fall of sand I call "this one" is the present. "The present" is therefore adjectival; it needs completion, as in "the present fall of sand in the timer," "the present course of the sun," "the present sweep of the second hand." In this context, it would be incorrect to consider "the present" to be a noun.

In order to mark a motion as the present motion, we must have begun counting the motions. We must see this one as discrete,

as having a start and a finish, as being one in a series of repetitions. In any such series, one of the motions is always privileged,
the one that is actual. It stands out against those that have been
actual and those that will be; there are always "the past motions"
and "the future motions." Even if we stop using the timer, so
that one of the falls of the sand becomes the last motion in that
particular series, we still see that last motion as profiled against
other motions that carry on, like the motion of the clock on
the wall, motions that could be taken as sequences in turn. The
running down of one clocking motion always occurs against the
steady running on of others. "The present" thus floats ambigu-
ously between a precise "one" that is going on, like the fall of the
sand or the course of the sun, and an indeterminate "one" like
this argument, this excursion, this visit, or this heat wave, which
are less exact in being counted and repeated.

We may feel somewhat dissatisfied with such ambiguity about
what is to count as the present and may attempt to fix a motion
that somehow underlies all the rest by being more exact, unfail-
ing, universal, and final, in the sense of permitting no motion
more basic than itself. We may be led in three different directions in our attempt to find this ultimate vehicle for time. (1) We
may look for an ultimate, regular, and universal physical motion,
such as atomic vibrations.[2] (2) We may turn to our flow of consciousness and try to find the ultimate pulse that underlies all
the acts of consciousness and the things presented in them. (3)
We may, as Newton did, try to establish a pure flow of time itself,
absolute time, a movement and sequence independent of any
motion, whether material, psychic, or biological, one that carries
on everywhere along with the events and processes that occur
within it.[3] One or other of these three possibilities will, it might
seem, provide a backbone for the various clocks of convenience
that we use here and there; we would then have "the ontologi-
cally real time" as opposed to the conventional times that come
merely from our agreement on a local instrument of measuring.

But such an attempt to get at the "real" time is misguided.
It is a confusion of philosophical explanation with the enterprise of finding better ways to measure time. We will clarify this
confusion gradually as we proceed through this essay, but some
remarks can be made now. (1) The most ultimate motion, such

as atomic vibration, is clearly only a more precise measuring apparatus and not a definition of what time is; to find the smallest unit is not to show what something is. Furthermore, such an ultimate unit of motion is not perceivable as a motion. We need counters to enumerate it, and a counter functions after the fashion of a digital watch and not as an hourglass or a chronometer. This form of time does not clarify the original of clocking, in which two observable motions are held together and one is measured by the other. (2) To turn to the pulses of conscious life is misguided not only because it is a hopeless task to determine how large the specious present is (each pulse of consciousness is determined as "one" not just by its own internal structure, but by what is presented to us in it), but also because this is the wrong place to look for the elements of time. Time is both inside and outside consciousness, and we cannot find what time is simply by looking within. (3) To postulate an absolute time running along with the processes and events occurring within it, with one chronon constantly following another, is to fall into the typical philosophical mistake of making a thing out of a dimension of things. It involves an unnecessary doubling of events and processes: while this car goes from here to there, the sequence of chronons goes along with it; at the moment John wins the race, another event, a shadow event—the ending of a chronon— is also supposed to happen. To make time into such a new series of events and processes is to turn the elements of measuring into the elements of being. But the fact that someone could have postulated absolute time can tell us something about time, provided we can disentangle the dimensions that are confused in such a doctrine.

The issue of the present raises the question of how a motion can be broken up into units, one of which is present while others are past or yet to come. It might seem that the unbroken motion is there first, while the cuts that break the motion up into countable units are added by the mind. The motion seems to be real and true, the units seem to be conventions we impose on it. But this Kantian-like interpretation of time makes the units far too external to the motion; a motion can be counted as one because it presents itself somehow as one. We have to do the counting to let the motion emerge as one, and also to let it emerge as "third" or "eighth," but the motion can and does so emerge. If it is the third, it is not the fifth. The mind is involved in marking time, but time is not just mental, since it is a numeration immersed in motions that both are and are counted. Slabs of wood that are cut and made part of a house are parts of a house—they *are* a window frame or the edge of a roof—and the house *is*, even though it would not be if a mind had not been at work in it. The house is not just in the mind, even though it is partly of or by the mind. Likewise the fifth passage of the sand *is* the fifth passage, even though it would not be such had someone not counted it.[4] It is the fifth passage because even apart from the work of my mind, by virtue of what it is before it is counted, it can be presented as one, and as the same as many other such motions in a series. It is countable before being counted.

And although this motion is continuous, both within itself and with the other motions, with the other passages of sand "before" or "after" it, its "being one" or "being fifth" is not continuous. Hence its being now or being present is not continuous either. It is continuous as a motion but discrete as "the present motion" or "the motion now," no matter how large a present we are dealing with: a day, a minute, a second, this turn of the sand timer. Also, each present motion, as present, is contiguous to its neighboring motions and not continuous with them. The present motion or the motion now has the kind of discreteness that a sentence has, which, in contrast to the continuous flow of sound that sustains it, comes forward as one at once as a single statement.[5]

However, because the "one" of the present motion rests upon a motion that is continuous beyond the present one, the motion that is prominent as "now" is always trailing some motions and running ahead of others. To the extent that these are counted, the present is between past and future motions. The involvement of numbers, repetitions, and sequences establishes a definite past and future, as contrasted to a vague mythical time in which no real othering of present, past, and future takes place. But the numbers alone do not make up time, not without the motions they number: there is a future not just because we expect one, but because things are always moving on. And it is not just *things* that let there be a future and a past, but things moving and counted as moving. We cannot disengage the present, past, and future from the motions and events they qualify; we cannot make the adjectives *present, past, future* literally into nouns.

But it is possible for us to take some distance to a particular instance of present, past, and future when we move into calendar time. If the temporal form of present, past, and future is especially involved in clock time, the temporal form of *before and after* is especially prominent in calendar time. Calendar time is defined precisely by not being enmeshed in the motions that are going on now. The one who uses calendar time refers to a period—already packaged by numbers—different from the countable motions in which he presently lives. Even if he refers to the day or week or hour he is enmeshed in while he uses the calendar, say the 7th of September, he refers to it at a distance and not as submerged in it. Thus the same words, "September 7," can be used differently by the speaker who is clocking and by the one who is calendaring. The difference lies not in what is identified but in how it is presented.

Although the person who clocks is riveted to the present and has the past and future motions spreading from there, the one who uses calendar time can take any period of movement as his focus, whether now, future, or past. He has that much freedom from his present station. But he can only take that period as being before or after others. He cannot consider it without such a setting. However, "before and after" are essentially only two, while "present, past, future" are three. And before and after are pliable: the same period (June 5) can be before this other period (June 6) and after that one (June 4); the same period is thus before and after simultaneously. But present, past, and future are fixed: when the present is the present, it cannot be the past or the future, and the future and past cannot "at that time" exchange places or be the present. The distance that calendar time gives toward the motions it refers to moves us from the triple but riveted form of the present, past, and future to the dual but moveable form of before and after.

It is true that "before and after" also occurs within the form of present, past, and future; *this* clocking motion is before the future motions and after the past ones, the future movement is after the past and present ones, and so on. But again, before and after can shift from one to the other; no one of the three is ineluctably only before, or after, the way the present is inescapably the present. And the before and after, although so mobile, remains even when this instance of present, past, and future elapses into the past: it always remains that this clocking motion, this third hour, is before that fourth one, and that fourth one is always after this third. Each is stamped with its before and after. Hence we can later, when we use calendar time, refer to this or that period as being before and after, and we can even anticipate or plan a before and after that will occur later. What is going on now can become calendared; what is now calendared can go on later.[6]

Can we clarify how the before and after can be implicated in and yet detached from the present, past, and future? Being before and after is involved in the simple ordering of motions, without yet introducing numbers into their order. Ordering motions by before and after is analogous to ordering, say, pieces of wood of various sizes, ordering them progressively by size. This piece becomes ordered as smaller than the next but larger than the previous. This motion now is before the one coming but after the one finished. But there is no number yet: this piece of wood or this present motion is not yet marked as the fifth or the ninth. Being before and after is prior to enumerated time, and it helps introduce the demarcations that let us number a sequence. (The analogy between time and spatial size and position—as in the row of pieces of wood—is not accidental. As Aristotle observes, "before and after," or "before and beyond," "fore and aft," are first used to name spatial relationships, and indeed their temporal application depends on a spatial sequence: the motion is first here, in the fore, and then there, beyond or afterward, and so we can distinguish two motions, one coming after the other.)[7]

Now when a motion gets a number (the third hour; January 20), it keeps its ordering of before and after, even though the number is more than the order. The ordering of before and after is inseparably bonded to the number the motion has, so if one keeps the number, the before and after has to be kept with it. And if we are very precise and very "scientific," as one might say, we might be activating these numbers and orders in our present activity: we might be clocking exactly when it is we are doing whatever we do (clocking the fall of a body, clocking our reaction time). We normally do not do this, but if we are being extremely careful, say for legal reasons or for reasons of scientific experiment, for military maneuvers or for accurate timing in sport, we may in fact explicitly activate the clocking numbers and the ordering of before and after, in our present, past, and future motions. But then we can refer to those motions when they no longer are *the* present and immediately past and future motions. We may refer to what happened in the experiments as a function of real time, or to what the accused did on that date just after the close of business in the bank. *That* present, past, future is no longer active—we are in "another" one now—but it can be referred to in its absence in our reporting. It can be brought to mind as absent, and this is done in the present to which we are unavoidably fixed, which we cannot be out of—as long as it lasts.

When we are thus with the absent motion by referral, before and after take on a prominence they did not have when the motion was present. The number of the motion, that by which it is identified in our discourse about time, is no longer the name of what is going on now, but the name of what is now exhausted by being before the next motion and after the earlier one.[8] Thus the articulation of before and after lets us speak about a timed motion that is in a context distinctly other than that in which we have present, past, and future; it lets us enjoy calendar and not only clock time. Furthermore, calendar time not only lets us hold on to passages that have occurred, it also lets us think ahead, in absence, about what is to come and is not yet in the offing. It lets us order not only the past time but our distant future as well; and it lets us order not only the motions we will be immersed in, but those through which other men will pass at another time and another place: "Thus strategists hesitate over the map, the few pins and lines of colored chalk, contemplating a change in the pins and lines, a matter of inches, which outside the room, out of sight of the studious officers, may engulf past, present and future in ruin or life."[9]

In this enjoyment of a reported time, we refer to an elsewhen, but we do so in the present, with its tailing past and coming future. The activity of calendaring, although it gets us out of what we are immediately present to, is enmeshed in our present motions, just as the act of speaking about an absent context occurs in the context in which we presently live.

4

We have associated the form of present, past, and future with clock time, and the form of before and after with calendar time. We now introduce the temporal form of *now and then*, which occurs especially in what has been called inner time, the time of remembering and anticipating and imagining.[10] This kind of time mediates to us clock and calendar time; it lets us be able to use both calendars and clocks. And the form of now and then functions in the interaction between the two forms of present, past, and future, and before and after.

The perception of the difference and the bond in "now and then" occurs in remembering, imagining, and anticipating. In each of these activities we "now" place ourselves, or are placed in, a "then." When I remember, I appreciate that what I am remembering is not in the present of my life; I present earlier motions and events as having been lived through, but as not being lived through now, except as absent and "there again." Yesterday's dinner is not being eaten now, but I am now remembering and reidentifying not an image of the dinner, but the dinner itself again, as absent. This is not calendar time because in calendar time I merely refer to another context. In memory I make the other context there again, represented and identified, lived through again, not merely lived through. No matter what neurological activity my brain is carrying on, presentationally the earlier scene, with its motions, is being reenacted:

> It played for him—certainly in this prime afterglow—the part of a
> treasure kept, at home, in safety and sanctity, something he was sure
> of finding in its place when, with each return, he worked his heavy
> old key in the lock. The door had but to open for him to be with
> it again and for it to be all there. . . . Wherever he looked or sat
> or stood, to whatever aspect he gave for the instant the advantage,
> it was in view as nothing of the moment, nothing begotten of time
> or of chance could be, or even would; it was in view as, when the
> curtain had risen, the play on the stage is in view, night after night,

for the fiddlers. He remained thus, in his own theater, in his single person, perpetual orchestra to the ordered drama, the confirmed "run"; playing low and slow, moreover, in the regular way, for the situations of most importance.[11]

Essential to remembering is the fact that I am there as both the one who remembers and the one who is engaged in the center of the remembered scene. This displacement of me is one of the differences in which my self is identified, in which I and my career become actual.[12] And the "now" and "then" are correlated with the "I here" and "I there," the "I now" and "I then." Remembering, anticipating, and imagining slip back and forth into each other as I move from recalling what I did to projecting what I will do, or to simply fantasizing what I might do. These patterns of duplication and displacement, of myself and my context, are not extraordinary events but go on all the time, implicated with our being directly with the things around us, with our perceptions, actions, and decisions, as we are, even sensibly, always both in our immediate context and beyond it. And it is not only within ourselves that we encounter this form of now and then; when we look at someone else we see another as so "selfed," as being not just what is bodily there now, but the one who was and still is what he did before, who is somehow already what he will do later: the one who bears his memories and expects his future.

Inner time, displacement time, is different from calendar time also in being mobile. What we remember or imagine is going on: we remember and imagine not inert things, but things in motion. Moreover in memory their motion is represented as the same motion that occurred before. We reidentify not just Paul, but Paul performing: Paul arguing or Paul running *then*. Hobbes claimed that imagination and memory were a continuation of the motion of sense. He said that an object causes sensation in us by bringing about a motion in our organs of sense, and that this motion continues when the pressure of the object is removed, just as water continues rolling after the wind that moves it stops or after the paddle that strikes it is taken out. Imagination and memory, he said, are decaying sense.[13] Hobbes is correct in stressing the mobility of imaginations and memories but incorrect in saying that the imagined or remembered motion is *continuously* the same as the initial parts of the motion we call sense. Hobbes does not describe correctly the form of sameness or identity that occurs here. What we remember is numerically the same motion we once perceived, not the same motion continued. Indeed only in memory can we have the same motion—as opposed to the same thing—appearing again; motions are riveted to their present and cannot be in another. Only memory presents a present again.

Thus in calendar time I can refer to the quarter hour from 1000 to 1015 hours on Monday, October 6, 1980, when I engaged in that heated public argument with Peter Smith; but in displaced time I can go over the scene again, catching snatches of its motion over and over again, each time having the same motion yet once more. Calendar time refers, displaced time represents. Calendar time refers to the clocking motions that framed the original process, it gives the time and date and then adds, "which is when X happened." Thus it refers to the event through the clocking motions that have been deposited and settled into our records. But displaced, remembered time gives the "then" without the calendar frame; it represents what happened in its happening, not through its calendar. There will be occasions when we examine our calendar record and suddenly, reminded by what we find, fall into reminiscence about the events reported there; we then engage two sorts of time, the time of calendars and the time of displacement, of now and then, and all this occurs in the time of present, past, future. Fantasy, of course, is a calendar-free version of what happens in memory, and anticipation is a version which expects to be calendared.[14]

The past and future in the form of present, past, future, in clock time, are the immediately trailing or immediately coming numerated motions. The use of "past" and "future" in the form of now and then is at a greater distance. If we must displace ourselves into them, they are neither continuous nor contiguous with the goings-on now. There is an interruption between them and what is happening now. The words *past* and *future*, and even the words *now, present,* and *then,* are used analogously in clock, calendar, and displacement time.[15]

No one of these forms of timing can be said to be absolutely prior to the others. Each reaches its definition against the others. And there can be a condition of mind, and a level of being, in which the three forms are not to be distinctly differentiated, when for example a traumatic event cannot be let go as being only *then* and not *now;* when something going on now cannot be clearly enumerated into its partial motions or measured against the steady repetitions of a clock; when we refer to events that cannot be placed in a calendar because their beginnings, ends, and differentiations are not contrasted enough one from another. What calendars, what before and after, can apply to what T. S. Eliot names when he says, "In my end is my beginning"?[16] In what we could call *mythical time*, the processes we encounter are also not discretely differentiated into now and then, present, past, and future, and before and after, just as in mythical action an agent may not be clearly distinguished from his image or his name. Such temporal indifferentiation, such uncharted becoming, always lies as the matrix beneath and within the distinctions and numbers that make up the three forms of time.

If we did not enjoy the difference between now and then, it would not be possible for us to refer to another period in calendar time. The sense of "another temporal context" is originally given to us when we memorially or imaginatively place ourselves at a time, at a then, different from the one we are in now. Having sensed this difference, we can go a step farther and refer to the then without remembering or imagining it; and subsequently we can refer to a then that was never now for us, a remote past or future beyond our lifetime. This calendaring of time has an effect on our present involvement in motion and on our current clock time. It provides a more general context and more rigorous units by which we can clock our world and remember or anticipate our actions in it. The calendaring of time also has an impact on our differentiation of now and then; once we enter into calendars, we can remember with a more definite placement, since we realize that the then we are remembering can also be referred to through its time and its date.

5

There are motions and times that fall between the margins set by clock, calendar, and memorial time. Rhythmic motions, mythical time, and the right time for action are not reducible to the numbers of clocks and calendars or to the displacements of now and then.

Rhythmic motion comes between simple continuous motion and clocked or clocking motions. Continuous motion, such as the fall of an object in space, goes on with no sense of repetition: there is always just more of the same. In clock time, however, a motion is identified as one—one sweep of the hand of a watch— and is taken to be exactly the same as other similar motions— other sweeps of the hand—in regard to being counted. We keep getting one just like the others, over and over again, and each gets its number. The number fixes a distinct identity on each of the motions, an identity that can be used later to refer to that period in its absence: "during the fourth hour." In rhythmic repetition, however, a motion is gone through again but its number is irrelevant. Whether this is the fifth or the tenth time we go through the routine does not matter. Also the routine is not meant to serve as a measure for other motions; it does not clock anything else, we just do the same once more. It is not placed against another motion, it draws other motions into itself: the monastic hours sung in choir do not serve to enumerate other activities during the day, they absorb and qualify the rest of the day; meals do not simply divide, measure, and clock the day, they are prominent parts of it. We are immersed in the rhythm for its own sake and do not acquire the detachment of holding one motion against another, the distance to movement that clocking gives to us.

The important thing in rhythmic routine is that we are engaged in the same motion again: the thing moving$_1$ and the thing moving$_2$ and the thing moving$_3$ are all "really" the thing moving$_0$. And the repeated motion seeps back into the thing in motion, so that the identity of the substance is also established and confirmed by its rhythms. Rhythmic motion occurs in religious ritual, but also in sports (the preliminaries of an event, the standardized motions during the game, the gestures when a player scores a goal, the awarding of prizes), in public ceremonies, in daily personal routines, on the stage and on television (the beginning of each program), in work and in play. In contrast to clocking motions, rhythms obscure time, but without allowing it to fall back completely into undifferentiated continuity. Rhythms are something like memories and anticipations, but in rhythms we do not fall into the "abstraction fit" that reverie and fantasy entail; we do perform the routine now, even though we sense that this doing is not all that different from earlier ones, or all that different from the exemplary one. The melody is actually sung again, it is not just dreamt about.

And although rhythmic motions tend to obscure the difference between the performance now and the performance then, they do introduce an articulation within the routine to be performed. The "internal" time of the motion can be richly and rigorously differentiated. The routine is to be followed exactly, with each part in its proper sequence. This train of partial motions inside a rhythm is an anticipation of the formal sequences we reach in clock time. The internal parts of rhythms thus anticipate clocking motions, while the repetition of rhythms anticipates memorial and calendar time.

Whereas rhythms are performances, myths are narrations. Myths are the discourses that clarify what rhythmic rituals are said to repeat; rituals "have" to be done because of necessities revealed in myths. Myths talk about the past, but it is not a calendared past: to want the date for what the myth describes betrays a fundamentalism which takes the mythical events as events to be framed by clocks and calendars. There is memory in myth, but the then it discloses is not simply the then of what I was doing earlier. It is rather a then that always was and always will be around: the events in a myth disclose necessities and exemplarities. Strife and justice, for example, did not begin at a certain date in the calendar; strife and justice always were and always are. Memory, Mnemosyne, as a possibility of being, does not begin at a measurable moment, nor does Eros. The archaic events, the beginnings described in myths are not simply starts: they are the establishment of what always is. "One is always contemporary with a myth, during the time one repeats it or imitates the gestures of the mythic personages."[17] This is so not because we project ourselves elsewhere, but because what the myth reveals is there always to be originated and revealed again. It is always at work.

We might think that we first establish our personal selves through memory and action, and then construct myths to help us to deal with the world; but in fact it takes something of an effort on our part to distinguish, and to keep distinct, our own remembered past, with its capacity to be placed against clock and calendar time, from the mythical past we pick up in the stories we hear when we are first able to listen, when we have very little of a past of our own. What begins to be clarified for us in these stories is the way things are and the way they have to be, and we get a sense of ourselves and our own past only within the possibilities that are there before we come about. We can be only because of the possibilities that there are.

In rhythmic motion we are assimilated into patterns that have been going on before us, and in mythical time we come across what always is. In both these cases, we go along and do not initiate. But in choosing and acting, we stand out much more prominently. We begin something that would not have been had we not been there. What we choose and what we do leaves a record of ourselves. Even the light we shed on what ought to be done is our own. Here we do not just fit into the ancient and the permanent, we must clarify the situation which is, inescapably, now and not then, now and not always. We must determine what is the right thing to do, and the right thing can become clear only at the right time, which is also ours—and only ours—to recognize, if indeed we are capable of choice and action.

Although the situation in which we are to act cannot be dissolved into the archaic possibilities disclosed by myth, the situation is determined and must be resolved in the light of such possibilities. Whatever we choose to do ought to be done in accordance with the way things are. The stories we live by disclose exemplarities. Our simply analytical understanding of the natures of things, an understanding based on our own experience, on our own thinking, and on the counsel of others, also reveals necessities and exemplarities that bear on what should be done, but this understanding itself is first articulated in mythical form, and its mythical form always conveys a more vivid sense of the good, the noble, and the obligatory than a purely analytical evaluation can provide. Action will almost always invoke myth. However, it will never disintegrate into myth, because moral timing is never

simply a matter of necessities: it responds to the particular conjunction of necessities and possibilities, and to the accompanying
contingencies, that are there now.

It might appear that the right time could be dissolved into
clock and calendar time: that on the basis of what we know about
physical, social, economic, and psychological laws, we could calculate when a particular action would indeed serve our interests
with "maximum positive feedback." But to interpret "the right
time" in this utilitarian way is to reduce it to something like the
right time for adding eggs when one is baking a cake. We are not
choosing and acting, we are serving when we perform in this way.
Choice and action are precisely an intervention we make against
the background of the natures of things, against the necessities
and possibilities that are there apart from prior human decisions.
When we choose we are under the sway of the way things are and
the way they should be, not merely under the sway of what others
have done; and in our actions and choices we define ourselves
in relation to the way things are. To fit our performance simply
under a goal set by another, or under a good sought by passion,
is to obey a command, not to choose and to act. Clock and calendar time help us calculate and serve, but by themselves they
do not disclose the right time to act. If they alone were sufficient, something like the astrologers' charts would be the best
guide for success in life. But in fact recognizing the right time
to act depends on the moral perception provided by virtue, the
knowledge of natures and necessities provided by thought, and
the appreciation, provided by moral imagination, that things can
be better than they are.

The kind of calculative time used in science, furthermore, does
not aim at shedding light on the particular situations in which we
find ourselves. The form of time used in scientific analysis, a form
that combines digital-clock time in experiments and calendar
time in reports, puts us at a distance from the motions and things
we talk about in our science. It does not allow us to discuss the
situated time in which we must act and does not even clarify the
situated time in which we carry out scientific experiments and
state scientific truth. To cultivate the habit of calculation does
not as such make us fit to choose; to figure the correct time *of*
something is not to know right time *for* something.

Finally, knowing the right time and knowing what is the good thing to do are made possible by rhythmic practice. We do not begin suddenly to choose and to act; initially we do things in imitation and in assimilation of the behavior of others. We imitate simply because we want "to do that too," not for any utilitarian purpose. Rhythmic repetition is the runway for action. When we gradually introduce our own clocking and calendars, our own understanding of how things have to be, our own appraisal of what is going on in the situation we are in and what can be done about it, when we gradually appreciate that what we do now will be with us later, just as what we did then is still with us now, we then acquire enough distance to see contrasts between things and their shadows, between here and there and now and then, and at that point the choices become ours.

6

There is a sense of "now" that cuts deeper than the now in the memorial or imaginative now and then, deeper also than the present of clock time. The word *now* can be more reflexive than either of these two forms of self-reference permit.

In clock time, "the present" refers to the unit of clocking motion—the sweep of the second hand, the fall of sand—that is going on. But even in such clock time, we must distinguish between:

1. having the present motion (having the fifth sweep of the second hand in the fourteenth hour of October 5, 1981), and
2. having this sweep as now.

What is the difference between:

1. having the actual *motion* and giving it its number, and
2. having it as now?

What is the difference between:

1. being, now, the actual and fifth sweep of the second hand, and
2. being the *present* motion?

It is hard for us to get at the "being present" or the "being now" or the "having as now." When we try to get at this we almost always are deflected into something less final, into the motion which is present or into the having of the motion which is present. It is as though we wanted to get at our eyeglasses but always were deflected toward what we see through them. Whenever we try to get at what it is to be in the present, we slip into getting the motions that are present.

It is not just that we get "external" motions, like the motions of a second hand or the flow of water instead of "being now." We may also try to find an "internal" motion to show us what "being now" means. We may turn to psychological processes and take them as the motions for a kind of universal and ultimate clock. We may, insidiously, take our short sweeps of attention as the determination of what it is to be now. Here we focus on the having of something present. But this maneuver is inadequate: it does not clarify what it means to have something as now or as present; and it does not clarify how the having is itself now and present. It does not clarify how we have the having as present. This maneuver toward an internal motion amounts to taking ourselves as being spotted and being measured, in our motions, by someone else. It looks like the decisive and final maneuver, the catching of our present, but it is not. What else are we supposed to do?

The structure of remembering may bring out more clearly what we are after. In remembering we *now* remember ourselves as doing something or experiencing something *then*. The then was then a now, one different from the now in which we remember. This structure makes us notice the peculiarity of being now. Thus while we remember, our attention is primarily drawn to the motions remembered (to the baseball game, to the boat ride); it is marginally drawn to the "motion" of our experience then (to our watching the game, to our feeling the boat move); but it is also, somewhat explicitly, drawn to the "thenness" of the motion and the experience. The then of that makes us aware, by a kind of contrast, of the being now that will later be a then. It makes us aware that the then of the past once was now. Thus memory gives us the then, but it also gives us an inkling of the now. It is in the space of such differences that we are to look for what it is to be now.

The now that we are trying to get to is often expressed sym-
bolically in myths that speak about the origins of the world. The
beginning, the eternal awakening they speak of, is not a start in
the past once and for all, but the perpetual upsurge of things
as time moves on. In reading stories about this we appreciate
that they do not describe any mundane process or any particular
psychic experience, but something underlying every experience
and every motion, the elusive origin and passage of time. Myths
can thus help us direct our attention toward what we are trying
to describe philosophically. We may also have an inkling of this
final form of time when we recognize the right time to act or to
choose. What we are now after is deeper than moral timing, but
we get hints of its immediacy and irreplaceability in our experience of the moment for action.

Calendar time seems to draw us away from the peculiarity and
the priority of the final sense of "now." We seem to be able to
refer to any and all epochs of nature and history, all at a distance
from us. Our present station seems quite unprivileged, flattened
out with all the rest. Calendar time seems to place us in what has
been called a block universe, one in which becoming is not a real
dimension. But even in calendar time we dare not overlook the
now in which we execute our calendral reference. That activity
at least, and the now in which it occurs, is not just one more of
the calendared motions and dates, not if we want to catch it in
its original form. We have to stand somewhere, somewhen, if we
are to pretend to scan everywhere.

There are two approaches we must use to get to the form of
"now" we are now describing, the form that Husserl calls "the consciousness of inner-time." One approach is the one we have been
using: listing some hints, contrasts, and leads in clock, memorial,
mythical, moral, and calendar time that point toward it. The
second approach is to observe that the form of "time" we are
after straddles the difference between continuous and discrete
changes. It would, for example, underlie both the sweep of a second hand and the flip of a number on a digital clock. It is therefore neither a continuous motion nor an instantaneous change,
but it is related to both in regard to their being timed. (The difference between continuous motions and discrete changes has
to be kept alive. There is a temptation for us to think that as
our clocking motions get shorter, they become discrete clicks; or

that our psychological experience of time introduces clicks while the world has only sweeps. But both clicks and sweeps have to be preserved, and the level of timing we are after now has to let them be preserved; it cannot itself be either of them.)

Memory and imagination give us a sense of the strangeness of the identity of a moment in time. Suppose I am involved in a difficult interview. First I anticipate it and rehearse it in imagination; then I go through it; then I remember it over and over again. I have various slants not only on the interview as a process, not only on the persons and places involved in it (I could always go back and see *them* again bodily), but also on the "being now" of the interview and of me in it. I anticipate, go through, and remember *that* also, however marginally. That "being now" seems so empty and so formal (in contrast to the interview as a motion and the people and places involved in it; they are "stuffed" with content and easy to differentiate one from another). And despite seeming so empty, that "being now" is different from the "being now" in which I remember or anticipate. How can there be so many of them when they seem so much alike? Each is differentiated from the others not just by what goes on or happens in it (something very different could have happened, with different ingredients, and the same then—"that now"—would still have occurred). How are the nows different from one another?

The issue is sharpened because we do not need the distance of memory and imagination to discover sameness and difference in being now; a rapid othering takes place right now. It seems both continuous (uninterrupted) and discrete (each part is abruptly over as the next begins). It seems to be like one of those strange mathematical curves that has a sharp corner at every point. We must clarify how this going on of the now can be beyond both the continuous and the discrete, and also clarify how it can be the final margin, the final form, not to be located in any further "when."

7

Our issue can be clarified by being expanded. Instead of speaking about the now, it would be better to speak about succession.

Besides the things that endure, besides the motions that go on, besides the changes that happen, there is also, simply, succession. Succession is not a thing, not a motion, not a change: like the now, it is on the margin of all of these. Even if one were to say, in an attempt to define cosmological time, that the universe is made of up static states that follow one another, the succession of such states is itself not one of the states. And although succession is marginal to things, motions, and changes, it could not be without them: it is a dimension belonging with them, even though it is not equivalent to them.

To speak about succession gets us away from thinking about the final now as a kind of contact lens, a rigid entity with the tabs of anticipation and primal memory attached. It gets us away from thinking about a now-point with extensions into the immediate future and immediate past. Even Husserl's subtle analysis of the now-point and of protention and retention imposes such a misleading image, and turning to succession instead of speaking about the now can help us formulate the issue more adequately. Succession is the whole within which the marginal now is to be placed. However, we must avoid projecting the now into succession as though the now were a small version of the kind of present motion that is used in clocking. Succession does not contain enumerable parts, "nows," the way a clocking motion contains parts: the motion being counted now, the motions already enumerated, the motions still coming. Succession has to have something like parts, but they must be worked out on their own terms.

And somehow or other we have to formulate how there can be a difference between this succession and that succession. We also have to show how several of us can be engaged in the same succession, and how several motions can occur simultaneously in the same succession. How do sameness and otherness work in regard to succession? Succession, furthermore, straddles both the subjective and the objective, the domain of minding and the domain of things. [18] It straddles the continuous and the discrete and lets each of them be what it is: it is itself neither continuous nor discrete, but it appears like something continuous when it underlies a discrete change, and like something discrete when it underlies a continuous motion or rest. It lets there be othering and parts in a continuity, even if the continuity goes on with no perceptible change whatever; and it lets there be a context, an encasing sameness, for the discrete.

But the most perplexing issue in regard to succession is that there is a difference between this succession and that one: not between this succession here and that one there, since two spatially separated successions really are only one, even allowing some of the difficulties introduced by the theory of relativity; but between this succession "now" and that succession "then." This difference implies that we have not reached the end of analysis when we move from things, through motions, rests, and changes, to successions. Successions themselves succeed. But successions are not motions, changes, or rests, so we cannot say successions themselves move, nor can we say they themselves are subject to succession.[19] We will therefore modify the word we use to name them and say that they succeed.

Now this success is simply the form of succession, and we cannot say about it that it in turn is differentiated into this success and that success. Success, the form of succession, is always the same, whatever *same* may mean here and whatever sense of *other* can be played off against it.[20]

Analysis thus requires that we work out the contrasts and identities, the metaphors and the descriptions, that will bring out both success and succession, and will show their differences with and their relationships to things, motions, and changes; to thoughts, feelings, and perceptions; to numbers, equations, and spaces. But this effort is not merely analytical, not merely mathematical: since the succeeding in question is the equivalent of Plato's One and Indeterminate Dyad, it is also the origin of the goodness we find in things and the elegance we admire in them. Our analysis is therefore a reminder that the point of all timing is success.

6
Measurement

A helpful and important distinction can be drawn between two kinds of measurement that are used in science. I will call the first kind *external measurement,* and the second kind *internal measurement.*

In external measurement the units used in measuring are brought to the object measured from outside the object. For example, I may measure the length of a wall by placing a meter stick down, say, five times along the wall, or by stepping off six paces along the wall. In such cases I have used measuring units— a meter stick and a stride—that are external to the wall itself. I measure the length of the wall by using something other than the wall.

In internal measurement, however, one part of an object is used as a unit to measure some other part. I may, for example, use one edge of a table as a unit to measure another edge, and I may find, let us say, that side B is twice side A. Then I may go on to say that the entire surface area of the table is side A multiplied by twice side A, that is, it is $2A^2$. In this case we are not using meter sticks or paces with which to measure; instead the measuring units come from within the object itself whose parts are being measured.

In this essay, I will be interested not only in elaborating each of these two kinds of measurement, but also in showing how they interact with one another. The features and the force of each are defined and accentuated in their interaction, and some important procedures in science are achieved not by just one of these types of measurement alone, but by the interplay of the two.

For the sake of simplicity, I will develop these two concepts of measurement by using as an illustration the spatial measurement of bodies and figures. Once the concepts have been developed, I will show how they apply to other cases. But just to anticipate the scope of these applications, let me mention now that an external measurement system can be considered to be the framework for a scientific experiment, while an internal measurement system can be considered to be the framework for a scientific theory. Thus the contrast between the two kinds of measurement will help us understand the relationship between experiment and theory in science.

1

We first explore the external measurement system as it occurs in spatial measurements. Suppose I want to measure the length of a wall. By using a meter stick I find the wall is five meters long. Each placement of the meter stick is not a merely bodily performance; it is permeated with categorial form. When I put the stick down the first time, I appreciate this as the "first" placement, and I already anticipate a "last" placement. The first is the first of a series, the third is the third in the series, and all are what they are as against the last in the series. The placements are involved in a syntax of summation. Thus when I place the stick down, I do not *just* bodily place it down. I place it down *as* the first, third, or last placement.

Furthermore, each of the placements is appreciated as part of a whole, but the last one is special in that it "edges" or "closes" the whole. There are no anticipations of further placement-parts when the last is given; the whole is now presented, and has been presented, at the moment the last part is given. The whole stops going on when the last placement occurs. That is what "being the last part" means: that when it is presented, the whole is and has been presented as well.

However, the whole is not given in the way that any individual part—even the last—is given: we experience each placement all at once as it occurs, but the whole encompasses placements that are absent and are no longer, or are not yet, experienced. When the last placement is given, the whole is presented as much as it ever will be presented; it is presented at the moment of its completion, but also as having been parceled in the earlier placements, as having been anticipated when the measuring process was begun, and even as having been more remotely anticipated when we set out to measure. The fact that the whole is given in a way different from the presence of each placement does not mean that the whole is not given at all; it is just given in a different way.

In fact there is an interesting analogy between the process of external measurement and the process of formulating a sentence. A sentence is never presented in the way each of its words is presented, but it is given as a whole in its words and it is finally stated when the last word is said. And each word is involved in syntax precisely because it is part of the sentential whole, just as each placement in measurement is involved in syntax because it is appreciated as part of a measurement whole.

When the measurement is completed, the result is stated simply as "five meters." The result is not normally stated as an equation. However, something like an equation is implied in the result.

In measuring the length of the wall, we deal not just with five placements, but with five placements against the wall. The wall has been there all along as marking the whole to be measured. We stop with five placements because the *wall* ends where the fifth occurs. Thus the anticipated, parceled, and completed whole that spans the five placements is itself equated with something outside itself, with the length of the wall. Therefore we can state, "The length of the wall is five meters," or "The wall is five meters long." In measurement we do not deal only with the categoriality of summation, but with this categoriality and its placements as equal to something outside themselves.

Thus the process of external measurement is bidirectional: (1) it moves toward a sum of placements, but (2) it also positions

these placements against a wall and equates them, in their summation, with the length of the wall. And because the units (the
meter stick or the strides) are other to the wall, we could replace
them with many different kinds of units, such as a twelve-inch
ruler, a piece of string, or a yardstick. We should also observe
that the sum of the units is equated not with the wall as such
but only with a "part" of the wall, with its length. The whole that
is being measured is itself only a part, an aspect, of the thing
in question.

Let us now turn to the internal measurement system. Here we
say, for example, that side B of a table is twice side A, and that
the surface area of the table is $A \times B$ or $2A^2$. In such a case we
cannot bodily use side A to measure side B; we cannot pick up
side A and place it twice against side B. Side A is not useful for us
as a unit of measurement in the way a meter stick is useful in an
external measurement system. If we wanted to introduce a bodily
procedure, we would have to use a tape measure or a meter stick
to find the relationship between sides B and A, that is, we would
have to go back to an external measurement system. But this
move to external units would be only provisional. Ultimately we
rest with the internal relationship and consider B as equal to $2A$,
and the area as equal to $2A^2$.

In other words, in our internal measurement system, the process of placements, the bodily procedure, evaporates. We move
into a more purely thoughtful procedure. We contemplate a
whole (the table) in which one part (side B) is related to and
measured by another part (side A). These relationships may have
been discovered by the use of an external measurement system,
but they are now considered simply in themselves.

We should also note that we never measure the entire object, the entire internal measurement system, by means of one
of its parts. We only measure one part—a side, a surface, a
volume—by another part. The object as a whole becomes a kind
of background or horizon or frame for the achievement of
measurement.

When an internal measurement occurs, the table or whatever
object we are measuring becomes a small world unto itself, and
many internal relationships can be determined with no reference

to anything outside. Besides determining the surface area, for example, we can determine the length of the lines from one corner to another, we can determine various features of angles generated by various lines, and so on, and all this can be done with units provided from within the whole in which these angles, lines, and surfaces are all parts. This sort of isolation of a system is not possible in the case of an external measurement system, because there we have to import units from outside the object being measured. There we cannot eliminate the meter stick or the paces, nor can we eliminate the bodily activity of placement or stepping.

Because the internal measurement system becomes a world unto itself, it can be changed into a purely mathematical object. The table top can be thoughtfully transformed into a rectangle, the box into a cube, the ball into a sphere. The cube is a box that has become exclusively and exhaustively determined, as a whole and in regard to all its parts, in terms of its own parts. The idealization of a box into a cube or a ball into a sphere is equivalent to transforming the box or the ball into an independent internal measurement system.

Let us now introduce a third factor, the diagram, as an addition to the two measurement systems we have distinguished. Diagrams play an important role in scientific writing. They are not just memory aids; they help us think scientifically. They help us generate the concepts used in internal measurement systems. And of course, in the case of spatial measurements, the diagrams in question would be sketches of the rectangle, the sphere, the cube, and other geometrical forms.

A diagram is a presentation of an object as an internal measurement system. It represents the idealized body:

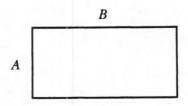

in which one side (B) is twice the length of the other (A). The diagram given above will, as we all know, be inexact. If we treated it within an external measurement system and calibrated it exactly, we might find that side A is, say, 1.9 centimeters long and side B is 4.0 centimeters long, but this inaccuracy does not matter. The diagram really represents the perfect relationship $B = 2A$; it does not present the inexact relationship that we calibrate when we measure the diagram itself.

But the diagram also represents, in another way, the external measurement system. It can be taken as a picture of the thing—the table top, the pyramid, the box—that we perceive and start with and bodily measure. The diagram mediates between the external and the internal measurement systems.

And it does so not only in regard to geometric objects. There can be diagrams of electrical circuits; of optical phenomena such as reflection, refraction, and diffraction; of harmonic oscillators; of hydraulic systems; of cellular structures; of neural networks; and of molecular, atomic, and subatomic systems. There can also be diagrams for organic and behavioral wholes: for immunity systems, prey selection, and behavior generation.[1] In all such cases, the diagram serves as more than a pedagogical device; it serves to help us isolate and express an internal measurement system in an area in which none was established before. It shows us which factors are to be considered in treating this object or network as a scientific theme, and it also excludes other factors. The diagram isolates as well as it illustrates and defines. It is surrounded by empty space. It helps us make our theme into an internal measurement system, a whole in which only those units and relationships are admitted that are permitted to survive in this idealization.

The heuristic use of diagrams is more obvious in journal articles than in textbooks. In textbooks, the writers discuss established scientific laws and the diagrams seem to be mere illustrations of well-known relationships. But in journal articles, where fresh research is being done, the writers are attempting to isolate the relevant factors and establish the functional relationships, and here diagrams serve not just to illustrate but to constitute a theory. They help us hold the relevant factors in mind, to see the relationships among them, and to appreciate the units that are being used in correlating one part of the whole with another. They help us determine the whole in question and its parts.

2

We have distinguished (1) the external measurement system, (2) the internal measurement system, and (3) the diagram. Let us now look at all three together and consider some of the characteristics of scientific measurement that occur in them.

First, the internal measurement system is an idealization of an external measurement system, and the diagram helps us to move toward this idealization. Edmund Husserl, in his account of the origins of modern science, describes idealization as a process in which we imagine an object being projected toward a limit of exactness: we imagine a surface being made smoother and smoother until it reaches the ideal form of a plane; or we imagine a dot becoming smaller and smaller until it loses all spatial dimensions and becomes a point.[2] Husserl's description is accurate; such idealizations are found everywhere in science. But his description is incomplete. Besides moving toward ideal limits, we also incorporate such ideal forms in measurement systems. We never just have lines, surfaces, points, point charges, and frictionless masses. Such things emerge in and are codefined by measurement systems and specifically by internal measurement systems. The forms are ideal because they are measurable and definable by other ideal forms along with which they make up a whole. If we tried to handle the idealized line with units from an external measurement system, it would stop being a line and would become the length of a body. It is an ideal line not only because it is projected to a zero limit in its second dimension, but also because it can be exactly twice another line. It is not that we first generate lines and then place them inside an internal measurement system; their being part of such a system is part of their being lines.[3]

Furthermore, incommensurability occurs only in an internal measurement system: the diagonal of a square is incommensurably related to one of the sides only in an idealized square, not in an "empirical" one, not in an external measurement system.

In the latter we could always use a ruler to measure both the side and the diagonal. Only when the diagonal is to be measured exactly by one of the sides does the ratio become strictly incommensurable.

Second, although the geometric transformation from bodies to shapes is the clearest example of idealization, this process occurs in regard to many other natural phenomena. In each case we begin with an external measurement system, with a procedure carried out on something occurring in the world. After enough observations and measurements have been made and enough functional correlations have been observed, we can begin isolating the external measurement system and project it toward an internal measurement system, and we will often use a diagram to help us in this isolation and determination. We have to purify our system of anything that is external to it and its internal measurements.

Different kinds of things generate their own measurement systems. There are appropriate systems, both external and internal, for bodies and spaces, mechanical forces and motions, electricity, weather patterns, neural networks, immunity systems, chemical states and reactions, prices, income and taxes, and demographic trends. In the various external measurement systems we use such instruments as thermometers, Geiger counters, barometers, tuning forks, voltmeters, anemometers, and electroencephalographs, and we use such techniques as price surveys, census reports, and the statistical analysis of population trends. In some of these we measure the objects directly, in others we measure indirectly through the reading of scales or dials. Each system develops its own appropriate kind of units: the units used in mechanics are different from those in economics. Each system computes some sort of sum of its units and then equates the summation with the object of measurement. These various measuring units would be analogous, in our earlier example of spatial measurements, to the meter stick and its placements along the length of a wall.

When these systems are transformed into internal measurement systems, the units are also idealized as units, but the important measurements in the internal measurement system are no longer the particular sums of units; the important measurements now are the relationships among the parts. For example, in resolving a parallelogram of forces, we do not measure a particular force; instead we now determine the resultant as being equal to the forces that compose it, multiplied by appropriate values (sine, cosine, or tangent) of the angles between the resultant and those forces. In the model of an electrical circuit, we can formulate a "circuit equation," in which the current, resistances, and electromotive force are mutually related in a certain way. We can attempt to model the central nervous system and its activity by idealizing it into an internal measurement system made up of variables such as neuronal groups, signals, repertoires, synapses, synaptic alterations, and neural circuits. Econometric models are systems made up of equations that express the relationships between economic variables; some small models may include only a few variables and contain a few equations, others may be much more complex, with many variables and thousands of equations. The variables in econometric models are factors such as the gross national product, the money supply in its various forms, the rate of inflation, the cost of energy, profit and expenditure, and so on. These factors would be analogous to side *A* and side *B* in our geometric model.

In the internal measurement system the important thing is not any particular sum or value, but the relationships between parts of the system, and the equations that express these relationships. The important thing is to determine how the variables are related, not to determine what the actual values of the variables may be in any particular case.

However, when numerical values are inserted in the place of variables, the values are the idealized units that are the sublimation, so to speak, of the units that were used for sums in the external measurement system from which our internal measurement system was derived. So long as we remain in the internal measurement system, the "ten meters" or "sixty volts" we mention as values of variables are idealized units, not simply empirical ones.

Third, what we call *models* in science are internal measurement systems. Models are often considered to be some sort of mental creation, purely conceptual beings that are put together in our minds as tentative, putative copies of what exists in the so-called outside world. Models are often understood in the context of an epistemology that separates the internal and the mental from the external and the real.[4] But a model is just an internal measurement system; it is not a mental entity, nor something assembled only in the mind, not just a mental construct. It is outside us, as much outside as the rod or the step that is used in external measurement. A model may carry more of our thoughtful achievement, more sedimentation of our transforming activity, but it is still a transformation of something in the world. A model does not need to be matched to an outside world, but it does need to be blended with an external measurement system. It has to be brought back to measurements such as six meters bodily measured, the increased clicking of a Geiger counter, the actual rise or fall of prices, a statistical decrease in the frequency of an infection, and so on. The transition is not from something inside the mind to something outside the mind, but from one form of measurement in the world to another. And a model fails to be valid not because it cannot be matched or mapped onto something outside the mind, but because we find that not all the relevant internal measurement factors have been accommodated in the model, or because we find that we have included some that are really not relevant. A model fails because we find that we have modeled too little or too much or not the right things into our internal measurement system.

Fourth, a theory is a network of algebraic equations; the equations express the relationships holding between various parts of an internal measurement system, or various parts of a model. The various dimensions in the internal measurement system become the variables of the equations in the theory. Moreover, the equations in the theory are ordered into a deductive whole. Some of them serve as axioms and others are theorems derived from the axioms. If the theorems or conclusions are particular enough, values can be introduced in place of the variables and an experiment can be made to confirm or disconfirm the theory.

But what does it mean to carry out an experiment to confirm or disconfirm a theory? We are inclined to think of the theory as a mental construct, a lattice of propositions in the mind, with some of the propositions reporting about things that we can observe in perceptual experience. The perceptual observations, we are inclined to say, serve as a kind of crossover between our mental theory and the real world. They would inform us whether things "out there" really are something like the descriptions we have constructed "inside," in our theory.

But this way of thinking does not do justice to the intentionality or the presencing of scientific theories. A theory is not a mental lattice. It is a series of algebraic formulas that relate various parts of an internal measurement system. The theory expresses and describes the internal measurement system.[5]

However, since the internal measurement system itself is a transformation of an external measurement system, the theory can also be said to describe its base, the external measurement system—the box, the falling body, the nuclear reaction, the activity of the cortex—but it describes this object only as having been transformed into an internal measurement system. Thus there is a staggered, indirect application of the theory to the "real" world. The theory works its way through the idealized internal measurement system that issued from the original object; and in this indirect way the theory returns to the object itself, as the object can be measured by our various bodily activities.

When the theory works its way through the internal measurement system to the external measurement system, what it does is to suggest a result that we would get if we were to measure the object. Because of the numerical processing that has gone on in the theory, we think we should get this or that reading on the seismograph, on the thermometer, in our placements of the meter stick, or in the leading economic indicators. The measurement we carry out may be a normal counting or summation, or it may be a numerical reading of an instrument, or the determination of a yes-or-no response within a range set by our procedure of measurement.

This is the experiment. A quantitative experiment is not just making something happen, but making it happen in a measurable way, in a way that will confirm or disconfirm a theoretical statement of a functional relationship.[6] Sometimes the experiments are made when the theory is just being formulated; they then serve to suggest a functional relationship. More often, experiments are made in the light of a theory. They are suggested by the theory. Even the instrumentation that is required for the experiment may be called forth by the theory, and it may take a long time, even decades, before someone invents the instruments that are suitable for testing a particular theory. As Thomas Kuhn observes, "The first direct and unequivocal demonstrations of [Newton's] Second Law awaited the development of the Atwood machine, a subtly conceived piece of laboratory apparatus that was not invented until almost a century after the appearance of the *Principia.*"[7]

The power of discovery in science is the ability to distinguish new dimensions in things, new dimensions that can become correlated into functional relationships, idealized into an internal measurement system, and captured in the formulas of a theory. The power of discovery is the ability to articulate wholes into new kinds of parts and new kinds of relationships among parts: to articulate a moving body into mass, acceleration, and the force that it undergoes, or to distinguish "heat" into the two factors of "quantity of heat" and "temperature." When such parts are articulated, the thing in question itself becomes seen as a new kind of whole. And progress occurs by zigs and zags: the new theory suggests new measurements and instrumentation, and these in turn suggest new wholes and parts and new theories.

Fifth, it is commonly recognized that a theory can be detached from that which it is a theory of. The lattice of equations or propositions can be taken merely as a formal system and no longer as the expression of Euclidean geometry, harmonic motions, or neural networks. Theories are liftable. They can be transferable goods. Some can be lifted from one domain and found, surprisingly, to fit quite well in another. Pure mathematicians can work out purely formal theories for their own sake; and sometimes a pure mathematical theory may be found to be just the thing for some new area in theoretical or applied science. And when a purely formal theory or axiomatic system becomes interpreted, it does not apply immediately to an object or to a system that can be bodily observed or measured; it first applies to an internal measurement system, which in turn can be transformed into an external measurement system. Only in this staggered way does the axiomatic system find its way to empirical verification.

And if a formal theory can be taken from one set of phenomena and found to apply to another (if we can have one model fitting many different kinds of things), the opposite can also occur: a single set of phenomena may be found to be consistent with many different models or theories. The astrophysical phenomena of gamma-ray bursters, for example, are said to be consistent with up to forty different models that have been proposed to account for them.[8] In this case, the detection and measurement of the gamma-ray bursters are done through an external measurement system, and the many models that are used to try to explain the bursters are the internal measurement systems into which the bursters are to be transformed. As the measurement of the bursters becomes more exact, many, and perhaps all, of the models will be disqualified, but the movement between the two kinds of measurement systems will still occur.

Sixth, in doing science, one shifts constantly between external and internal measurement systems. The applied scientist, concerned primarily with external measurement systems, still sees his work in the light of at least tentative functional correlations, and he always tacitly engages the formal theories that are well established in his field. The theoretical scientist always appreciates that what he is working on must sooner or later be verified by some sort of experiential measurements.

When we shift from the external to the internal measurement system and back again, we may use some words in an ambiguous way. Terms such as *side, angle, fifteen meters, gross national product,* or *neuronal columns in the cortex* may be capable of occurring in both the external and the internal measurement system. In one case the term names something empirical, in the other it names an idealized form or unit. The same word is used in two contexts. And the same word must be used, because we are indeed talking always about the same thing. It would not do to have different names. But the word does undergo a slight shift in meaning, because the same thing is being taken in two slightly different ways, once as part of an external measurement system and once as part of an internal measurement system. The term is systematically ambiguous, and it must be so. There is a difference in presentation between the thing taken as bodily measurable and the same thing as idealized and measured by the other parts of its internal measurement system.

Seventh, computers have introduced some interesting new possibilities in regard to diagrams. Before computers were available, one could introduce values for the variables of a theory, but each such introduction of a set of values gave a static description of a possible state of the internal measurement system. But with computers it becomes easier to insert sequences of values for the variables in the equations. It then becomes possible for us to see how the state of the system progresses as these values are introduced. We get a sequential, discretized numerical description of the system in motion. The changes and the progression of the system may furnish new information that the individual static descriptions alone do not provide.

The possibility of a dynamic analysis also occurs in regard to visual computer simulations. Such simulations are like a living diagram, a diagram in motion. A diagram, as we saw earlier, is an attempt to isolate the relevant factors and relationships of an internal measurement system. But in computer simulation we see immediately how the diagram changes as the relationships in the system progressively change. A visual computer simulation can thus serve as a kind of verification of the theory or the internal measurement system. It shows how the system works.

But neither the diagram nor the visual simulation are the empirical object itself. The diagram and the simulation stand between the external and the internal measurement system. For final verification we cannot rest with the computer, whether in printouts or in graphics, but must move to the external measurement system and the interactions—the measurements—we carry out upon it.

Finally, any theory of measurement has to mention the problem of indeterminacy in measurement and the uncertainty principle. So far in our exposition we have not treated this problem. The issue arises especially in regard to external measurement systems: (1) In some cases, the bodily activity of measuring, or the instruments used in measurement, interfere with the object measured. (2) In other cases, we cannot be sure that our measuring instruments remain invariant: that a measuring rod does not, for example, change as a unit when its direction is reversed, or that the measuring rod does not shrink or expand in function of temperature in a way in which the measured body does not. (3) In still other cases the object being measured may not be stable enough or distinguishable enough to be measured accurately, or, as occurs on the subatomic level, the more accurate measurement of one of a pair of conjugate variables may force a greater imprecision in the measurement of the other.

One way of dealing with indeterminacy is to use several different types of measurement in external measuring, or to carry out the measurements in different circumstances. This can help to cancel out, as much as possible, the indeterminacy that belongs to any one type or to any particular circumstances. Another way is to use internal measurements to control and correct external ones, that is, to use theory to override imprecisions in actual bodily measurement. These procedures do not eliminate indeterminacy and uncertainty, but they help to bring it under control when it can be brought under control. In those cases in which the object measured is itself undetermined, obviously the measurement can reach no more precision than the object itself will allow.

A special problem arises in the measurements of quantum mechanics, because according to some interpretations, the observer must be taken into account in determining the object being measured. The problem here—in the terms we have formulated in this essay—is that the observer and the observed, or the measuring and the measured, seem to have to be combined into a new kind of whole, one that should generate its own internal measurement units and relationships. But the observer and the object observed, or the measuring and the object measured, seem to be incommensurable. How could internal units be formulated that would straddle the difference between observer and observed? How can the sheer act of measurement be combined with the object measured into a new kind of internal measurement system? This problem, which is known as the measurement problem in quantum mechanics, has been interpreted in various ways, and we cannot pursue it further in this essay. But it does not seem to violate the distinction between internal and external measurement systems, and perhaps that distinction may provide some resources for the treatment of this perplexing issue. The immediate task would be to unravel the layers of idealization that have occurred in ancient mathematics, in classical mathematical physics, and in relativity and quantum theory, and to begin to examine what sort of "object" can still be presented through them all.

The difference between external and internal measurement systems sheds light on other issues. For example, the British measuring system of inches, feet, and yards operates within an external system; these units are derived from parts of the human body—the inch is derived from the width of the thumb, the foot is derived from the length of a human foot, and the yard is derived from an arm's length—and therefore they imply a bodily activity of measuring things, a process in which we bring our own bodily units to the things being measured. But the metric system is quite different; the meter, the basic unit, was originally determined as one ten-millionth of the distance between the equator to the pole measured on a meridian. Thus the whole world is turned into a kind of internal measurement system when metric units are introduced. The world is much more rationalized or mathematized by this metric system than it is in the more human and external scales of British units.

In addition, it would be interesting to examine how integrals and differentials of functions can be related to the internal measurement system, and how they apply to external measurement systems; such a study would clarify the sense of the calculus. It would be interesting to examine how set-theorical analysis is related to the algebraic formulas of internal measurement systems, and to examine how graphs, especially those plotted against Cartesian coordinates, can be compared to diagrams. One could ask whether internal measurement systems really are adequate in the social sciences, psychology, and neurology, since the opinions and expectations of the persons being studied must be taken into account, and such intentional aspects within the system turn it into a different kind of whole. One could examine more fully the nature of the equations that occur in internal measurement systems, and ask if there is anything analogous to an equation in the measurement procedures followed in external measurement systems. These problems and many others remain to be worked out, but the distinction between external and internal measurement systems gives us a new perspective on the forms of intentionality at work in science.[9]

7
Exact Science
and the World
in Which We Live

As it is described in Husserl's *Crisis*, the life-world, the *Lebens-welt*, is not simply the world in which we live; it is the world we live in as contrasted to the world of exact science.[1] Furthermore, it is this world, so contrasted, as named by phenomenology. *Life-world* is a word expressed in transcendentalese, not a word expressed in ordinary language. The turn to the life-world is a philosophical move, not simply a relapse into prephilosophical and prescientific experiencing.

A philosophical turn to the life-world is called for because the world we live in has been called into question and its truth has been interpreted as mere appearance by the kind of exact science carried on since Galileo. Philosophy is to allow us to repossess critically the world of our immediate involvement by showing us how this world is the foundation for what is achieved by exact science. The world we live in is changed into the world of exact science by a special handling of appearances, and only a kind of thinking that examines appearances as such, only phenomenology, is capable of telling us how the two worlds are related to each other. This issue could not be treated either by prescientific experience or by the experiences of exact science, which are constituted by different forms of appearing but which do not make appearances themselves their theme.

1

Husserl uses geometrical forms as examples of exact, ideal essences, but such exact essences are found in many areas of the study of nature. Newton's definition of a ray of light is an interesting example: we are to imagine a light beam being partially occluded up to the point at which any further occlusion would cut off the light entirely. A test charge or test particle, one which is imagined to have no effect on the field in which it moves, is another example, taken from electromagnetism. Another is a heat reservoir, a body whose temperature is not raised or lowered by the addition of heat to, or by the withdrawal of heat from, the reservoir. We are to imagine, for instance, a glass of water that is somewhat cooled by an ice-cube; then imagine the ocean being practically unaffected by the addition of an ice-cube; then imagine a body totally unaffected by any such subtractions or additions of heat. Still other examples of exact essences are the ideal gas, the incompressible fluid, the perfectly flexible string (in which the stiffness is reduced to zero, the mass is taken as uniformly distributed along its length, and the tension is taken as uniform), the ideally efficient steam engine (whose energy output depends only on the temperatures of the hot source and the cold sink, with friction and dissipation reduced to zero), and the ideal voltage source (which, in contrast to any real battery, has no resistance between its terminals).

In all such cases the ideal structure is appropriate to the kind of thing we are involved with. The features of a ray of light are not the same as the features of the ideal gas; we begin with empirically different kinds of things and come to different kinds of ideal essences. Inventive genius in each domain consists in having the insight to know what sort of ideal is appropriate to the thing in question. Inventive genius consists also in seeing what variable can and ought to be projected toward a limit in the kind of thing we deal with. Carnot, for example, had to see that dissipation of heat ought to converge to zero in the case of steam machines, while Newton had to see that the thickness of the light beam should converge to a limit in the case of light.

Ideal forms therefore have to be achieved by someone, and Husserl attempts to describe what this achievement is like. He distinguishes several elements:

First, in the disclosure of an exact essence, we begin with something we experience directly, then we imagine a projection, toward a limit, of some relevant variable factor in what we experience (*Crisis* 25–26, *Ideas* 1 §74). We imagine making the surface smoother and smoother until we reach the geometrical plane, or we imagine less and less heat modification until we reach a heat reservoir. Imagination is a necessary element in this process; we cannot actually reach the limit we imagine we approach. Furthermore, we cannot imagine what it would be like to reach this ideal limit; the ideal essence itself is not given even to imagination. We imagine the process of approximation, not the arrival at the limit. Also, we imagine only one or two steps in the process of approximation; we do not go through the whole process of approaching the limit. Once we define the ideal form, however, all "imperfect" but actually experienced forms become identifiable as versions of the exact essence. They can be understood in contrast to the ideal essence we have reached in thought. When we now experience a steam machine, for example, we do not just have another engine, but an approximate version of the ideal steam machine. Exact essences give us a new way of taking the things of our direct experience (*Crisis* 32–33).

Second, according to Husserl, such limit-forms are determined in order to exclude imprecision and to make exact identifications possible. We become able to identify something that is perfectly the same always and everywhere and for everyone. The things we directly experience are always imprecise, and are therefore not given as exactly the same when we perceive them again or when others perceive them. Husserl observes that even the similarities of such things are not exactly the same (*Crisis* 25). One actual surface will always differ in surface measurement from another even though both appear to be congruent; and even the same surface will be slightly larger or smaller or more or less irregular at different times because of its inevitable reaction to its surroundings. The ideal excludes such indeterminacy and change (*Crisis* 27, 29). Furthermore, every object we directly experience presents different profiles at different times and to different observers, depending on the condition of the medium through which we perceive it, the condition of our own perceptive faculties, and the point of view from which we experience it. Even the yellowest yellow will look orange in certain kinds of light. But the ideal essence excludes all such subjectivity and relativity, and seems to exclude any reference to an observer at all. It seems to be the most objective of objectivities, and to achieve sameness to an ultimate degree.

Third, the ideal structure is not separable from the approximations through which it is established. It is not the case that the ideal essence drops off, like ripe fruit from a tree, from the imagined sequences of appearances that come ever closer to it as to a limit they never reach. Husserl says that idealizing thinking "conquers the infinity of the experiential world" not by excluding the imprecise identities, but by arranging them in a convergent infinite series (*Crisis* 346–48, 41; see all of Appendix 5). The ideal form cannot be understood except as the point toward which all such imprecise forms converge. It is not separable from them. However, the person who develops and deals with the exact essences may forget this and take the ideal form as if it were concrete and separable from its approximations, as if it could be presented apart from them. He does this because he is lost in what Husserl would call positivity; he is concerned with objects and oblivious to the way objects are cognitively given and possessed. A new object seems to be presented to him in the process of idealization, this new object seems more durable and more exactly identifiable and more precisely measurable than the objects we normally encounter, and so it seems to him to be more real than the things he experiences (*Crisis* 43–44). Only if he were more alert to the working of appearances would he be able to appreciate the presentational dependence of ideal forms on the things we experience in imprecise identifications. Only if he paid attention to the process of identification itself, and not just to what is identifiable through it, could he avoid the dilemmas that arise when the ideal forms enter into ontological competition with what we experience.

For the ideal essences escape the imprecision of directly experienced objects not by separating themselves from such objects but by a kind of omnivorous inclusion of all the objects in themselves; or, to change the metaphor and the direction of inclusion, by a kind of ghostly presentation of the ideal essence in all the "deficient" cases we experience. The circle is in all rings, not separate from them, and the ideal voltage source is in all batteries, not separate from them. When we experience a ring as a ring, we do so by seeing it against the circle, and, if we are theoretical physicists and not locomotive engineers, when we experience a steam engine we see it against the ideal engine described by Carnot and others. And somehow the "reality" of the ring seems to be the circle, and the "reality" of the coal-burning locomotive seems to be the ideally efficient steam engine.

2

In contrast to things that can be interpreted as instances of exact essences, there are other kinds of things that simply cannot be projected toward an ideal form (*Ideas* 1 §74). No matter how far we let our imagination range over various instances, no pattern of approximation can emerge. Examples of such "morphological" essences are what are commonly called secondary sense qualities, like tastes and colors; also, living things—trees and elephants—cannot be conceived as converging toward an ideal limit; and objects related to people, like tables and houses, are also morphological in kind, because people themselves are always different from one another. It is possible to register essential elements and distinctions in such things through the process Husserl calls eidetic intuition, but the essences of such things include inexactness, and they cannot be transformed into ideal, exact essences. Imprecision is built into such things and cannot be overcome by making it converge toward a limit at which it would disappear.

Because ideal, exact essences rid themselves of all involvement with human viewpoints and perspective, it would seem to be impossible to find exact essences in the structure of human existence itself, whether social or individual. Husserl claims that his own science of phenomenology examines morphological, not exact, structures in subjectivity (*Ideas* 1 §75, §145). In the work of both Marx and Hobbes, however, we find something like exact essences used in the analysis of the human estate.

As described in *Capital*, Marxian unskilled human labor, which is used to determine the value invested in things by the laboring process, is an exact essence. In fact—and Marx is well aware of this—every human being has some skill in whatever he does, and of any two people one will be at least slightly better or worse than the other in performing a particular task. But in order to establish units by which the labor invested in objects is to be measured, Marx lets the differences in human skill converge toward zero and formulates the exact essence of totally unskilled human labor.[2] All human labor is then charted against this ideal, just as every ring is seen against the circle. The need for such an exact unit of measurement arises in a commercial economy, where objects are produced not primarily to be used, but to be exchanged for other objects.[3] Units of human labor are used to explain the origin of exchange values in commodities. The notion of unskilled human labor, furthermore, must be seen in the context of industrialization, in which a complex process is broken down into simple motions so that each agent in the process needs less and less skill to perform his part. The person acting in this process is therefore treated as if he were unskilled, or is made to be unskilled, by the nature of the process he has entered. It is easier to imagine the limit case of totally unskilled labor in such an economy than it is in the case of a society of craftsmen or farmers, where the imprecision of morphological essences could not be thought away. It is interesting that the concept of unskilled human labor is achieved because of the need for measurements and identifications, of determining how two things can be exactly the same. This is the same need that prompts us to determine exact essences in the science of nature. So we have not only the perceptual world replaced by the world of ideal physical forms, but also the world of human making replaced, in principle, by the idealized forms of undifferentiated, unskilled human performance and the exchanges that it makes possible; and in each case the ideal form is presented as the truth of what appears to us as approximation.

In Hobbes it is political life that is interpreted against a pattern of exact essences. The state of nature, for example, and the social contract, are both ideal forms. All human agreements depend on some prior agreements and sympathy, and all human conflict depends on some recognition of common rules. But Hobbes's state of nature, this war of all against all, this maximum agitation, reduces human agreement to a zero point. Then the social contract is the sudden agreement that is preceded by no other agreements. And once in this world of ideal essences, we run into other strange entities, like infants that make contracts with their mothers and sovereigns who cannot do injury to their subjects, the political analogues of lines that intersect at a dimensionless point and machines that have no internal friction.[4] Just as Marx knows that all human workers do differ from one another in skill, Hobbes realizes that legal and political matters are different from mathematical ones; but he still begins to insert idealized structures as a factor in political understanding and thinks about human affairs against the background of exact essences. And we may ask whether the exact essences of Hobbes's mathematics of morals, essences which keep trying to come to life in the modern state, have not had as distressing an effect on the possibility of natural political activity as Galileo's exact essences have had on the possibility of living and working in the world which we perceive. Later thinkers have tried to soften the harsh ideality of Hobbes's forms, but their efforts are like efforts of people trying to make circles and planes more accessible by adding qualifications to them.

3

Husserl frequently observes that in the science built upon exact essences, the world we live in and the world we directly perceive, with its imprecisions and perceptual qualities, is relegated to the condition of a merely apparent world. The mind that is fascinated by exact essences and oblivious of how they have come about considers the appearances in the lived world as merely subjective views which are to be discounted in a final description of what is and of how things are. But other things besides perceptual perspectives are also played down in the world dominated by exact science.

The world in which human skill is needed and recognized is also relegated to mere appearance by exact science, and therefore skill and its achievements are not considered ultimately real. Skill in performance is required only when there is ambiguity in regard to how things will turn out: not merely an ambiguity in our ability to foretell the future, but a real imprecision in the things themselves. Skill consists in being able to bring about determinations that are for the good of the thing in question. In medicine, for example, certain states of an organism are likely to lead to further states that are dangerous, and medical skill consists in being able to determine the organism in such a way that the dangerous states are avoided and good states are brought about. But there are no better or worse states in an exact essence, and nothing we can do can change what an ideal essence is. To use an ancient principle, the good is not a cause in mathematics.[5] The sheer identifiability of ideal forms, which is so attractive to the theoretical mind, excludes the imprecision in which skill is called for. The mind correlated to exact essences is the mind of someone to whom skills are indifferent.

Furthermore, the mind correlated to exact essences is also indifferent to virtue and vice. Human actions are always executed in a concrete situation that calls for action. People act generously or selfishly, in a courageous or in a cowardly manner, in a temperate or self-indulgent way, or justly or unjustly. The agent's character, the kind of person the agent has morally become, makes it possible for him to recognize an opportunity to act, constitutes his ability to know what to do and how to do it, and makes him capable of carrying out the action. Just as a settled ability is needed to execute a skillful achievement, a character is the source of being able to act morally. But in the world of exact essences, there are no situations that call for human action because there are no situations that need to be determined one way or another by a human being, and the sheer objectivity of exact essences precludes any reference to an agent and an agent's character as a measure of what ought to be done.

Both the exercise of skills and the performance of virtue or vice involve a reference to the agent and to his perceptions of what is going on. Not everyone sees what ought to be done in a situation calling for action. A skilled person or a virtuous person will interpret a situation differently from the way an unskilled or a vicious person, or someone who is simply morally obtuse, will interpret it. The correct measure of a situation calling for action inevitably involves the agent as a measure of what ought to be done. Ideal essences strive to exclude any reference to an agent or observer; they are to be ideals that are absolutely the same for everyone who can go through the method that generates them. Therefore a world in which exact essences are taken to be the final reality excludes what seems to be most important to human beings: human skills and human virtues "do not count" in such a world. The only human reality left in this ideal world is the mind that generates the exact essences, and perhaps also the residue of unskilled human labor, which seems to be the only possibility of intervention left to man in this new world he has achieved. This bleaching of the world of the need for human deliberation, both in regard to skill and in regard to virtue, this underlying conviction that human beings "don't count" except in a mathematical sense, is even more demoralizing than the disorientation induced when we are told that the world we perceive is not the true world.

And of course the two issues are related to each other: the reason why skills and action and deliberation are eliminated is that the world in which such things can be real, and in which they can make a difference, has been disqualified. In fact there is a tendency for people who deal primarily with exact essences to invoke the sentimental and the capricious when they attempt to say anything about the nature of action and skill. They do not know the categories appropriate to deliberation, choice, and action, and are usually unwilling to admit that there are any true necessities, any morphological essences, in the world we are immediately involved with. The only necessities they tend to acknowledge are the mathematical necessities in exact essences; all others are considered to be cultural or linguistic conventions.

Besides skill and character, another element that becomes dismissed in a world modeled on exact essences is the opportunity to take risks and to discover new alternatives in regard to the production and distribution of goods. Economists have shown that uncertainty in business and industry actually improves productivity and distribution because it provokes imaginative, more efficient responses to problems. But the problems, with their uncertainty and risk, have to be allowed to make an impression on the people who are supposed to deal with them. To shield individuals and groups from risk may make their immediate future more secure on a small scale, but it makes the large-scale future—that of the country as a whole, or that of the industry as a whole—more unstable, because the many small adaptations that are necessary are in fact never made. Competition and uncertainty improve economic performance and even reduce unemployment, thus contributing to long-term stability. Uncertainty and its attendant risks are therefore beneficial for modern economic life. However, economic theories that employ exact essences will tend to neglect uncertainty and the possible response to uncertainty by imaginative individuals. When such theories become the basis for economic policy, the policies will tend to suppress imprecision and will not tolerate uncertainty. Bureaucracies and regulatory agencies are much more at home in the world of exact essences than in the world in which uncertainty must be acknowledged.[6] And governmental policies that try to eliminate ambiguity also discourage, and finally prevent, groups and individuals from taking risks, that is, from making choices. Ironically, therefore, the very habit of idealized abstraction that makes modern industry and commerce possible finally threatens to stifle this economic life by suppressing the uncertainty and imprecision that characterize the life-world.

Skills, virtues, and the ability to handle risk are required because there is imprecision and indeterminacy in being. It is not just that we are confused or ignorant about how things are; indeterminacy is real, and the things themselves are truly undetermined.[7] For this reason what we do if and when we act does make a difference in the way things will be.

4

Why do exact essences exclude imprecision? Not all necessities or essences exclude indeterminacy; if we determine a morphological essence, our eidetic intuition discloses necessities, but it does not exclude imprecision and vagueness; on the contrary, it shows that certain kinds of imprecision are essential to particular kinds of things. We can work out eidetic necessities for morphological essences, for things like perception and memory, houses and animals, sport and war, things that cannot be made into ideal forms. And since imprecision is left in the essences

we so determine, what we discover can be applied directly to
the things we experience. Rover is an animal, and whatever is
essential to animals is found in Rover. The eidetic necessity does
not exclude the imprecision that comes along in actual experience. In contrast, an exact essence does not apply directly to the
things we experience; nothing we experience can be a circle or
an ideal voltage source the way Rover can be an animal. Ideal,
exact essences are distinguished from the world we experience
in a way eidetic necessities are not. In projecting certain variables toward a limit, the process of idealization does not merely
abstract from such variable factors; it positively excludes them
from the object it establishes. Idealization excludes imprecision,
it does not—as eidetic intuition does—merely leave the imprecision undetermined.

But why are exact essences distinguished in this way from the
things we experience? What are the presentational "motivations"
that make them not immediately predicable of ordinary objects
(*Ideas* 1 §47)? Exact essences are involved with *measurement* in a
way that disconnects them from things. Eidetic necessities belong
to the nature of a thing, but ideal, exact necessities belong to the
thing as subject to being measured. Eidetic intuition treats the
thing as to be understood, while the generation of exact essences
treats the thing as to be measured. In idealization we transform
the thing exclusively into a thing to be measured, and we exclude
from it that which cannot be counted, or that which impedes
accurate counting; we exclude imprecision. When we do this we
are not left with the whole thing and all its necessities, but only
with what in it is subject to exact measurement.

When we establish an exact form, when we go for example
from a table top to a geometrical surface or from a pointed hill
to a cone or to a pyramid, the ideal form itself does not become
a unit of measurement; it becomes an ideal form of something
measured. Part of the sense of such an ideal is that ideal units of
measurement are also established in function of the form to be
measured. That is, we not only have the ideal projection toward
a surface, but also the ideal projection of units that measure the
surface and its sides. We begin to operate with "the" meter and
"the" inch. The exact essence and the units of measurement are
moments to one another. And when the ideal form and its ideal

units are generated, the ideal essence, "the" triangle or "the" cone, remains the "object" to be measured. The ideal essences are not mental constructs in the sense of being something psychological. They are a possibility in the world, a possibility of presentation. They are a special kind of profile or "look" or *eidos* of things, the kind of look things have when they become taken as instances of a geometrical or other ideal form. The intentionality of the mind, its work of making present, is not interrupted when we deal with exact essences.

We can appreciate exact essences better if we examine the units of measurement correlated to them. Using spatial measurement as our paradigm, we can distinguish four levels in the activity of measuring. (1) Measurement begins with units like an arm's length or a step which a man can pace off. (2) Then the human scale can be replaced by something like a rigid body, like a piece of wood, that escapes the indeterminacy in the size of people's arms or strides. However, this rigid body still has to be placed down over and over again against what is to be measured, so there is still a physical human gesture involved in using a rigid body. This gesture is like the activity of stepping off the length, the activity described under (1). But then (3) the measuring stick itself can be replaced by "the" meter or "the" yard. And when this occurs, the physical gestures of either pacing off or placing the rod down over and over again are sublimated into the sheer categorial activity of totaling. Furthermore, the thing measured is now no longer a field or a table but a rectangle. So three things: the object measured, the unit of measure, and the gesture of measuring, are transformed at this stage. We cannot clarify any one of these without involving the other two; we cannot for example clarify what exact essences are without also clarifying the ideal units and the sublimated gesture of measuring. (It should be repeated that although the gesture of measuring has become mental, we do not measure something mental.)

One more change in the measuring process can occur. (4) Instead of using units we bring to the measured object, units like the inch or the meter or the step, we can use one part of the object as a unit for measuring other parts. We can use one side of the rectangle and say that the other side is twice this one. We would express this "proportionally" by stating $B = 2A$. This kind of measuring still involves the measuring gesture, for we still "place" the shorter side "down" twice against the longer side. Also, we still have the object being measured: we continue to measure the rectangle or the circle or the cone, even though we are using one part of this object to measure the other parts. The object measured is measured by parts of itself. We have what we might call an internal system of measurement, one in which we determine the proportions of one part to others. But even when we use such parts of the ideal essence to establish equivalencies, which are expressed in equations, we still do not use the form or the essence itself as a unit of measure: the rectangle or the triangle is still the thing measured, not the unit by which we measure.

The establishment of an exact essence, like a geometrical figure, is therefore linked to the establishment of exact units by which that figure is to be measured. We must not suppose that a geometrical figure is generated simply by a kind of visual purifying of actual shapes into perfect forms: we do not just imaginatively "polish" the surface more and more until we get a plane; the process of smoothing the surface into a plane is correlated to the process of measuring the plane with exact units or with parts of its own self. The geometrical figure is not there first and only subsequently measured by us; it is there by being measurable. Furthermore, other ideal essences, like light rays, ideal machines, voltage sources, perfectly flexible strings, and the like, are likewise established not just by an imaginative projection toward a limit but also by the determination of exact units by which the object is measured, units appropriate to the kind of thing in question. To complete what we said before, inventive genius in a particular area of exact science involves not only seeing what kind of ideal is appropriate to the thing studied, but also seeing what sort of measuring units are appropriate to it.

We have distinguished between measuring units that we bring to an object (like the steps or the meter stick or "the" meter we use to measure the side of a field or rectangle) and measuring units that are taken from the internal structure of the object measured (like one side being used to measure another side, or one vector used to measure another in a parallelogram of forces). Equations that are used to express the relationships in an exact essence employ the second kind of unit, the units of internal proportions. This occurs, for example, when we say that side *B* of a rectangle is twice side *A*; or that the square of the hypotenuse of a right triangle is equal to the sum of the squares of the other sides; or that the efficiency of a Carnot engine is formulated as:

$$\text{Eff.}(\%) = 100 \, \frac{T_2 - T_1}{T_2}$$

where T_2 is the absolute temperature of the heat input and T_1 the absolute temperature of the heat output; or when we say the force exerted on a charge *q* moving through a uniform magnetic field is expressed by:

$$F = qvB\sin\phi$$

where *v* is the particle's velocity, *B* is the induction of the field, and ϕ is the angle between the directions of *B* and *v*. In all such cases we express a whole or a system by showing how its parts or dimensions are internally related to one another. It is significant that such expressions are *equations;* that is, they show how parts combine to make up an identity or a whole, how the parts become equal to other parts when they are taken together.

Now when we put values into the equations, when we say side *A* is five feet long so side *B* is ten; or that T_2 is 480°F and T_1 is 102°F, so the efficiency of the Carnot engine is 78.75 percent; then we shift our measuring units from those that are internal to the system to those that we bring to the system; we move toward the meter, or the meter rod, or even the step; we move toward the thermometer or even the freezing of water or the melting of ice. In the levels we distinguished earlier, we move from (4) to (3) or (2) or even to (1). It is, of course, at this point of shifting to units we bring to the system that instruments are employed as factors in measurement.

Obviously units like the step and the meter stick, those used in (1) and (2), are parts of the life-world. And obviously the structures in (4), the internal system of proportions, are not parts of the life-world. They belong to the world of exact forms. But what about (3), the exact form measured by "the" meter and by other ideal units? The forms found in (3) are a transformation of the types found in (1) and (2), a transformation which occurs because the measurements in (1) and (2) are now seen to anticipate the internal system of measurement found in (4). When we move from (1) and (2) to (4), we move from using units we bring to the object, to using units provided by the object itself. The idealization of the object is the legitimation of this move; it is an identification that asserts the object is the same object no matter by which of these two methods it is measured.

Finally, it may be claimed that exact essences no longer play a role in physics, that no one now believes in any sense in the reality of ideal voltage sources or frictionless machines or other ideal forms. Instead, physicists are interested in functional dependencies of one part of what they examine upon other parts. In such physics we seem to move beyond what we earlier described as step (4). But the equations and relationships expressed in algebraic formulas and in computer printouts are still determined by the transformation in the forms of measurement that takes place between stages (1) and (4). The formulas and the data are taken to refer to something, and the exact essences still mediate their reference. It is only because the things we experience have been transformed into ideally measurable things that algebraicization can work for them. Exact essences are still around to give sense to our figures and calculations, to provide the horizon within which such calculations can occur, and to determine that *these* figures refer to one kind of thing (like electrical circuits) and *those* figures to another (like subatomic particles). Once we have gone through exact essences to get to functional relationships, we do not leave the ideal forms entirely behind. We may be less tempted to take exact essences as a sort of depiction of what things really are like, but they still function to mediate the reference of numbers and formulas; they are a factor in the mind's intentionality, for even in exact science the mind is with things and not simply with its own constructions.

The mathematical, economic, and political ideal essences become more self-sufficient as they cut the ties that bind them to the everyday world, and as they formulate their own exactness in terms of the internal relationships of their parts. The exact essences become independent, and yet remain applicable to the lived world from which they arise. As they become more self-sufficient, they can be used more thoroughly to dominate the ordinary and the imprecise. The combination of independence and applicability gives these essences great power over the source to which they owe their being.[8]

IV

8
Exorcising Concepts

1

Ferdinand de Saussure says that a word is composed of two parts, a sound-image and a concept: "The linguistic sign unites not a thing and a name, but a concept and an acoustic image."[1] The sound-image signifies the concept: the sound-image is the signifier, the concept is the signified. De Saussure is only one of a large company of thinkers who describe words in this way. Most philosophical and semiotic analyses of words claim that words have two components, a dimension of sounds and a dimension of concepts.

But to look at words this way can be very misleading. It inclines us to believe that the concept *is* something: that there is some sort of entity in our minds, or perhaps in our brains, that we can call the *concept.* De Saussure himself speaks of concepts as "facts of consciousness" found in our brains.[2] And when we take concepts in this way, we become inclined to consider our minds or even our brains as the kind of thing that contains ideas and concepts. Because of the misleading way in which we have described words, we generate a population of strange entities, and then we construct a place in which they can dwell. We tend to substantialize both concepts and the mind. We may even go on to add a process of ideogenesis, a natural process in which impressions cause images which in turn cause concepts; thus new concepts are said to be brought into being and to take their place in the mind along with those that are there already.

Mental entities, as the significations of our words, have been postulated under many different titles in the history of thought: as *concepts, mental words, interior words, intelligible species, ideas, notions, cognitive contents,* and *abstract entities.* Under these and other names they have been accepted by Neoplatonic philosophers and theologians, by various Scholastics, by Descartes, by the classical British empiricists, Kant and the Neokantians, as well as by many recent thinkers. But other writers have argued against the existence of such mental entities. William of Ockham, for example, in his later philosophy, denied that a concept could exist as something distinct from an act of understanding. Earlier in our century Ryle argued against mental entities, and the general drift of recent theories of meaning and reference has also been negative.[3] But such entities still keep coming back, just as they have throughout the history of Western philosophy; recently John Searle has launched a vigorous counterattack against the critics of mental states and intentional contents. In a chapter entitled, "Are Meanings in the Head?" he claims, "Some form of internalism must be right because there isn't anything else to do the job. The brain is all we have for the purpose of representing the world to ourselves and everything we can use must be inside the brain."[4] Searle's own position is "a kind of biological naturalism," but he does feel compelled to posit intentional states as the only possible explanation of consciousness, thinking, and language.

It is interesting that the writers who posit concepts do so as a result of argument and because they see no other way of accounting for the way we experience the world. No one directly experiences concepts or abstract entities or ideas. Those who believe in them are backed into accepting such things; they are forced by argument to posit them. And when we do posit concepts, we find that their way of being is troubling and embarrassing. It is not surprising therefore that there have been many arguments against them.[5]

But none of the arguments against the existence of mental conceptual entities will rid us of our tendency to posit such entities until we can get a better analysis of language. We need a positive description of words that is more adequate than the one that leads us down this false trail. Just to argue against the existence of mental entities is like treating the symptoms of an illness without treating the illness itself. The ailment will keep coming back. We remain left with the misunderstanding of words, the inadequate description, the bed of infection that generates the symptoms we chronically suffer from. Until the understanding of words is set right, we will continue to fall back again and again into positing the imaginary mental kingdom with its population of ideas.

Furthermore, we tend to posit ideas and concepts, not just because of philosophical confusions, but quite spontaneously under the sway of ordinary language and experience. It seems so plausible to say that our words bring out something that is somehow in us, and that they convey this same curious thing to someone else, to the one who hears and understands what we say; that we then share the idea that was previously possessed by only one of us. Even primitive descriptions of what goes on when we speak appeal to such ideas "in" us, whether in our heads or in our hearts.

I will try to provide a philosophical description of words that will not force us to posit ideas or concepts as mental entities. My approach will expand the number of factors that must be taken into account in a description of what happens when a word exists. My description requires four elements: (1) the speaker; (2) the sound, the phonemic dimension of the word; (3) the thing being named or referred to through the use of the word; (4) someone who hears and understands the word.

The position I argue against would claim that a word can exist when only the first two of these four factors are present, (A) the speaker and (B) the phonemic dimension, and that these two factors require the presence of (C) the mental thing called a concept. The position I argue against would claim that the concept in the speaker's mind is activated—it begins to "glow"— as the word is spoken or imagined. The thing spoken about could be dispensed with; it could be absent, or it could even be nonexistent. The interlocutor or listener could also be dispensed with. A word comes into being when someone blends a glowing idea with a phonemic stream. As de Saussure says, "A linguistic entity exists only by the association of the signifier and the signified; once one keeps only one of these elements, the linguistic entity disappears."[6] The sound alone could not make the word; by itself it has no meaning and does not count as a word. The glowing concept alone would not constitute a word either; that would be only wordless thinking, if indeed it could happen at all. But a word does come into being when sound and concept are generated together, and for this to happen, the concept must somehow exist. This is the conclusion I wish to destroy.

2

I maintain that the concept as a mental entity is a transcendental mirage, something analogous to the mirages we occasionally encounter in our experience of things.

In an ordinary, worldly mirage, we think we see something when no such thing is there. What we seem to see appears to us because of the refraction of light waves, a refraction that displaces and distorts the looks of distant objects. One of the causes of our false seeing is the point of view from which we observe; if we were placed elsewhere, the refraction would not strike us the way it does and the distortion would not take place.

A transcendental mirage occurs to us not when we look at objects but when we try to talk about words and thinking. Here again we think we "see" or must posit something. However, that something is not there, at least not as we think we must posit it. And one of the causes of our false positing is the point of view from which we think: it is the position from which we reflect. It is because we want to talk about words and thinking—which are strange things to talk about indeed—and not merely to talk about ordinary objects, that we are subjected to this mirage. My task is to unravel some of the perspectives at work here, and to show how they bring about the mirage of entities such as concepts and ideas.

Even an ordinary mirage is not nothing: it *is* a mirage. A mirage is not what it seems to be, but that, precisely, is what a mirage is. Also a mirage is not a dream, it is not a memory, it is not a pine tree or a beaver. It can be distinguished from other kinds of being. It is as a mirage. Likewise, the entity called a *concept*, the thing that we want to show up as a transcendental mirage, *is* as a mirage, and there are factors that go into making it to be such. There are reasons why we are so strongly inclined to posit such a thing. The mental entity is interesting, philosophically interesting, precisely in its being a transcendental mirage. I will attempt to demystify this issue, to exorcise ghosts and show they are only shadows; but also to show what such shadows are, and why they look like ghosts. My procedure of demystification will not be all negative, therefore. In eliminating concepts as mental beings, I will have positive things to say about the ontology of appearance. And my first step in doing this is to insist on the four factors I cannot do without: the speaker, the sound, the thing spoken about, and the hearer.

3

John says "persimmon" and Mary understands what he says. We want to avoid appealing to concepts as explanations of what John expresses and Mary understands. How are we to clarify what is going on?

Mary has been acquainted with persimmons. The sound John utters makes her think of persimmons. Persimmons become the target of her attention (whether they are perceptually present or not). But they become present to her in a special way. They become present to her *as presented by John through what he voices*. This slant is the new and important dimension, and it makes persimmons into the meaning *persimmons*. Persimmons taken (by Mary) as presented by John make up the meaning of what John has said. The only "thing" added to persimmons is their being taken as presented by the speech of John. This formal dimension is all that is "layered" onto persimmons. This way of being taken transmutes a persimmon into a meaning, and it gives a meaning to the words that are voiced.

Thus there is no need to appeal to a concept or idea as a mental entity, distinct from real persimmons and expressed by the words. A new slant, not a new thing, is all that is added. To postulate a mental entity, a concept or idea, is to undergo a mirage; it is to substantialize a slant or a way of being taken. We do not need such entities; all we need are the verbal sound, the object, the speaker and his achievements, and the interlocutor and her achievements. And underlying all these, of course, is the ability we have to take a presented object as being presented to us by a speaker in the words he voices.

My interpretation brings words and things more closely together (there is no concept mediating between them). My interpretation of meaning seems to paste a meaning right on the thing that is meant, instead of locating it in the mind or in the psyche. My interpretation almost seems to go back to the kind of identification of word and thing that is said to be typical of primitive cultures, in which the name of something or someone is thought to contain the "soul" of what is named. But there may be something to this primitive understanding. We in our sophistication have psychologized the use of words. In a Lockean spirit we have allowed words to range only over the domain of our ideas, and we have tacitly taken ideas to be some sort of internal things. But philosophically this is terribly naive. An idea is not an internal entity and in an important sense it is really not other to the thing of which it is the idea. An idea is a thing presented or understood. Only the slant of being taken as presented or as understood needs to be "added" to a thing to give us the idea of that thing. So a linguistic sound should indeed be blended more closely with that which it presents. The sound is the vehicle by which the thing is presented and also taken as being presented by the one who makes the sound. The meaning of the sound is the thing, but the thing taken as presented by the speaker. And the word does indeed possess something like the "soul" of the thing: it draws attention to the thing's possibility of presenting itself, of being itself in its many ways of being experienced and understood.

To bring out the peculiarities of words and their meanings, let us contrast them to signs that indicate an object but are not used to mean the object. Suppose that every time I hear tires screech, I think of Avery, who is a terrible driver. Sometimes, indeed, the sound of screeching tires is a sign that Avery is coming. But although this sound indicates Avery to me, it does not have the meaning Avery, the way the sound "Avery," or some other name of the same man, does. The difference lies in this: the indication-sign makes me think of Avery, but not as presented by anyone to anyone. The screeching tires only draw my attention to Avery. But the word *Avery* draws my attention to Avery as being presented to me by whoever voices the word. Another dimension is added in words, one that does not function in indication-signs. The presentational intitiative of the speaker and the presentational achievement of the listener come into play and the thing is presented as presented by someone to someone: the thing becomes a meaning, and the sounds acquire a meaning (whereas the screeching tires, strictly speaking, do not). And once we take an object as being presented by someone to someone, we naturally want to find out *how* the object is being presented: we go on to hear *what* the speaker has to say *about* the thing.[7] But we do not wait to hear what else the screeching tires have to say about what they suggest, because no saying and no meaning are involved in them. Thus an indication-sign just turns us toward an object, while a word turns us toward an object to prepare us for what is to be said about it.

A sign that merely indicates a thing, such as the screeching tires that indicate Avery, brings that thing to mind and then lets go; it simply lets the thing be presented. But a sign that is used to mean a thing brings that thing to mind and then holds on; it lets the thing be presented as presented by the sign and by the one who uses the sign, to the one who "takes up" the sign. Thus the name of a thing does not just present the thing; the name stays around as presenting the thing, and the thing remains suffused as being what the name refers to. The thing and the name belong together in a way in which the thing and its indication-sign do not belong together. And once the thing has been presented by its name, we can go on to inquire *how* the thing is meant by the use, even by *this* use, of the word. When we do this, we inquire after the meaning of the word.

4

My interpretation of meaning has some affinities with the account given by Frege. Frege says that a name has both "sense" and "reference," *Sinn* and *Bedeutung*.[8] The names *morning star* and *evening star* have different senses but the same reference, since they are both used to refer to the same celestial object. Frege defines *sense* as the "mode of presentation" of the object, the description under which the object is presented, while the referent is the "bare" or "mere" object. In my analysis also a name has both reference and sense: a word turns our attention to an object, but to the object as to be presented in a specific way by the use of this particular term. However, there is a difference in the import of Frege's account and my own. My account tries to show how the very domain of sense is differentiated from the domain of objects. It tries to bring out the various contexts and achievements within which the domain of meaning is established: it brings into play the object, the sound, the speaker and his achievements, the listener and his achievements, and most of all the capacity we have to take an object not just directly but as presented by someone to someone. Frege does distinguish sense from reference, but he does not explore the being of sense and the differentiation of sense from object by the achievements of the speaker and listener. He provides the statics but not the dynamics of sense. Frege takes the difference for granted whereas I wish to treat it as a philosophical issue.

I have limited my description of an act of meaning to a rather simple case, the case of one speaker using a single term to express something to a listener. But the important thing is not whether there are only two conversationalists or many, and it is not whether the meaning stated is simple or complex: the important thing is that a new dimension, a new slant is opened. We have not only things, but things taken as presented by someone to someone. This is the domain of meaning. In this dimension we enjoy great flexibility. There is a wide range of *ways* in which a thing can be presented by someone to someone. It can be presented in its individuality (Avery) or it can be presented as an instance of a kind (this case of smallpox). The kind itself can be presented (smallpox damages the complexion). And besides changing the formal registers in the ways the thing is presented, the speaker can bring out various features and relations in the object. All these possibilities are not simply psychological permutations of an impression, existing simply in the speaker's mind. They are not simply ways in which we can mean; they are ways in which the object can be presented. They are not merely eccentricities of language, nor merely mental mechanisms or psycholinguistic possibilities. They are ontological. They are ways in which things can become meaningful. They are ways in which things can be presented, and as such they are part of the being of things. One of the most destructive effects of the tendency we have to psychologize or mentalize meanings is the withdrawal of the formal possibilities of presentation from beings and the confinement of these possibilities to our mental and psychological makeup, as though our minds were something else besides the presentation of things.

Furthermore, linguistic grammar and logical syntax do not affect merely our speech and the subjective, psychic arrangements of our ideas. They pattern how things can be presented. In ordering our meanings, we order *how* things seem to us and *how* we present them to others, because meanings are precisely things as presented. Through our syntax we do not merely link a subject-idea with a concept, we do not merely combine mental representations into propositions, making them into complex mental entities. Rather, we make moves within the dimensions opened up when things are considered as being presented by a speaker to a listener. To say, "Persimmons are sour when they are not ripe," is not to rearrange our mental concepts, but to articulate a small part of the world, to arrange its wholes and parts, its things and aspects, and to present it as so arranged through the words we voice. Syntactical composition is a special kind of achievement made possible in the domain of presentability we call meaning.

And although we have used the simple case of John and Mary speaking to one another, the new slant on things can occur both when a speaker is alone and when the speaker is generalized or depersonalized to such a degree that we reach, not John's or Mary's meaning, but "the" meaning that everyone or anyone would have of the object in question: in the case of the anonymous meaning, we still acquire the dimension of meaning by virtue of the object's being taken as presentable to everyone and anyone. The slant does the trick. Even dictionary meanings are how certain things are presentable in a certain language; they are not expressions of possible mental entities. And in the marginal case of the solitary speaker, the speaker, though alone, still introduces the slant of how things are presentable to himself and how they could be presented, by what he says, to others. There is always some incipient conversation even when we think by ourselves.[9]

5

I have noted that we seem inveterately inclined to think of ideas or concepts as things in the mind. Perhaps we can spell out why we tend toward this psychological interpretation of meaning, why we are inclined to posit concepts as mental entities and the mind as the repository of such entities. One of the reasons is philosophical, perhaps metaphysical. It is the great difficulty we have in coping intellectually with presence and absence. One of the great advantages language gives us is the ability to deal with what is absent: with the future, the past, the distant, even the forgotten, the sought, the misunderstood. We as language-users can react not only to what is immediately before us, but also to what is not there before us. We become involved with the absent through our memory and imagination and through pictures, but certainly language is the primary vehicle by which we deal with what is not there before us; language may even be the dimension that permits the specifically human forms of remembering, imagining, and picturing. And when we deal with the absent, we do become cognitively involved with what is away from us. If I tell you about a meeting I had yesterday, or about a building that is a thousand miles distant, you and I are truly concerned with that meeting or that building; I present that object in its absence, and even *as* absent: as "yesterday" or as "far away."

Now we seem to resist the view that we truly deal with the absent. We seem desperately to want something "here" as the true target of our discourse. So we posit ideas, concepts, mental contents, perhaps even images or "mental pictures" as what we are truly concerned with. But in fact we do deal with the absent; we present and intend what is past or distant. Meaning also functions in such intending of the absent; in fact most of our speech and meaning is about what is absent. And when I speak about the absent building and you listen and understand, you can take that absent building and what I say about it as being presented by me. *That* is the meaning of my words: the absent building being taken as presented to you by me in the words that I voice and you hear. The meaning is not something here in my mind as a psychological concept; it is not a substitute for the building that is not there before us. It is what I am stating. It is a small part of the world, an absent part, one being taken as presented by me to you in the sounds I make.

The existence of false statements and of statements that are mistaken in their reference is another reason why we are inclined to posit mental entities as the meanings of such statements. There may be nothing, or there may be something else, "out there," but, in this mistaken interpretation, the concepts are said to exist "in here" and their falsity or failure of reference is said to consist in their somehow not matching what is "out there." How does my interpretation, which seems to locate meanings in the presentabilities of things, account for falsity and reference-failure? Would my interpretation not make falsity and failure of reference impossible?

It would not. The fact is that things can be presented as other than they are. Presentability is such as to allow false appearances. This happens even in ordinary perception when, for example, a bush looks like and is taken as a man, or a piece of ice looks like and is taken as a piece of glass. It happens even more intensely when we deal not with simple perceptions but with the way things can be presented—usually in their absence—in words. Anger, for example, may be talked about as hatred, or friendship can be talked about as exploitation. The thing presents itself in speech as other than it truly is, and the speaker who presents it in this way is false in what he says. Even a failure of reference—as when I talk about Peter's second sister (he has only one)—is an attempt on my part to present a small part of the world; it is not a failure of something in my head to be correlated to anything in the world. My attempt to identify fails, but I am still engaged in processing the world, and my meanings are how I try to present the way things are.

Yet another reason why we are inclined to posit ideas and concepts as mental things is the fact that this domain seems to subsist apart from our voluntary control. As long as we are talking, there seem to be ideas around; these ideas seem to surface, to begin glowing, even before we talk: they seem to be what stimulates us to speak. But we do not need to substantialize ideas and concepts to account for the phenomenon at work here. We are constituted as human beings and as speakers not by the emergence of mental entities, but by our persistent ability to take what we experience as presented by, or as presentable to, someone in speech. It is this ability, and its almost perpetual activation on the border of all our experience, that allows us to deal not only with things but also with things as stated or as statable, that is, with meanings. As users of language we are always incipiently reflective. Indeed it is this sensitivity to things as presentable that opens the possibility of speech to us: it is not simply the learning of words and grammar. Words and grammar rush in to fill the space opened by this new slant on things. Without the slant, the composition of words would be only a game.

Once we have the ability to shift from things to things as presented in speech, we can exercise it in various ways. Sometimes we may do so in serious work, as we try to verify whether what is said is true or not: we experience things in order to confirm or disconfirm the way they have been presented by someone, the way someone said they were. But we can also just flick from one to the other, from thing to meaning and back, for the sheer enjoyment of it. We can simply delight in the difference between thing and meaning. We can, for example, think of eating, and think of eating as presented by John Jones, and think of eating as presented in Italian, French, German, and English, for the nuances of meaning it can have in these languages. It is only because eating is somehow the same and yet differently presented that, say, a French comedian can make jokes about British cuisine. And if we extend the scope of our enjoyable shifts to cover even the voiced sound, we can delight in puns, double entendres, insightful metaphors, and amusing incoherences, as when Mr. Rude is put in charge of hospitality, or when we meet a plumber named Flood, or when a man named Forget edits a book on hermeneutics.[10] In such cases we sink down into the word itself and we stir up the other meanings it carries, the other presentations of which it is the vehicle. We allow these other senses to be played off against the one we are engaged in now, and thus allow things (as presented) to be compared and contrasted with one another in an enormous variety of ways. We can be far more clever in speech than we can be in simple mimicry or imitation.

But when we move from thing to meaning to word, whether in work or at play, we do not turn from that thing there (an object) to this thing here (a mental entity) to still another thing coming forth (a word); we simply shift our attitude and go from the thing to the thing as presented to the thing as presented and as voiced. And concepts as mental entities, the transcendental mirage that occurs so persistently, are simply reified or decontextualized meanings. They are modes of presentation that have mistakenly been taken as mental things.

I have, in other places, claimed that philosophy is the analysis of the forms of presentation, the description of the ways in which things can be presented.[11] The philosophical reflection that issues in such analysis is not, of course, the same as the kind of reflection we are discussing in this paper, the kind that establishes human existence in language. But unless there were the reflection that opens the possibility of meaning, there could not be any philosophical reflection either. Philosophical thinking brings to a new level the distancing to experience that is begun in all human speech.

9
Referring

1

When words appear, they interrupt the dense continuity of things. Pictures do so as well, but in a different way. The things surrounding me form a dense continuum: my attention can move from one thing to another without leaving what is immediately there. I can go from the table to the rug to the chair to the lamp and to the wall. But if at some point I come to a picture, this plain sequence is broken, and although it may quickly be picked up again, it is interrupted by the picture. When I hit the picture, I am no longer just with what is immediately there. I am with the depicted as well as with what is itself there. It is as though a fourth spatial dimension suddenly came into play, not effacing but being added to the three that were and are there all along. A new horizon appears and is blended with the one in which I am engaged.

Likewise, if there is a continuum of mere sounds and suddenly the word *Tristan* intrudes, the continuum is broken and the dimensions of sound are supplemented, for as long as the word lasts, by the dimension in which I am with Tristan and not just with the mere sounds, not even just with *Tristan*. The word carries me somewhere else; it "refers" me to Tristan.

But in their interruptions, words and pictures differ. A picture pulls the depicted into the context in which the picture is found, but a word does not bring its referent to where the word is stated. It does the opposite: I am referred to the thing and taken out of my immediate context. A picture is an amplification of presence, a word is a more explicit invocation of the absent. Pictures also bring something absent to mind, and make us aware of its absence, but they do so with a kind of overcoming of absence. They make the thing to be as though present. Words are more resolute and abrupt. They renounce any likeness and carry us away, away from themselves as words and away from ourselves and our context. They erase any presence of the thing, and yet they make the thing the object of our thinking; in doing so they help establish thinking as devolution into absence. Words make us think of the thing as it is in itself, wherever it may be, whereas a picture makes us think of the thing as it appears to us in the picture, as it visits our context. Thus words and pictures have much in common: both mix the "to us" and the "us to"; but their emphases are different.

Words exercise their referential function as soon as they appear within the sound and silence that surround us at all times. The words themselves can relapse into the flow of sound, when they belong to a language we do not understand—and make up, say, "Polish chatter" or "Italian melody"—or, if they belong to a language we know, when we ourselves stop paying attention to them as words and allow them to blend into the background. We then just rest in the phonic presence and stop making any effort to go to whatever they would refer us to. We reseal the dense continuity of things and close down the horizon the words try to open. This dimension, the involvement with the absent, can come and go as words flash on and off in the mere sounds that surround us.

But reference is never indiscriminate. It is never only a reference to "anywhere else, just not here." It is always specified, even though we may be unsure of the specification. Sometimes, given the context in which the word is spoken, and given the target to which the word is used to refer, the simple occurrence of the word is enough to identify the referent. If I have an uncle named Tristan and my aunt utters "Tristan," I just wait, without perplexity, for what else she has to say. But at other times more words will be needed to organize the reference: "A customer bought a bicycle from our store in Annapolis yesterday; he . . . ."

Thus within the dimension of reference as such, which has been added to the simple dimension of immediate sound, we can distinguish two ways of achieving reference: by means of a simple name and by means of a description.

And we can use a particular locution to refer to our target in two ways. We can use a description to identify a referent, then allow the description to fall away once we have locked onto our target. This is a throwaway description. We might begin with, "The customer who bought the bicycle from us yesterday . . .," but what we go on to say about him has nothing to do formally with his being a customer: ". . . lives on Tilghman's Island and has been a fisherman since he was a boy." The field of force of the first, identifying description is neutralized. Although we do say more about him, we do not speak about him as the customer who bought the bicycle. The identifying phrase is like a cloud of words that materializes only to spot the object behind it, then dissipates and leaves us with our target.

On the other hand, we can also let our identifying phrase remain in effect: "The customer who bought the bike: he found out it was used for a month by somebody else. He's bringing it back." We go on to speak of him precisely as the customer. The field of force, the semantic magnetism of our first, identifying description stays in effect and provides a context for the rest of the things we go on to say about our target. In this case the identifying phrase is like a frame that remains around the referent and provides the basis for what is disclosed about it.

This contrast between getting to our target apart from the way it appears in our identification, and getting further into it as it is already presented in the identification, occurs not only in the use of descriptive phrases. It can also occur when we use simple names. We can be concerned with Tristan as an individual and use the name *Tristan* to get at him as such, or we can be concerned with Tristan precisely as named "Tristan": "Tristan was named after his grandfather." The name can be used as the identificatory cloud or as the encompassing frame.

There are then these two formal possibilities in reference: just locking onto our target; and dealing further with our target still under the characterization by which we locked onto it. They are like two purely logical possibilities. In our actual speech, we may invoke one or the other, or we may oscillate between the two. The distinction between identifiers that vanish and those that remain as a context for description will be examined further in section 4 of this essay.

2

We introduced the problem of reference by contrasting words and pictures and by discussing how words are used to refer to something absent. When we speak about the absent, we are in possession of the words and the object must be brought to mind. But this way of formulating the problem of reference must be played off against the other possibility, the one in which the object is present and the word is to be introduced. The "referent" is already there and the word or the words are brought to mind.

Suppose I am dealing with Topper, in his presence, and Margaret says "Topper. . . " A word surfaces in the ambient rush of mere sound; it arrests me as words arrest those who hear them; it opens the new dimension in which something other to the word is brought to mind. But what is the "something other" that is introduced? Topper does not need to be *brought* to mind; he is there and has been there all along.

But he is brought to mind in a new way. The word is not just more of Topper, not merely one more of the things I experience as I go on dealing with him. In and through the word, Topper now appears to me as being targeted by Margaret.[1] Moreover, he surfaces for me not just as the object of Margaret's activity—as to be picked up or fed or brushed—but as to be disclosed in some way. Margaret is going to say something about Topper, and Topper now appears as "about to be manifested" by what Margaret is going to say. He emerges as a referent. This dimension into which Topper has been moved, this "presentational form," arises for me when and as Margaret says "Topper. . . " The occurrence of the word in the rush of sound turns on a new dimension in Topper, even though Topper has been with us from the start.

The ellipsis in "Topper. . ." is what makes *Topper* into a referential expression. The ellipsis indicates that there is more disclosure to come, a disclosure that will be expressed in the words that follow.

Determining what we refer to is not very difficult when the thing is present to us, especially if we are already attentive to it. Often a demonstrative pronoun is enough ("This is such fun") and sometimes no special term is needed, only the feature need be mentioned ("Frisky today!"). But the ease of identification should not make us overlook the fact that a new dimension is introduced: we do not just have more of Topper, more of what we had before there was a word, but Topper is now appreciated as referent and as to be stated and manifested; we have the same Topper identified in a new dimension which is added to those that were there before there was a word. The fact that there is no problem about what we are discussing should not blind us to the fact that there is still an issue here: the shift between Topper and Topper as referred to has clicked into place, and this happens when "Topper. . ." occurs.

When Margaret talks about Topper in his presence, the object is there and the words intrude to pry open a new dimension. If Tristan is absent and Helen says "Tristan. . .," the object is absent but the same dimensional change occurs. I could have been thinking about Tristan all along, but when the name occurs, I think of him in a new way, as being referred to, as about to be displayed by whoever uttered his name. The reference in the word is a modification of the way Tristan is taken. And if I have not been thinking about him all along, the word brings him to mind, but it does not just bring him to mind. It brings him as about to be articulated by the one who refers to him, by Helen.

There is a difference between a word, with its reference, and a signal. Suppose Margaret and I had agreed that she would ring a bell when Topper returned home. This ringing does not refer to Topper in the way that "Topper. . ." does: it puts me in mind of Topper, but not as to be distinguished and articulated by Margaret, the one who rings the bell. Reference is not the same as mere association.

However, the associational substrate remains a part of a word. The word *Topper* can function like the ringing of a bell, merely to put me in mind of Topper. When this happens, *Topper* is not fully active as a word; it is something like a word that has collapsed into being a signal. It does not exercise reference because it only makes me think of Topper, not of Topper as targeted by someone to someone for display. "Topper . . ." has been reduced to *Topper*. Words can degenerate into being mere signals. But the associational substrate is not just a danger, not just a threat to the being of a name. It is a necessary condition for reference, just as perceptual association is a condition for inference and for intelligent anticipation, and not only a substitute for logical thinking. Without the associational base as a kind of awakening, the more discrete and thoughtful accomplishment of reference could not occur. Reference incorporates its associational basis into itself, it uplifts and perfects the association of word and thing. Reference is a new form, an intentional or presentational form that completes its associational substrate.

It has often been observed that words, even simple names, function only as embedded in sentences. In speaking about the relation between a name, its object, and a speaker, Donald Davidson says, "It is inconceivable that one should be able to explain this relation without first explaining the role of the word in sentences."[2] Our discussion of reference provides the presentational structure behind this linguistic fact: a name does not stand alone because through its reference it targets something as to be further disclosed, and the rest of the sentence expresses this further disclosure. A signal, on the other hand, does not necessarily need other signals to complete it—it is not syncategorematic— because it only brings its object to mind, it does not introduce it as to be further manifested.

Reference therefore does not occur simply between an entity called a word and another entity called the referent. Reference occurs when a word is used by someone to refer someone to something as to be disclosed: Helen makes Tristan a referent by saying "Tristan . . ." to me. I am the dative of reference. As such, I think of Tristan under a double slant: (1) I have him in mind; but (2) I have him in mind as targeted, for display or articulation, by someone in speech. I do not just have Tristan in mind: that would be mere remembering or thinking or association or the result of a signal. But I also do not have *only* the second slant on Tristan either: I do not see him *only* as referred to *by Helen*. It would not be possible for me to have only this slant on him, because for this slant to occur, Tristan must *also* be an object of *my* thinking. To have him as the object of my own thinking is something like a basis for having him as the target referred to by Helen, just as the association between *Tristan* and Tristan is something like the basis for the reference between the word and its target. Tristan is presented to or intended by me under a double aspect, and this dual aspect makes Tristan a referent.

And in describing the structure of reference, we have to blend the two cases we have discussed, the introduction of "Topper . . ." to refer to something present and the introduction of "Tristan . . ." to refer to something absent. Reference straddles presence and absence, and its power lies precisely in being able to do so. The importance of referring to and articulating Topper in his presence lies not just in being able to enhance a perception, or in being able to say the same thing again when the thing perceived comes back; it lies in the capacity to accomplish the same reference and articulation when the target is absent. We can inform one another, clearly and distinctly, about what is absent to us. And the absent thing I am told about can be brought to presence; I can confirm in its presence what I was told about it when it was absent, and I can be prepared to cope with it when it comes into view. The structure of reference allows me to deal with an object as an issue across presence and absence, to negotiate a unity in the difference between presence and absence.[3]

Human rationality is sometimes thought to lie primarily in the power to grasp universals. But the ability to rise to a unity above the difference between presence and absence, and to recognize an object as the same, in its identity and its articulations, across presence and absence, is a more fundamental constituent of rationality. It is a condition for dealing with universals, which are a special form of identification in absence. And it is the form of reference that allows us to straddle presence and absence in regard both to individuals and to kinds, and to do so in public, with the involvement of others. The resolute and abrupt way in which words allow us to deal with the absent, the way words allow us to function in a context that is discretely other to the one that surrounds us, is what makes human speech different from animal signaling.

3

If Helen says "Tristan . . . " and establishes a reference to Tristan for me, it is true that I could be replaced by some other listener and Helen could be replaced by some other speaker who says the same thing, and the same relationship between "Tristan . . . " and Tristan could be established. Because this is so, we may be tempted to conclude, at least surreptitiously, that reference is a matter simply between words and things, that the speaker and listener are mere accessories. We may then try to treat reference as such an "objective" relation, independent of the "subjectivities" of speaker and listener. We may be especially inclined to treat reference this way in the case of scientific terms. *They* seem to be purged of any and all subjectivity; they seem to hold their reference almost by natural and automatic necessity. Indeed science itself seems to be the discovery of formulations that maintain their reference and truth quite independently of anyone, any place, and any time. It is easy to forget that science has to be spoken and stated by someone.

And when we as analyzers of reference try to treat it as such a purely objective relation between words and things, we place ourselves outside the relationship itself. We do not see ourselves as somehow coconstitutors of it; we do not see ourselves as the same ones who are referred, say, to Tristan by the "Tristan . . . " uttered by Helen. We see reference only as a line strung between *Tristan* and Tristan, and we try to describe what makes the line to be what it is.

But there is no such automatic line between "Tristan . . . " and Tristan. Reference cannot be described except by invoking Helen and me, or someone, even someone in general, in the places of Helen and me. And when I as a philosopher analyze what reference is, I do so not by examining only the relationship between *Tristan* and Tristan, but by thinking about myself as the one who has been Helen's (or someone's) interlocutor, the one

for whom the reference was made, the one who helped constitute the reference by taking the Tristan I have in mind as also
being targeted by Helen in view of a display. In clarifying what
reference is, and how a thing can be a referent, I also clarify
my own being as a dative of manifestation; not my being as a
philosophical analyst, but my being that which is analyzed philosophically. Alternatively, of course, I could have seen myself as
in the place of Helen, as the one who makes the reference for
and before someone else, the one who is "behind" the word; or
I could have seen myself as an onlooker to an exchange of reference between two other persons. Whichever place I see myself
occupying, whichever mundane role I think about, in my philosophical reflection I not only reflect on the word and the thing,
but also on myself in my prephilosophical being, as one of the
engaged constitutors of reference and referent. Thus the analysis of reference yields also an appreciation of self-identity as it
occurs between myself in my worldly engagements and myself as
reflecting philosophically.

The philosophical problem of reference cannot be discussed
by examining just the words that are used in reference; reference occurs rather in the way a thing is presented or intended.
But of course the word must be around and alive and effective
when the thing is taken in such a way as to become a referent.
When a thing becomes a referent, when it vibrates in the two
planes we have described (being in mind and being in mind as
targeted for display), the word has to be vibrating as well. I have
to hear Helen's "Tristan . . ." for Tristan to be appreciated by me
as targeted for display by Helen. Both object and word, as well
as speaker and hearer, belong to the whole we call the mode of
presentation of reference.

4

Now that we have discussed reference as an intentional form
that requires words, object, and interlocutors, let us return to
the distinction introduced in section 1, between terms that serve
to identify a referent and then dissipate, and terms that remain
in force as a context for what we go on to disclose. Since we

now understand reference to be a presentational achievement between speaker and addressee, we can take the first kind of reference as one in which the speaker uses any convenient means whatever to get at the target that is to be disclosed. The speaker is pragmatic; any name or description that makes the audience think of the target will do, and whatever term is used is dropped once the target is spotted and set up for manifestation: "The customer—or Tristan, or the man with the red hat, or Jerry's cousin—lives on Tilghman's Island." But in the second case the speaker is under greater constraint. He sets up not just the target but also the context for disclosure along with the original referent. Indeed his reference is the beginning of the disclosure; it expresses the first thing that is to be said about the target: "The customer is returning the bike and is angry with the salesman." It is as the customer that he is angry and is returning what he bought.

But is this, after all, a genuine distinction? Does the first case really occur? Do our original identifications ever totally dissipate? Does not at least part of the identifying phrase always remain in effect as a context for what we go on to say? If we identify someone as the customer and then drop his being a customer and talk about his boyhood and his domicile, we have not dropped everything from the reference: as a customer he is also a human being, and this provides the basis for our going on to talk about his childhood and where he lives. We have dropped the surface level of our identifying phrase, but not the levels that lie below the surface. These deeper levels seem to straddle both the reference and the disclosure that follows the reference. And even simple names seem to contain such implied characteristics: *Sue* implies being a woman, *Tristan* implies being a man, and *Topper* implies being a dog, and such connotations usually remain as a setting for what we go on to say about our referent.

Moreover, there is not just one level of sense, that of being a man, folded in beneath the surface of being a customer. There are many. If I said, "The customer . . . broke his arm," I would be moving down beyond his being a man to his being a living organism; and if I said, "The customer . . . weighs two hundred pounds," I would move down to his being a body. In all these cases I would have discarded the setting provided on the surface of my referential phrase, but I would have taken advantage of senses implied in the phrase, so I would not have entirely abandoned the term by which I identified my referent.

Indeed I could not drop all the senses from the subject of my statement because the disclosure that follows needs some sort of "kind" as a context within which to occur. It seems that when we talk to one another we cannot attach a predicate just to a bare particular. The structure of reference and disclosure seems not to permit it. Suppose I try to target a referent with as little qualification as possible; suppose that instead of speaking about "the customer" I referred to "the mass x that traversed path p at time t" and then went on to say, "It is the mayor's brother." I could not just do this. I would have to rebuild the reference before I could attach the predicate and make the disclosure. I could not just say, "Mass x is the mayor's brother," but would have to say, "Mass x is a man and that man is the mayor's brother." "That man" is the proximate or appropriate matrix for this disclosure, not "that body" or "that mass."

Furthermore, *man* is not merely attached to *mass x* as one predicate among many, as one predicate added to the predicate of *being the mayor's brother*. *Man* is not just annexed to *brother*; it is the matrix for *brother*. The more remote reference, *mass x*, could not serve as a proximate and appropriate setting for the disclosure of *brother* to take place. It is not the case that "*Mass x* is brother to the mayor," but rather that "*Mass x* as man is brother to the mayor." Thus the referent has to be sufficiently built up to manifest itself in this way. But I could, of course, say that *mass x* weights two hundred pounds, because weight attaches to it precisely as a body; or because it is precisely as a body that it shows up as weighty.

Furthermore, even by using the terms *mass x* or *that body*, I qualify the target somewhat and do not refer to it as a bare particular. I could not get beneath *mass x* to some sort of still more elementary referent, to "just plain x, the bare particular." Presentationally we do not have the referential resources to be able to say, "X is a body" or "X is a mass." The reason we cannot do this is that we could not pick out an object as one being and as a "this" or a "that" unless we specified what sort of thing we were referring to. The referent has to be qualified as some kind of thing if it is to be presented or intended as one. We always deal with this man, this house, this sentence, that red object, that piece of lead, this drop of water, that atom. "This" and "that" are syncategorematic and call for a kind. We have to qualify our object at least accidentally, at least as "that red thing," if we are to identify it at all. And the requirement of specification is not just a subjective necessity for us; the thing itself has to present itself as somehow specified if it is to be identifiable.

We do come close to referring to a sheer "this" without any specification when something conspicuous intrudes on us in our common situation and we "refer" to it as "this" even though we have no idea what it is. The intrusive object has to differentiate itself from a background, but its kind may be quite indescribable. We might use a demonstrative to indicate it, but the demonstrative verges on being an exclamation: the "this" is very much like "look!" or "hey!" We just draw attention to what intrudes.[4] However, such a "reference" without specification is abnormal: it could not function in the absence of the intrusion (in the absence of the object we would have to specify it as, say, "that looming thing that surprised us"), and it depends on the aggressivity of the object. The object is not picked out through our initiative as speakers, because we do not strictly refer to it: we do not take the responsibility of establishing it as a target of disclosure; this is shown by the fact that we cannot perform such "calling to mind" in the object's absence. The object itself does all the presentational work; it intrudes itself on us; we do not "call" it.

Another presentational activity that comes close to referring to a bare particular is the activity of signaling. The one who signals does take an initiative, and he can signal to someone to whom the target is absent, but he does not specify, in his signal as such, what kind of thing is being signaled. If Margaret rings a bell when Topper comes home, the bell does not connote anything; it does not even imply that Topper is a dog or a living thing. It only connects to "that"; it is close to being a sheer pointing gesture, except that it can work in the absence of what it signals. Furthermore, the signaler need not specify a kind because he is not setting his target up for disclosure. He does not need to establish a matrix for what is to appear. The signaler's work is done when the object is just brought to mind.

Thus signals and the demonstratives or exclamations that are a response to an intrusion both seem to "refer" without any specification. Signals are able to function in the absence of what is signaled, while the demonstratives are bound to the intrusive presence. However, both fall short of being genuine references because they do not establish a target for disclosure across presence and absence.

But although we do not seem able to refer to bare particulars when we speak in ordinary conversation, it might seem desirable to construct a special language in which such reference could occur. For example, instead of saying, "My uncle is boring," we might want to say, "There is an x such that x is my uncle and x is boring." This is the form of reference used in the notation developed for quantificational logic. There are two reasons why such a transformation of reference seems desirable.

First, this procedure seems to secure accuracy of reference. Different persons identify an object in different ways: I may know Tristan as my uncle, but someone else may know him only as the unnamed clerk in the post office. When each of us uses his own way of identifying the referent, we may not know we are speaking about the same person and our predicates may not find their proper attachments. The artificial notation we have described uses a reference that is purified of any particular description or name. It flushes out any subjective viewpoints we may have on the target of our discourse. It seems to be more objective and accurate. And second, besides securing accuracy of reference, this transformation of our ordinary statements prevents us from making illicit inferences. In the ordinary way of referring, one person may make inferences based on certain senses implied in the reference while another person may not. In the rigorous notation, only what is explicitly stated as a predicate can be a premise for an inference; everything is up front.

In the artificial notation, all the sense is distilled out of the referential expression, which becomes simply "an x." All the sense is put into the predicates and is explicitly spelled out. Sense and reference are notationally distinguished. This yields accuracy of reference and rigor of inference. It makes our speech more objective and scientific, it eliminates indexicality and clears away the varied viewpoints and understandings that the speakers bring to the thing being talked about. It seems to clear away all prejudices.

Such a purified reference to a bare particular, to a pure x that receives predicates, is an idealization of language. It is a special kind of projection to a limit, analogous to the mathematical projection of a flat surface into a plane, a box into a cube, or a ball into a sphere.[5] It has proved very useful in the development of quantificational logic and indispensable in developing languages for computer programs. It has the advantage of basing all inferences on explicitly formulated axioms and rules of inference, not on the material content of the terms used in the notation or programs. Languages that are formalized in this way can handle logical inferences of great complexity. However, their logical strength is accompanied by what we could call a material weakness. It is difficult in such languages to draw inferences based on the nature of the things being referred to and on the meanings of the terms used in the language. Programs used in artificial intelligence are now running up against this "barrier of meaning," as it has been called by Stanislas Ulam and Gian-Carlo Rota: the barrier posed by the network of inferences that can be made very easily by a human being who knows the sense of terms such as *key* or *passenger* or *customer*, but that are very difficult to program into a computer because they are based not on formal operators but on the sense of what is being referred to.[6]

However, this limitation of idealized propositional form and pure reference should not be taken as a reason to condemn the formulation of such languages. Such languages have their uses. Indeed their very purity can be used as a foil against which ordinary language can be studied philosophically. Rather than discredit ordinary language because it does not attain formal purity, and rather than condemn formal notation because it does not do justice to natural languages, one should simply think about the movement from ordinary to formal languages and back as one of the transformations that can be carried out on human speech. But we should refrain from thinking that the formalized notation gives something like the essential core at the heart of natural language; it does not do so, no more than the geometric sphere provides anything like the essence of a ball. But we can still find it rewarding to consider how we can move from the ball to the sphere and back, and why we enjoy thinking and working with the sphere as such. Likewise, we can contemplate the differences between natural and formal languages and better understand each in contrast with the other.

In contrast with the use of formal notation, in which we "refer" to bare particulars that are initially devoid of sense, a reference achieved between two users of natural language always involves some characterization of what we refer to.[7] We do not, in our conversational references, scan the universe and pick out sheer x's, monads which we would then begin to unfold. Furthermore, the senses that function in our references have layers and blends that can be exploited in our disclosures. If we target someone as a customer, we imply, as we have seen, that he is a human being and also that he is a living thing and a body, and each of these levels could become the proper substrate for our further disclosures if his being as a customer dissipates: "He is the mayor's brother," "He caught tuberculosis," "He weighs two hundred pounds." Our further predications rest on the deeper, unstated levels and not on the surface level, not on the level on which we explicitly stated our reference; but they do rest on part of the content of our reference.

No reference is sheer surface, sheer explicit specification with no implied substrate and no connotation. All references, whether names or descriptions, are blends of sense. Consequently, every reference has depth, and we show how well we understand our reference by the versatility with which we are able to exploit the unstated layers and connotations that underlie what we say when we set it up as a target of discourse. The name or description by which we establish reference thus has far more importance than that of its utility in achieving a simple identification. Besides being used to target an object, it helps us begin to say what we have to say about the object and it sets a context for what else we have to say. The connoted levels in the blend of sense that belongs to every reference are thus not a deficit of some sort, not an undesirable shadow that trails our reference and threatens its accuracy, not something we might wish to remove in the interests of scientific or conversational rigor. The connoted parts of the blend of sense serve as the unstated context for what we go on to disclose in our referent.

Sometimes we as speakers can be coy in exploiting the blends of sense. I can, for example, talk about the customer returning the bike and mention that he is the mayor's brother. This may seem like only a matter of incidental fact, a disclosure in which his being a customer dissipates and in which I let the predication rest on his being a man or a citizen in our town. But when I say he is the mayor's brother, I may be also engaging, cleverly, his being a customer: I may be indirectly warning my interlocutor that the customer can be a tough customer because he is the mayor's brother. His being a customer may not have dissipated after all. But if pressed I could retreat from this insinuation and say that I was only mentioning a fact about him, not saying anything relevant to his being the dissatisfied customer. The blends of sense in reference are a resource, not an obfuscation.

When we formalize our reference and purge it of all sense, when we develop the notation of a mere x which has these and these features, we try to purify ourselves of ourselves as speakers. We try to clear ourselves of our situations and our addressees, and also of the contextualized manner in which even the most independent issue appears to us, even as independent and objective. We try to divest ourselves of discourse about what is present and restrict ourselves to speaking about the absent, where we claim the power to scan everything in the universe in our search for the appropriate x's. The effort to do all this is philosophically rewarding because, by virtue of the impossibilities it bumps up against, it sheds light on what we as speakers necessarily are.

In summary, we can distinguish three forms of reference: (1) that in which the identificatory phrase stays fully in effect as a basis for what we go on to disclose; (2) that in which the surface sense of the identificatory phrase dissipates and some unstated connotation becomes the substrate for what we go on to disclose; (3) that in which the expression of reference is reduced to a pure x and drained of sense. The third form is an idealization found in logical notation and not in actual speech. Another related possibility is (4) the activity of signaling, which is no longer a form of reference because it does not bring the object signaled to mind as to be further disclosed. Still another is (5) the unspecified use of demonstratives or exclamations in response to an intrusion. This also fails to be a reference because it cannot function in the absence of the target and, like signaling, does not specify the kind of thing being indicated.

5

Until now we have been discussing the reference of terms that serve as the subjects of sentences, but not that of predicates or, in general, of the verbal parts of sentences. What sort of reference occurs when words such as *is blue, is hard, grows,* or *is larger than x* are used?

In particular, do predicates have a reference in the way that subjects do? If reference is an establishment of a target as to be disclosed, it would seem that predicates or the verbal parts of sentences do not have reference, because they express the disclosure occurring in and to the original referent. If the predicates were to have their own reference, speech would be just a series of acts of setting up targets for disclosure. But in a sentence the subject is used to identify what is to be disclosed and the predicate is used to show how it is manifested. The predicate is used to execute the manifestation that is anticipated in the reference. A word like *blue* or a phrase like *is blue,* in the sentence "My car is blue," is used by the speaker to let the car appear to someone in a certain way; it does not set blue up as a target to be manifested.

And yet *blue* must mean something objective. It must enjoy some sort of reference. How can it refer?

Blue and other predicates ride on the reference of their subjects. They do not refer independently. If they did refer independently to some sort of entity, then disclosure would be the joining of two objects, the thing and a feature. But features do not exist in such an independent way. A disclosure is merely a thing manifesting itself in a certain way and any reference we make to the feature is really a reference to the thing showing up in the feature and as so featured. When I use the word *blue,* the term is parasitic for its reference on the reference of the word *car* or whatever word is used to express whatever shows up as blue. Predicates and the verbal parts of sentences do not have their own reference.

Frege says that the reference of a word like *blue*, which he would call a concept-word, is not an ordinary reference to an independent thing but a reference to something that has "a predicative nature" and an "unsaturatedness."[8] What *blue* refers to must come along with something else, with the original referent, which serves to complete and saturate the concept. Our explanation of the reference of predicates agrees with that of Frege but stresses even more strongly the dependence of the feature on the object. Frege moves from the word to the feature or concept which he then attaches to the thing, whereas we move directly to the thing and see a feature as merely the thing showing up in a certain way, not as something to which the thing is joined. Furthermore, whereas Frege analyzes such reference in terms of logical and propositional structure, we analyze it in terms of the activity of targeting and disclosing in speech, in terms of presentational forms, which are more elementary than the structures of logic.[9]

For the subject to provide the independent reference in a sentence, it is not necessary for it to appear as the first term linguistically in the formulation of the sentence. I could start with the predicates. I could say, "Blue, sleek, wedge-shaped, fast . . . my car." The predicative nature of the first few terms is palpable; the listener realizes they express manifestations and waits to learn what is showing up in them. The dependence of the mode of presentation on the referent is a presentational (or protological) dependence, not simply a linguistic or grammatical one. And as sentences succeed one another in a speech, we find the recurrent movement between reference and sense, the disclosive ballet between "what" and "how," whether in the presence or the absence of what we are talking about. The skill of the speaker lies not only in forming linguistic patterns that please, but also in the intelligent way in which targets are brought forth to be seen by others, alternately named and disclosed, as words are used to present things.

Of course a term like *blue* can also become the subject of a sentence: "Blue can take on such subtle shades and intensities." We can manifest not only cars and trees, but also colors, shapes, styles, or other ways of being presented. When we make *blue* into a subject, we take away the predicative nature of its referent.

Here the referent is treated as though it were independent, but this transformation is only provisional. The original and normal way in which the referent of *blue* appears is as a manifestation of something that is already determined, as an aspect of a bonnet, of a piece of wax, of a car. When a speaker makes *blue* the subject of a sentence, he targets as to be further disclosed something that is itself originally a way of appearing.[10] And these shows of prior showings also depend for their reference on the original referent underneath them all.

To make a predicate into a referent, to make a way of appearing into what appears, is a movement in the opposite direction from the idealization of reference by reduction to a bare particular in quantificational notation. In quantificational notation we move toward the ideal of something that is stripped of any way of appearing, but here we make the way of appearing itself into the referent.

6

Intelligence in discourse does not involve just saying and understanding a lot of things; it also involves being able to sustain a reference through a long period of disclosure, that is, being able to bring out a lot about the *same* issue, or being able to let the same issue present itself through many manifestations. Allowing a reference to slip out of place, not being able to hold on to a single theme, is a form of failure in thinking. Since our disclosures sometimes work within the explicit descriptions we use to target our reference, and sometimes dip down into the unstated connotations that accompany our original identification, holding a single reference in mind as the theme that is being explicated may well require a flexibility that not every speaker or listener enjoys. It may not be easy to keep the same target in focus. Furthermore, the variety of features that we bring out puts a certain strain on our reference and may provoke us to lose our grip on it.

How are references sustained and changed? (1) In the best case, the same reference is kept alive through a disclosure that is sufficiently long, through as many sentences and fragments thereof as are necessary to show what ought to be shown about the referent. (2) The best form of a change of reference occurs when the change is explicit: when a new theme is named or described and differentiated from the theme that went before. (3) A form of weakness in thinking is what we could call *staccato reference*, in which the changes are explicit but too frequent, so that not much is disclosed about anything. (4) But the most obnoxious form of failure in reference is what we can call *slipped reference*, a condition as painful to conversation as is the slipped disc to our bodily movement: in this case the speaker thinks he is continuing to disclose the same thing, but he really is not. There are surreptitious shifts in reference, back and forth, and what is most infuriating to the interlocutor is that he cannot merely respond by saying, "That is false." If he could simply deny a statement, it would be relatively easy to correct the error. But he cannot do just this. He has to turn to a presupposition of what has been said, to the reference, not to the statement itself. He has to stop the conversation and unpack the machinery; he has to show where and how the reference slipped, and in doing this the conversational burden on him is enormous. He has to interrupt everything and change the focus. But if he does not take up this burden, his slippery interlocutor will get away with saying the wrong thing about one topic because he is confusing it with another.

For example, Jim may be talking about the president and his policies and may surreptitiously introduce features that show that his reference has slipped from the president as president to the president as a man of a certain character and style. He may introduce certain repellent mannerisms the president has. The mannerisms may have nothing to do with the political policies the president is pursuing, but they may be presented as having an impact on the policies, and they may seem to be points in favor of Jim's criticism of the policies, because Jim does not acknowledge a shift in reference. Jeff, his interlocutor, cannot just say that Jim is wrong, because what Jim says may be true about the president while having nothing to do with his policies. Jeff therefore has to interrupt the discussion and show where the reference slipped. The fallacy of slipped reference occurs especially in conversations about issues concerning which people have strong and passionate opinions, in which, for one reason or another, they want to say about one referent something that really belongs to another.

The possibility of slipped reference shows that there is a kind of truth and falsity in reference itself; the true and the false, the correct and incorrect, do not begin only when full propositional structures are reached. Thus within the formal structures of reference—the presentational structure of targeting something for someone for disclosure; the structure of using either an explicit description or an implied connotation as the frame for the disclosure; the structure of referring in either the presence or the absence of the target—in all these formal possibilities, we can achieve reference well or badly, correctly or incorrectly, and success occurs in two stages: first in establishing the right reference, and second in sustaining the right reference, in not letting the reference slip. This sort of success is not propositional truth, but it does enter into the truth of propositions as its condition.

One reason why references slip, one reason why we can talk about one thing but think about another, is the fact that any terms used to establish reference are made up of blends of meanings or features. Some of the elements of a blend may also be used in targeting other referents, and the similarities may cause us to shift from one to another. We can, for example, talk about jealousy but think about envy, or talk about authority but think about tyranny, or talk about artists but think about romantics, or talk about education but think about indoctrination, or talk about seventeenth-century Puritans but think about nineteenth-century Victorians. Furthermore, each word always retains some associational force, and the subjective associations instilled into the term may also work to derail our reference. They may pull us in another direction. And when our references slip, we confuse not only our audience but ourselves as well. Normally a speaker targets an object for the listener in order to manifest the object to him, but we also internalize this axis of speaker-addressee and speak to ourselves in order to set up a target of manifestation of features to ourselves. If our reference is unsteady, our own thinking also suffers.

The phenomenon of reference, although it involves words, is not a simple relation between words and things. It involves a constellation of elements: words, object, speaker, addressee, and the disclosure that follows the reference. Throughout this essay we have emphasized the activities of the speaker and addressee and the functions of words. But the entire constellation could also be described from the point of view of the target. Everything could be analyzed from that angle. In reference an object presents itself as to be explicated in many manifestations, and success in reference depends not only on the staying power of the interlocutors but also on the durability of the topic, on its capacity to reveal itself continuously in many disclosures. Not all topics are equally interesting; some practically scream for a change in reference. Intelligence in speaking does not necessarily imply sticking relentlessly to a theme; it requires knowing when to leave it and turn somewhere else. But when a theme deserves and gets manifestation, there is a stable referent that continues to appear through the derived referents that are incident to it: through the features that are meant by the verbal terms that follow the words used to establish the reference.

Besides being worthy of many manifestations, a candidate for reference must also be the kind of thing that can *be* a referent in the first place. It has to be targetable as a *this* or a *that*, and must therefore also be identifiable as a kind of being and as one being. Not everything is so identifiable. Some "things" are merely accidental conglomerations and do not hold up as a single referent but break apart into many; a superstitious conjunction, for example, is a purely accidental whole, not truly "one being." Also, Aristotle states that primary matter is not a "this" in itself.[11] And it may be the case that some of the paradoxes of measurement in quantum theory, such as those expressed in delayed-choice experiments, are due to the difficulty of achieving reference in regard to such elementary "objects." These paradoxes can be treated as problems of reference and not just as problems of measurement. There has to be something there that is capable of being targeted for disclosure if we as speakers and listeners are to be able to achieve reference.

When words surface, there can never be *just* words. When words come to mind they also bring something else to mind, something to be further disclosed. And words do not generate themselves; they appear as being stated, so the one who states them shows up behind them as the one who has taken it upon himself to target an object and to let it appear. We ourselves, those to whom the words appear, also surface as datives for the reference and as addressees for the words. The occurrence of words is therefore the activation in many ways of the difference between things and their presentations, the difference between beings and being.[12]

V

10
Grammar and Thinking

1

The purpose of this essay is to examine the relationship between grammar and thinking, and to discuss this relationship as it occurs in speech, in the written word, and in the artificial written languages we find in mathematical logic and computer programs.

Grammar is an aspect of language. There are grammatical features in every language, and there are also grammatical features in every *parole*, every activation of a language. There are grammatical features in English, German, French, and Chinese, but there are also grammatical features in the speech I am making now, in the conversation you had at breakfast, and in what the ticket vendor at the railroad station is saying to the passenger.

Grammar penetrates all the words in a language or a speech. It is not the case that only some words are purely grammatical while others are pure names or referential expressions devoid of grammar. All words, even simple names, are touched by grammar and have a grammatical aspect.

On the linguistic level, grammar has to do with the unification of words into larger linguistic wholes. The grammar of a language prescribes how the words of that language are to be combined into sentences and arguments, and the grammatical features of a speech are those features that have to do with the speech's being properly or improperly built up into a whole out of its parts. A speech is ungrammatical if it violates the rules of combination of the language in which the speech is given.

The grammatical aspects of a speech may be expressed in particular words, such as conjunctions or prepositions, in certain parts of words, such as inflections, or in the very position that words take in their larger wholes, such as the placement of the subject before and the object after the verb in the sentence, "Captain Ahab hunts Moby Dick."

The task of the grammarian is to study the various rules of combination that hold sway within a particular language or group of languages. The grammarian can carry out such a study synchronically or diachronically. Such a study would be what we might call an empirical grammar, the kind carried on by linguists such as Jespersen or Meillet. But a grammarian can also study what we might call the grammatical logic of a language and show how some combinatory rules can be derived from others and how some are related to others in meaning and function. He may also try to show how particular rules of combination can be derived from certain deep-seated combinatory rules that underlie all languages and seem to be the laws of thought; he can move from surface structures to deep structure in grammar. If he does so, he would be pursuing what has been called transformational grammar, with which the name of Chomsky has been chiefly associated.

But as philosophers we have an interest in grammar that is different from that of the grammarians, whether they be of the empirical or transformational sort. We are not concerned with the relationship between grammar and linguistic wholes, but with the relationship between grammar and human thinking. We are concerned with the relationship between grammar and the various intentionalities that occur in human awareness. And since human thinking and intentionality are correlated with manifestation and being, we could also be said to be concerned with the relationships between grammar and being and between grammar and presentation. The context within which we as philosophers study grammar is wider and more ultimate than is the context within which the grammarian carries out his inquiry.

2

Grammar is especially related to thinking. The grammatical aspects of a speech are especially related to the acts of thinking that occur when the speech is made. Husserl can help us make this clear. At the beginning of the first *Logical Investigation* (§1–5), Husserl distinguishes between two kinds of sign, expression and indication. He says that speech normally functions in both ways, as expression and as indication. A speech *expresses* a state of affairs or a situation, but it also *indicates* to the listener the presence of an achievement of thinking in the speaker. If I say, "The building is crowded," I express the crowded condition of the building, but I also indicate to you my act of predicating this feature of that object. Husserl goes on to say that in solitary speech, when I talk to myself, the expressive function of the words remains in place, but the indicative function does not, because there is no need to indicate to myself that I am carrying out this act of predication (§8). I do not have the act presented to me by a sign, because I have the act presented directly to me.

I want to use Husserl's concept of the indicative role of speech to clarify the relationship between grammar and thinking. And instead of using Husserl's term *indication,* I want to use the term *signal.* With Husserl we can then say that a sentence with subject and predicate, when uttered, signals to the listener that the speaker is predicating, that he is carrying out a particular achievement, that he is thinking what he expresses. To put this more technically, a sentence signals that the speaker is carrying out the categorial activity that constitutes what the sentence expresses. It signals that the speaker is constituting the state of affairs expressed in the sentence.

On this point we agree with Husserl. But Husserl's analysis is deficient. There is another aspect to the signaling function of a sentence, one that is not mentioned by him. Besides signaling that the speaker is accomplishing a certain categorial act, the sentence also signals to the listener to carry out the same categorial act himself. The sentence is not only a signal that the speaker is thinking, it is also a signal to the listener to think. The words are both a signal *that* and a signal *to*.

The signaling function occurs primarily in the grammar of a speech. The grammar of a speech does not only organize the words into a linguistic whole. It does not only serve as the linguistic mortar of the sentence or paragraph. In doing this, in performing this linguistic function, the grammar also signals that the speaker is thinking and signals to the listener to think. If I say, "The horse and the rider . . . ," I signal that I am taking the horse and the rider together, and I signal to you to do the same.

When we speak, we do not only combine words, and our grammatical abilities are not directed primarily toward linguistic combination. As we speak, we articulate things. The linguistic combinations are only on the margin of the combinations, distinctions, relations, and summations that we carry out on things. Our primary intentional concern is with the things we are thinking about. And the grammatical features of our language are the signals for us to combine, distinguish, total, and relate the things that we are thinking about. To put this in Husserlian terms, the grammatical aspects of linguistic signs are signals to the listener to execute the various categorial activities that constitute the higher-level, categorial objects, such as states of affairs, relations, and groups, that are the primary object of our rational intentionalities and that are expressed in the words that are spoken.

3

Now let us examine four different ways in which the grammatical elements of language carry out their signaling function. The first case is that in which the speaker is actively thinking or constituting the state of affairs as he speaks about it. For example, the speaker and the listener are in the presence of the object being discussed, and the speaker registers a fact: the fact, say, that the color of this cloth before them is faded. The listener hears, sees, and understands. Or the speaker and listener may be in the absence of what they are talking about, but the speaker still actively *thinks* what he says, and the listener hears and understands. In this first case the predicational grammar of the speaker's sentence signals that the speaker is articulating and predicating, and it also signals to the listener to do the same, and he does do the same.

But let us now consider a second case. Here the speaker is already convinced that the color in question has faded. He saw it or heard about it earlier; he constituted the fact earlier. Now he just tells the listener the fact by saying, "The color of the cloth is faded." It is likely that the speaker is not thinking the fact through as he says these words. He thought it through when he first discovered it or was told it, but now he is only handing it on. As he now communicates, he must begin to remember and repeat. Even though he uses the same words in both statements, his statement now is different from the statement he uttered when he registered the fact in question; his statement now becomes something like a documentation. It is almost—but not quite—like a written statement.

In this second case the grammatical features of the sentence being uttered do not signal that the speaker is carrying out the categorial activity that constitutes the fact expressed in the sentence. At best they indicate that the speaker has at some time carried it out, and that the expressed fact is therefore an abiding possession or conviction for the speaker. But the speaker need not be articulating the fact right now as he speaks. However, the same grammatical features do signal to the listener to carry out these categorial achievements. They do exhort him to constitute that fact as he listens. This part of the signaling function of the grammar persists, while the other part lapses. The words continue to signal *to*, even as their signaling *that* becomes weakened.

This second instance of grammatical signaling, in which the speaker communicates something he originally thought earlier, provides a transition between the first case, in which the speaker thinks while he speaks, and the third case, the case of writing. In writing, the writer detaches himself from the reader (in the second case the speaker did have to talk bodily to the listener), but now the writer in his bodily absence from the reader still signals to the reader to think, and he also signals that he, the writer, has thought, but not that he is thinking what the words

express while the reader is reading them. The grammatical signals in writing are like land mines or buried bombs. They are
buried in books. They can remain quiet for a long time. They
only explode or fire as signals when someone opens the book and
reads them. When someone becomes constituted as their reader,
he the reader thinks the same categorial objects that the writer
once thought. The reader categorially constitutes the same part
of the world in the same categorial form as the writer once did.

Writing gives the writer great reach and power. He is able to
place his little bombs throughout great stretches of space and
time, over distances that his own voice could never span, and
he is able to signal to crowds of readers to constitute the same
categorial objects he originally constituted and so to see the world
in the same way as he sees it. And it is particularly in the grammar
of his writing that he gets others to agree with him, to think as
he thinks. His writing is not merely a series of labels or names of
things. If it were only that, he would be inducing a daydream, not
communicating a thought. It is the way the names are organized
into wholes that signals how we as readers are to articulate and
believe what we are led to think about.

Let us now consider as a fourth case the kind of writing that
Frege called *Begriffsschrift*. Let us consider the symbolism of mathematical logic. In this case, whether in propositional or quantificational logic, the grammar becomes purified and isolated into
particular symbols, particular operators. It also becomes reduced
to a minimum, to very few operations, far fewer than the multitude of grammatical forms in natural languages. It is reduced to
those operations that cannot be reduced to any others, and that
are both relevant and essential to the truth of statements and
inferences.

Furthermore, the grammatical functions become very visible
as combinatory operators. Their role of combining terms into
larger wholes becomes especially clear because they are now expressed not as ordinary words or as parts of words, but as artificial
symbols for combinatory operations. The symbolism makes very
clear the fact that grammatical terms signal an operation: the
symbol "v" is much more obviously a signal for us to disjoin the
terms flanking it than is the word *or;* the symbol ".", like the symbol "+" in arithmetic, is much more obviously a signal to conjoin

the terms that flank it than is the word *and*. The artificial, symbolic character of "v" and "." make it much more obvious that they are signals, somewhat like the flashing of a light or the blowing of a whistle. They do not look like words and they cannot even be pronounced.

In fact the words *or* and *and* are also signals, and so are all the other grammatical aspects of a speech, but they do not look like signals and it is easy for us not to realize that they are. But once we realize that such words do have something in common with the logical operators in the symbolism of mathematical logic, and once we appreciate the signaling function of such operators, we can become more sensitive to the way the grammatical parts of natural language, whether spoken or written, also function as signals. The pure formalism of symbolic logic thus sheds light on natural language, just as the pure formalism of, say, Mondrian's compositions sheds light on what occurs in a landscape or a still life.

4

We have discussed the signaling function of grammar in four modes: in living, registering speech, in mere communication, in writing, and in the symbols of mathematical logic. Let us now subdivide one of these modes; let us examine more closely the phenomenon of writing and show how grammar functions as a signal in it. And let us start with an elementary form of writing, with pictographs.

Pictographs must be distinguished from pictures, and the distinction is not easy to make. Pictures are not yet writing. In principle, a picture can be taken simply by itself. A picture as such does not need to become part of a larger syntactic whole. Even if the pictures are arrayed one after the other, or if they are combined into a complex picture, they do not essentially, as pictures, call for completion, and they are not to be taken as forming a discourse.

But it is not so with a series of pictographs. A series of pictographs tells a story or makes a statement. It builds up a logical and syntactic whole, a pictographic analogue to a sentence or a paragraph. Each pictogram must be understood not only in relation to what it depicts, but also in relation to its position in the larger statement, the larger whole, which itself is not just another pictograph but a syntactic combination. A picture does not necessarily require this larger whole; it can be sufficient unto itself in its own depiction.

Because pictograms require completion into a discursive whole, they involve something like grammar. For example, consider a series of six pictographs, arranged something like a comic strip. The first shows a man leaving a house, the second shows the man walking on a road, the third shows the man being frightened by an animal, the fourth shows the man running back on the road, the fifth shows him approaching the house, the sixth shows the house with the door closed. In this series the spatial positioning of the pictographs, and the temporal succession of one being seen after the other, provide the grammar of this simple narrative. The spatial and temporal positioning makes us think the depicted scenes one after another. It makes us constitute the narration as *one* story, as *one* categorial object. There are no special pictographs to depict the grammar; the mere positioning is all that is necessary. But the positioning and sequence become meaningful, not as a representation of any distinct event, but as a signal to think the parts into a whole, to carry out the activity of thinking.[1]

After pictographs, the next stage in writing is ideographic, and here we have the introduction of explicitly grammatical terms. Ideograms are polysemic. A single sign can, for example, mean the sun, or heat, or light, or a ray of sunshine. Pictograms are not like this; they are univocal. They only signify what they depict. And because ideograms are polysemic, some ideograms can become merely grammatical terms, not representing objects or events but signaling how we are to arrange what the other ideograms represent. Simple pictographic writing has no such purely syncategorematic "terms." The only grammar is the slight grammatical form of spatial and temporal sequence.

And finally alphabetic writing, like ideographic but unlike pictographic writing, also has written terms that are specifically grammatical. But of all these forms of writing, perhaps the pictographic makes it most clear that grammar signals us concerning how we are to articulate the world in our thinking. The pictographs obviously present scenes in the world to us; we are not tempted to think they only bring words to our attention. Pictographs, being images, vividly present things, and by their sequence in space and time they instruct us to accept things as being in a certain way, as presenting themselves in a certain process. If we "read" the pictograms, we let things and events appear to us; indeed the things and events almost seem to appear to us in the pictograms themselves—and yet we know they really do not. The things and events, we know, are only written down in the pictographs. Alphabetic writing also presents a part of the world, but because it first symbolizes the vocalized word, instead of being a picture of a thing, alphabetic writing may seem more opaque and distanced. It may seem to be more concerned with language than with things, and its grammar may seem to indicate only linguistic combinations, not categorial articulations of the things themselves.

5

Having claimed that the grammatical features of speech and writing signal categorial activities, let us now explore what kind of signal the grammar can be.

Grammatical parts of speech are an unusual kind of signal. Consider a normal signal; consider, for example, someone's shouting the word *Go!* as a signal for the competitors to start running in a race. The word *Go!* signals *that* the starter is starting the race, but it also signals *to* the runners to begin running. But the runners must do two things as they respond. They must understand the word, and they must begin running. There is a mental achievement and a bodily performance; there are two different actions.

Now when we are dealing with grammatical signals, there is only one side to the response, not two. If in a speech I say the word *and,* all you have to do is to understand what I say. To understand the word *and* is to conjoin. We understand the word *and* by conjoining, not by doing something beyond the categorial achievement of taking together the things named by the words that flank the conjunction. When I hear and understand the word *go*, I have not yet gone, but when I hear and understand the word *and* I have already conjoined, I have already "and-ed."

Likewise, to understand the word *is* in a sentence that is being spoken is to predicate a feature of an object. It is not first to hear or understand the word and then to do something else, something different from the understanding. To understand the word *is* is to obey the word as a signal. It is to do something, to perform the categorial activity or achievement of predicating.

It seems therefore that when we obey a grammatical signal we do less than we must do when we obey the standard type of signal. We need only perform the categorial activity. But this obeying of the linguistic signal is still very complex. The words, when spoken and heard, serve as an intersection for many presentations. When we obey the grammatical signals, we as listeners perform the categorial activities that the signals indicate: we conjoin, predicate, relate, or total. In doing this we constitute the appropriate categorial objects. But we appreciate these categorial objects as being expressed in the words that signaled our actions. And in addition the same words also signal that the speaker is carrying out, or has carried out, the categorial achievements in question; that is, we also appreciate, on the basis of the words we hear, the categorial activities of the speaker. We apperceive him as a speaker and a thinker. And we also appreciate that the categorial object he is signaled as constituting is the same categorial object we constitute, the one expressed in the words that are uttered. Thus because of the complexity of our response to the words, the words are allowed to function in three ways: they signal us to think; they express what we are to think; and they signal to us that the speaker is mentally active. The words prompt these three intentionalities, which are the noetic correlates of words.

This complexity of response occurs when we experience living speech, the speech of someone who thinks while he talks. Let us now move away from the case of living speech and move toward the other extreme, to the written symbolism of mathematical logic. As we have seen, in such symbolism the grammatical parts of speech become simplified, formalized, and expressed in artificial symbols. But something else happens to them as well. It becomes much easier to take the symbol as an object. It becomes easier, in other words, to stop responding to the symbol as a signal, to stop performing the categorial operation that it signals us to perform.

It is much harder to treat the grammar of natural languages in this way. When we encounter the words *and* or *or*, it is very difficult for us not to conjoin or disjoin. But if we are dealing with the symbols "." or "v", it is easier for us to treat them as simple marks or objects to be manipulated according to certain rules. This is what is done in computer languages. The operators are taken as mere marks, and rules are established that govern how the strings of marks are to be transformed. The transformation itself is the running of a computer program. After the program has been run, however, after we get the output of the program, the operators become signals again. They once again signal to us to conjoin, disjoin, predicate, or to do whatever is necessary as a categorial activity to understand the "answer" the computer has given us—indeed, to constitute the output as an answer. Thus, after the excursus in which the grammar ceases to be grammatical and is reduced to structural manipulation, we come back again to the original condition in which the formalized grammatical symbols signal us to think.

6

The grammatical parts of a speech signal that the speaker is executing categorial operations. However, the grammar can sometimes be a false signal. Sometimes there may be no categorial activity, no thinking, behind the grammar, or perhaps there may be only a vague, languid, insufficient categorial activity behind it. This is the phenomenon of vagueness, which Husserl describes in *Formal and Transcendental Logic* (§16). In vagueness there is speech and grammar, but the speech and grammar are not sufficiently backed up by categorial achievements.

And in discussing vagueness we are not talking about the case in which our speech communicates an articulation that we made earlier, before the speech was made. We are talking about the case in which the running-on of speech masks failures in thought, the case in which there is inadequate thinking, whether at the moment of speaking or prior to it. The speaker only pretends to have thought; his grammatical signals are not true signals. They are not genuine signs that he is thinking.

And yet, even if his categorial articulation is vague, the speaker still signals the listener *to* think. The listener is being signaled to think by the grammar of the speech. If the listener does execute the categorial operations signaled by the grammar, it is very likely that he will find, sooner or later, that he is being signaled to constitute contradictory and incoherent categorial objects. The lack of thinking in the speaker may not show up in a single sentence, but it will almost inevitably show up as one sentence follows another: the speech will not build up a unified whole, it will not form a coherent and consistent argument. The confusion of the speaker will be recognized as confusion by the listener, and the listener will realize that the speaker is not in control of what he is saying.[2]

But the listener will recognize the confusion as such only if he is more thoughtful than the speaker. If the listener is also not able to carry out the categorial activities signaled by the speech, then both listener and speaker will be lost in confusion and vagueness and will not realize that they are lost. The blind will be leading the blind.

The phenomenon of vagueness in speech and thought is very important. Most of our speaking has elements of vagueness in it. Clarity and distinctness emerge out of vagueness and often lapse back into it. It would be philosophically misleading to describe speech as though it expressed and communicated only sharp, clear thinking. And vagueness, together with the inconsistency and incoherence that may be harbored within it, is possible only because speech can conceal as well as disclose. Speech, and in particular the grammar in speech, can signal the actual presence of thought, but it can also be a false signal, one that only seems to indicate thinking but really does not. Words can run on from one to another by mere association, the speaker's memories can lead associatively from one to another, and this associative inertia can smother the directive force of true thinking. When this occurs our speech may make it seem that we are thinking when we really are not.

7

We originally developed the theme of grammar as signal by appealing to Husserl's distinction, in *Logical Investigations,* between signs as expressions and signs as indications. The signaling function of grammar can also be related to another important theme in the *Investigations.* In the sixth Investigation, Husserl speaks about the reference of syncategorematic terms. He asks specifically about the reference of the copula *is* (§40). He points out that syncategorematic words seem to insert an "excess of meaning" into the sentences in which they function, because the words do not seem to correspond to anything definite in the world. In the sentence, "The house is yellow," there are, obviously, objective correlates for the terms *house* and *yellow,* but there seems to be nothing corresponding to the term *is.* The term seems to introduce a surplus of sense. Husserl goes on to say that all the grammatical aspects and terms of an expression contain such a surplus of meaning, even, for example, the noun form of the word *house* (§40), as well as words such as *a, the, and, or, if, then,* and the like (§43). He asks what could correspond, in the world, to such terms or aspects of speech.

Husserl answers that the objective correlates of such syntactic forms are not "real" moments of objects (§43). They are not features that could be presented to sense perception. Rather, they correspond to and are presented to categorial activities, not to sense perception. The objective correlates are presented in categorial intuition. In these categorial intuitions we disclose not just particular features of objects, but the articulations and presences themselves of the objects that are presented. Through categorial experience we enter into the issue of being and presence. Thus the linguistic grammar that signals categorial activity serves also to express various forms of presencing, various forms of being. And the same grammar that discloses to us the inflections and presences of being is also a signal to us as datives of manifestation, as agents of being and presentation. The categorial activities that we are signaled to perform are not just psychological events, but activities that establish us as *Dasein,* as the place for the interplay of presence and absence. Thus linguistic grammar is fully understood only in the horizon of being.

11
Tarskian Harmonies
in Words
and Pictures

Thoughts on seeing Matisse,
Harmony in Yellow

1

What do we present when we put words together?

When we put words together, we present the words themselves, and we present them together. We present them as a whole. But it is almost impossible for us to present only words, whether we present them singly or in groups. If I present *chairs*, I can hardly help but present chairs also, to myself and to whoever else may happen to be a dative for my presentation of *chairs*. Indeed, what normally occurs is that chairs come to mind when *chairs* is presented, and it takes some effort to bring *chairs* into any prominence at all. *Chairs* is there but it usually gets overlooked.

If we make the effort and if we do bring *chairs* into the foreground, we would normally still keep chairs in mind marginally. It would take not just some effort, but enormous effort to bring only *chairs* into presence, purged entirely of any presence of chairs. It would be like looking at a portrait and totally eliminating any presence of a face and figure, seeing only color patches and lines.

227

It may be possible for us to concentrate on the colors and lines, but a residue of the face and figure will almost always remain; it may be possible for us to concentrate on *chairs*, but something of chairs will almost always remain present.

It may happen that we look at an unfamiliar painting and cannot see it as a portrait, even though someone may have told us that it is one. For a while the face may not appear; we then do see only color patches and lines. Likewise, we may have *sedes* present to us and not have chairs given. We may know *sedes* is a word and know that something should be presented with it, but nothing particular can come to mind. We do not know what should be presented. But in both cases, when the face cannot be seen and when *sedes* does not present chairs, we do look for a face and we do anticipate a thing because we know that this is a portrait and that is a word.

But at an extreme, we may have the colors and lines of a portrait presented to us not as a portrait at all—we do not know it is one—and we may have the sounds of a word presented but not as a word. We just see colors and lines and hear sounds as configurations. They may not even stand out from what surrounds them: they may not occur as circles and squares or as distinct noises but only as blended in the general drift. They mingle with the colors and shapes and sounds that make up their environment. At this extreme there is only the presence of color and shape or the presence of sound. The color, shape, and sound do not of themselves present anything else besides themselves. They may in fact suggest something—a color may make me think of my car and a sound may make me think of the ocean—but this is only coincidental. We can rest simply in these colors, shapes, and sounds in a way in which we cannot rest simply in what we take to be a picture or a word.

Let us return for a moment to the case in which we know we are dealing with a portrait or a word, but cannot yet see the face or comprehend the word. We intend the face or the thing but we cannot see it. We do not rest simply in the color or the sound; we intend something else, something other, but we do not yet identify it. The strange presence of what is not yet identified deserves more attention.

In this strange condition, I know the picture is a picture, and I see the thing that is the picture, but it has not yet begun to work as a picture for me. It has not yet become actualized as a portrait. Likewise I know *sedes* is a word but I am not able to let it be a word for me. It becomes a word at work when it succeeds in presenting chairs, when it brings chairs to my mind. So both the picture and the word are themselves not fully presented until the other things—the depicted and the named—are presented as well.

2

But the picture and the word do their work in different ways. When we know these color patches are a portrait but cannot see the face, we look *into* the colors and lines to find the face. When we know *sedes* is a word but do not know what it names, we do not look into the word to find the thing; we inquire about the word or we may guess at the word from the context, but we try to think about something other than the word; in this case, we try, although we may not know it yet, to think about chairs.

There is one case in which we may at first look more closely into the word: we may try to figure out the word by discerning the words that make it up (if it is made up of other words). We can figure out *steamboat* by first discerning *steam* and *boat.* But even in this case, we must ultimately turn away from the words, to steam and boat, just as we had to turn away from *sedes* to chairs, whereas in figuring out a picture we never really turn away from it. We find the thing present, as pictured, in the colors and lines themselves.

It may be the case that we have to learn how to read a particular picture. We may need to be instructed how to look at the thing before us if we are to see it as an image.[1] Even when such guidance is necessary, however, we still look into the picture to find what it depicts; we do not think away from the picture toward something available somewhere else.

3

We must distinguish between presenting *chairs* and presenting chairs. When we present chairs, we often intend them not only

in themselves but also as being presented by the presentation of
chairs. We appreciate chairs as the meaning of *chairs.*[2] Is there
an analogy to this in the case of the picture? Can I not turn
from the portrait of my uncle to my uncle himself, standing near
the portrait, and even consider him as the one whom I just saw
depicted in the portrait? Can I turn to him as the "meaning" of
the picture? In addition, can I turn from the portrait to my uncle
even in his absence, and think about him wherever he may be
and whatever he may be doing? Is this not like going from *chairs*
to chairs?

Not exactly. There are two differences. First, when I have only
the portrait, I already have my uncle given, but when I have *chairs*
I do not at all have chairs given. The portrait is heavier with the
thing than is the word. I do not have to turn away to my uncle
to see him depicted in the picture, but I do have to think about
chairs to see them as the meaning of *chairs.* Secondly, when I
turn to my uncle, the picture drops away. Precisely because of
the heaviness of the picture, the picture must get out of the
way when I go to the thing itself.[3] But when I go from *chairs* to
chairs, I must keep *chairs* alive to have chairs as the meaning of
chairs. The very lightness of *chairs* permits *chairs* to be part of
the action when chairs are given. *Chairs* does not compete with
the presence of chairs in the way the portrait competes with the
bodily presence of my uncle.

The portrait does so much in making my uncle present that
it could not become transparent enough to let his simple bodily
presence shine through. But *chairs* does so little that it can remain
around to help the chairs become present. Pictures are obdurate,
words are compliant.

Let us bring this out with another example. If I used *kukuriku*
to mimic the crowing of a rooster, I would get in the way of someone's listening to the rooster crowing if I voiced those sounds
while he was trying to listen. I would compete with the rooster's
sounds. But if I used *kukuriku* as a name for the rooster's crowing, my speaking would be less intrusive. As a name the sounds
would fuse with the crowing in a way that as mimicry they would
not. The sounds as a name would somehow be the same as the
crowing; they would not constitute another crowing. As a name
they would direct my listener to the animal, but as mimicry they

would attract his attention to me. The ersatz presence in pictures conflicts with the genuine presence of things.

It is because of the difference between pictures and words that words are more useful than images in thinking about things. With words we can get more directly to the things themselves. The words do not compete with things as pictures do. Pictures draw us into themselves, words point to things. If words were like pictures, we would, whenever we used words, only be able to quote; when we mentioned *chairs* we would only be able to rest with *chairs*, and would never be able to move to chairs as such. We would be absorbed into the word as we are absorbed into a picture. But because words are what they are, they can allow us direct access to things. Even if the thing is seen as named by the word, even if the thing surfaces under the presence of the word, it is the thing and not a simulacrum that appears or is intended, that is brought to mind. The word gets out of the way. And since we can go from *chairs* to chairs, we can disquote and determine whether what is said is true or not, whether what is said is as the things are. We can shift from hearing "The chairs are soft" to seeing whether or not the chairs are soft.

When we disquote words, we go from hearing "The chairs are soft" to saying the same thing in our own voice, but we cannot disquote a picture; we cannot assert, on our own, what the picture "states" by somehow stating the picture in something analogous to a voice of our own. In this regard the portrait is more like the chairs themselves than like *chairs*.

4

There is another difference between pictures and words. A picture presents its subject in a certain place and in a certain manner of being and appearing. The picture presents my uncle in his study near the fireplace, and as sitting still and looking at me, the viewer. If I were to turn from the picture to my uncle, I would find him in a different place and manner: not in his study but in the living room, not sitting still but drinking tea. If he were absent and I were to turn to him in his absence, I would again have to contrast him there with him here in the picture: now he is driving his car or watching a baseball game, not sitting and looking at me. Wherever he may be and whatever he may be doing, there would be a contrast between the way he is presented in the picture and the way he is now. The picture would interfere with the way he is to be registered now.

But words are not wedded to one manner of appearing. *My uncle* is not bound to my uncle sitting in a chair, but to him no matter where he is, whether present or absent, and no matter what he is doing. Therefore I do not need to contrast my uncle with *my uncle,* and I can use *my uncle* to refer to him wherever he is and however he is to be presented. *My uncle* refers to my uncle without qualification, whereas his picture presents him in a certain light. This is a further reason why words are better than pictures for tagging things.

5

Let us now consider more closely how we assemble both pictures and words.

(1) If we were simply to put two color patches together, we could present only the colors themselves. The colors could, for example, be merely the beginning of our process of painting the surface in question. Likewise, if we merely combined two sounds, such as a rattle and a squeak, we could be presenting only the sounds themselves. The sounds would be phones and not phonemes. (2) Colors and shapes must come together as one to form an image: we have not just colors and marks but a bird presented to us, not just black lines but a stick man. Likewise, sounds become phonemes when they are made and taken as parts of a whole: the phonemes *sa* and *tis,* which when taken separately are neither mere noises nor meaningful, when combined (*satis*) are a word meaning "enough." (3) If we were to place two images on the same surface—an image of a leaf and an image of a bird—we could be presenting them simply as two pictures, not as one; they would not be presented as together, as one picture. Likewise, two words could be presented in such a way that they remain simply two, two that happen to be in the

same place: *man* and *tall* could be written on two pieces of paper that happen to be placed together or spoken randomly by two people who happen to pass one another. In such cases, a man would be presented and being tall would also be presented, but merely in unjoined succession. (4) The image of a bird could be presented *with* that of the leaf; then there would be one picture, of a bird before a leaf, and not two. The togetherness would be part of what is given, part of the picture. Likewise, *man, tall* could be presented as one. *Man, tall* is a presentation different from *man* and *tall.* Again, the togetherness, the being one, becomes part of the verbal presentation. And when I present *man*, a man comes to mind, but when I present *man, tall* more comes to mind than just a man first and being tall second. Man as tall comes to mind, as one arrangement. The togetherness of the thing and feature is part of what is given when the words are given.

What we have when we come to man as tall is a protological, a prepredicative structure. This combination arises for us when the words *man, tall* are presented; just as *chairs* always brings chairs in its train, so *man, tall* suggests a man *as* tall. But this preliminary articulation of part of the world leads on to (5) the full form of predication, in which "X is y" is stated and the man is asserted to be tall. The full predicative assertion is preceded by the prepredicative activity in which X is taken as y, in which X shows up as y.[4] The prepredicative does not have the explicit categorial form of the predicative; it mediates between simple perception and categorial predication. The prepredicative state of affairs can be expressed by joined terms such as X,y or *man, tall,* which are less than explicit statements such as "X is y" or "The man is tall."

We should observe that in predication, the togetherness of X and y is not only part of what is presented, as it is in X,y; the togetherness also receives its own distinct expression in the *is.* Moreover, since the togetherness becomes thematic and explicit in this way, various kinds of togetherness can be distinguished and expressed through the diverse grammatical particles, terms, and inflections that a language provides. Grammar amplifies the various ways in which the presence of things can be modulated and stated.

The prepredicative is more passive than the predicative. The precategorial verbalization expresses our *acceptance* of X as *y*, while the categorial verbalization expresses our *assertion* that X is *y*. X, *y* or *Man, tall* is more in the nature of a suggestion, while "X is *y*" or "The man is tall" is a declaration. The first has almost no grammar: while its words are combined and not merely juxtaposed, they are not grammatically combined, not as the words in "X is *y*" are. We are more responsible and we can be more explicitly quoted when we make a declaration than when we merely combine two terms precategorially, in a suggestive way. The categorial is more discrete, it has a more definite beginning and end, and the articulations are more exactly stated (there can be subordinate clauses, causal expressions, inflections, parts of speech); the precategorial is rather a simple continuum of theme and features, with things laid out flat, one item following another in parataxis, not syntax.

When we compose a picture, we put colors, shapes, and various images together. Is there in pictures anything analogous to the distinction between the prepredicative and the predicative? Are there "precategorial" and "categorial" pictures? I would say that this distinction does not hold for pictures.

One can speak of a "grammar" or "syntax" in images, but the terms are used analogously. In verbal categorial wholes, some words, such as *is* and *and*, explicitly express the syntax, but no element in the picture can express the syntax of the picture (just as no thing or aspect of things can express the syntax of a state of affairs). There are no grammatical "parts of speech" in a depiction. Things are placed next to one another, or in some significant relationships, or they are given some special posture or expression, but no part of the picture signals how the other parts are to be arranged and read. The viewer has to read the picture himself. In contrast with fully articulated speech, pictures are mute. They show themselves but they do not declare themselves. Even allegorical and other symbolic depictions have to be read directly by the viewer without the guidance that explicit grammar gives. "What is being said" by the one who makes the picture is never as explicit as a statement made in words.

6

And yet the one who makes the picture does say something, even though it may straddle suggestion and assertion. Photographs, sketches, and paintings can make statements that have powerful rhetorical effects: David's *Oath of the Horatii* helped shape revolutionary opinion, Jacob Riis's photographs of children working in sweatshops helped bring about laws concerning child labor, and Yousuf Karsh's picture of Churchill lets us see what kind of man Churchill was. In what way do pictures "state something" that can be either true or false?

Furthermore, the "statement" made in a picture is taken as having been made by somebody. The picture presents part of the world as it seemed *to* someone (the painter or the photographer) and as it has been represented *by* that same someone. In a picture we do not just have a part of the world; we have that part as depicted by some individual. We can appreciate a particular photograph or painting as the work of a given artist not only because of the technique, but also because of the understanding expressed, the statement made, in the image. It is the kind of thing that this artist—Fellini, Sanders, Gilbert and George, the early Rembrandt, the later Rembrandt—would say.

If pictures state something, and if they are statements made by someone, can we not quote pictures in the same way we quote sentences? Indeed, do we not necessarily quote a picture when we ask whether the picture is true or false? What are truth and falsity in pictures?

7

Tarski[5] proposes the following as a partial definition of the concept of truth:

"*p*" is true if and only if *p*.

Stated more concretely:

"Snow is white" is true if and only if snow is white.

The phrase with quotation marks at the beginning of the definition is a name of the sentence that is said to be true. The sentence is *mentioned* at the start of the definition and *used* at the end. It is used in order to state the conditions that must obtain for the sentence to be true.

A sentence that expresses a state of affairs belongs to what Tarski calls the "object-language." A sentence used to speak about other sentences, perhaps to say that they are true or false, belongs to what he calls the "metalanguage."[6] Specialized, partial languages, such as the language of the science of chemistry, can be sheer object-languages; they need not allow reference to sentences within themselves. They can simply let us state what is the case. A metalanguage could be used to speak about the sentences in the science of chemistry, but it would not necessarily become part of the science.[7]

Our ordinary language, however, is an amalgam of object-language and metalanguage.[8] It allows us to speak about both things and sentences. It allows us not only to use sentences but also to mention them, and allows us to shift between use and mention. It is a language *in* which we speak, but also one *about* which we can speak, and we speak about it with terms found in the language itself. A language which contains the resources to speak about its own words and sentences is said by Tarski to be "semantically closed."[9] Our common language is semantically closed. It is universal and comprehensive, not only because it lets us talk about any sort of object, but also because it allows us to speak about sentences in the language itself and to declare their truth or falsity.

Can Tarski's definition of truth be expressed in pictures and be about pictures? Can pictures somehow mention themselves or one another, and can one picture state that another is true or false? Does it make sense for us to make a distinction between "metapictures" and "object-pictures"?

8

Let us begin by discussing false pictures. What makes a picture to be false? Suppose a man is falsely accused of a crime. As part of the evidence against him, his accusers claim he met with a particular woman at a particular time. The accused denies meeting her, but his accusers bring forward a doctored photograph that shows him talking with her and holding a newspaper with the date visible. The photograph is "false": it purports to display a meeting, but the meeting never took place. Is there not a sense in which we can merely quote this picture and then say that it is not true? Is the picture not like a proposition, or even like a sentence?

The reason a photograph can be used as evidence is that the photograph is an effect produced by a situation. A photograph is normally made when light rays reflected from objects strike photographic film and cause chemical changes. After the film is developed, these changes produce a piece of mottled paper that resembles what caused it to look the way it does. The photograph counts as evidence not because it is a picture but because it is an effect. A photograph is like a vivid clue. To produce a doctored photograph is not different, in this respect, from, say, putting down false footprints that would indicate that the accused and the woman met at a certain time and place.

If instead of producing a photograph, the accusers had brought in a painting of the accused meeting the woman, the picture would not count as evidence. It is not as a picture that the photograph is false, but as an effect, as a clue.

We would get a better example of a false picture if we were to think of a painting that presented someone in a false light. Imagine a portrait of a mild, kind man that makes him look savage and cruel, or a picture that shows him doing violence to someone. The features would be his but the tone or the action would not. We could say that the painting is not him at all, even though it is a painting of him. A photograph could be false in the same way: it could capture a look which is uncharacteristic of the subject, making, for example, a solemn, wise person look silly. A photograph does this by isolating a momentary look or a profile from its context of looks and behavior before and after; the deception lies not in the photographer's taking the picture, but in the choice made by the person who selects this picture as the one to be used in representing its subject.

Pictures are put together to allow their subjects to appear in a certain way. There is both selection and combination in pictures, just as in speech. But while speech assembles words that are to shape a perception, a picture gives us something like the perception itself, it gives us a replica of a thing perceived. It shows us that we can and perhaps should see the object depicted in such and such a way, that the object has it in itself to become manifest in this way. If the picture depicts an action, it does not necessarily assert that the one depicted did what the picture shows him doing, but it does say he could have acted in this way, that he has it in him to behave in this manner. A picture displays at least a possibility.

If we think the picture brings out something false, if we think the depicted could not be seen in the way it is represented, we must make use of words to deny the picture. We can *say* that the picture is misleading, that it is a caricature, but we cannot paint another picture that would somehow contain the first one and indicate that it is false; we also cannot paint a picture of the artist falsifying his subject while he paints (even though we can paint a picture of the artist depicting his subject). Pictures cannot express falsity, even though they can embody it. Why is this so? Why do we have to move from pictures to speech when we wish to assert that something is false?

9

First of all, if we were to deny that a picture is true, it would not be clear what exactly we were denying. Suppose we agreed that an X drawn through a picture negated it; it would not be clear whether we were denying that the person depicted has these facial characteristics, or that he ever sat on this easy chair, or that he ever wore such clothes, or that the tone given him was appropriate, and so on. Speech is much more definite; it isolates more explicitly. If I deny a sentence, I deny exactly what is stated in it. It is not that a picture is vague; rather, so many senses are condensed into the one picture that we must resort to speech to spell out what it is we are negating. A thousand items of information could be registered in any picture. And in the case of a highly intelligent painting or photograph, the embedded senses are so subtle, complex and interwoven that even speech could not unglue them and pin them down for our confirmation or denial.

Secondly, the grammatical apparatus that permits negation is lacking in pictures. An X drawn across a picture is not part of the picture. It is almost like a verbal convention, a "no" stated about the picture. Pictures are densely positive; pictures as such have no grammatical room for explicit negation. The only thing that approaches grammar in picturing is the frame that encloses the picture.[10] The frame detaches the picture from its surroundings; it draws attention to the picture as picture. Likewise, the grammatical elements that structure speech draw attention to the other words as words, as involved in representation.

Grammar, however, does not only draw attention to the representational character of words; it also signals how these words are to be ordered (the frame does not do this for the picture).[11] In ordering the words, the grammar also signals how the things presented when the words are presented are to be ordered: *chairs* always brings chairs along, and *soft* brings the attribute of softness, so an *are* between the two words signals us not only to join *chairs* and *soft*, but also to present chairs as being soft. But any signal can be countermanded. A *not* added to the *are* cancels what the *are* normally does. "These chairs are not soft" prevents us specifically from presenting the chairs as soft.

Only a representational system that contains grammatical complexity, only a system that can in various ways draw attention to and arrange its own modes of presentation, can carry out explicit negation. Pictures do not have a grammatical system. They have some reflexivity—indicated by the frame—but they do not have the convoluted and involuted reflexivity of language. Through its semantic closure, language can work on itself and on what it presents in a way that pictures can only hint at. Pictures can best be compared with precategorial uses of language, the uses that allow us to say merely "man, tall" and "chair, soft." On this precategorial level negation is rudimentary even in language; because speech here moves on continuously in parataxis, without crisp beginnings or ends of sentences, it would not be clear how far forward or how far backward a negation would reach. And since there is practically no grammar in the precategorial and in pictures, there are no grammatical signals to be countermanded.

Why do pictures not have grammar? Their special strength—their imitation of a perceivable thing, their donation to us of a perception and a sensation—keeps them from having grammar. Grammar is not included in things; it appears when we come on the scene and articulate, modify, and speak about the presentations of things. We must make the presence itself of things thematic to some degree if we are to introduce grammar. We also are the ones who fabricate pictures, but in doing so we simply double the things we see; we do not declare in our duplication how we have imitated or disclosed what we have pictured.

10

Thus there are two factors that prohibit pictures from stating their own falsity and that of other pictures: indeterminacy of content and lack of grammatical resources. If pictures cannot declare falsity, they also cannot declare truth (even though they can embody both). Consequently, Tarski's definition of truth cannot be transformed into a procedure governing the truth of pictures.

In the spirit of Husserl's imaginative variation, let us try to imagine what it would be like to transform Tarski's definition—"p" is true if and only if p—into pictures. We would have to put a pictorial name of a picture on the left and place the same picture simply "stated" on the right. But then there would be no way of depicting either what is said by the words "is true," or what is said by the words "if and only if." Also, there would be no way of showing, pictorially, a difference between the picture on the left and the one on the right. And finally the picture on the right would not really direct our intentions beyond itself to the conditions that make it true; it would merely present itself, not its own truth conditions. In the verbal analogy, it would be as if we said:

$$\text{``}p\text{'' is true if and only if ``}p\text{''.}$$

If we cannot transform Tarski's entire definition into a pictorial mode, perhaps we could transform part of it. We might, for example, point to the picture and say, "This is true if and only if...," and then point to a situation in which something was going on that conspicuously verified the picture; if the picture presented James as cruel, the situation might be one in which he was acting cruelly to someone. In doing this, however, we diminish the role of the picture and make everything verbal or at least gestural: we point to the picture and perhaps say "this" or "this picture," and we point to the situation. We do not use the picture to indicate the situation. Pointing is not imaging. Pictures cannot name themselves and they cannot be used to name their own truth conditions, as sentences can; hence Tarski's definition of truth cannot be expressed in pictures and it cannot be applied to them.

Thus despite the harmonies between sentences and pictures, the two modes of presentation are different. Tarski's definition can be expressed in words but not in images, and it can be applied to words but not to pictures. Words and pictures represent in different ways, and the way each works can be better understood by thinking about the differences between them.

11

When we put words together, we also combine and arrange something else, but this "something else" is not ideas or concepts taken as "things in the mind." The "other things" we combine when we combine words are the things themselves in their presentation. We arrange the way things appear: we make the chairs seem soft, we make the man seem tall. The soft-seeming chairs are not mental chairs; they are chairs as minded, chairs as brought to mind, but not chairs in the mind as opposed to chairs themselves. Words bring things to mind but do not make them mental.

It seems more obvious to us philosophically that when we depict something, our combining of colors and shapes serves to bring things to mind without making them mental. The material density of the colored shapes helps to keep the thing "out there." But words, despite their transparency, also arrange the world and not just our concepts; they let things, whether present or absent to us, appear in a certain light.

VI

12
Moral Thinking

1

There have been many philosophical attempts to clarify what makes a human act to be morally good or bad, and to clarify what makes human behavior to be a moral action at all. I suggest that most of these attempts, at least in the forms they have taken in the past few centuries, can be divided into two kinds of theories, two kinds of moral philosophies. I further suggest that each of the two kinds of moral theory is determined by the kind of categoriality that the theory appeals to in explaining what moral action is. Each kind of theory tries to explain the being of moral action by claiming, implicitly, that a certain kind of thinking makes up the substance of a moral performance. And finally I claim that these two kinds of moral theory fail to provide a sufficient account of moral thinking, and that we must turn to another, to a third kind of moral categoriality for a more adequate philosophical description of moral thinking and moral behavior.

I use the term *categoriality* in the way that Husserl uses the term in *Logical Investigations;* it refers to logical structure or logical form, but to logical form as it is realized in states of affairs or in articulated things. For example, a car's being blue is more than

just a car and blue; as a fact or a state of affairs, it is permeated
with the syntax or the logical and ontological form of S's being p.
Husserl claims that we do not discover such categorial forms just
in the internal working of the mind; he insists that they modify
the presentation and the being of things as such. In a profound
opposition to the Kantian tradition in philosophy, he shows that
there is such a thing as categorial intuition: we can intuit not
only simple things or sensory givens, but states of affairs, groups,
universals, and other categorial objects as well.

I claim that categorial forms are also to be found in the moral
domain, and that they play a strategic role in determining the
morality of human behavior. I begin my analysis by saying that
there are two kinds of moral theory, and that each kind appeals to a special type of categoriality as the substance of moral
behavior.

The first kind of theory appeals to what I want to call the
categoriality of *judgment*. In a moral judgment, we subsume an
individual action under a moral category. Deontological and axiological ethical theories appeal to such judgmental categoriality
when they try to explain what makes a human action moral. According to such theories, an action is moral and it is good or
bad because it is identifiable as an instance of, say, generosity
or greed, courage or murder, or because it obeys or violates a
rule of behavior, or because it serves and instantiates a moral
value. The particular action comes under, it is subsumed by, the
moral category, rule, or value; the particular action is judged
according to that category, rule, or value. Its being judged in
that way makes it to be a moral action and not merely nonmoral
human behavior.

However, the categories, rules, obligations, and values are
themselves not derived from anything more ultimate; they are
not judged by anything beyond themselves. Nor are they established by empirical induction. They have a kind of irreducibility,
a presentation and force of their own. Somehow or other they
must be grasped on their own as obligations and as values. But
once grasped, they have to be applied, and the kind of thinking
that goes on when they are applied is judgmental thinking. It is
this sort of thinking, according to the moral theories we are now
describing, that constitutes human action as moral.

The second kind of moral theory I wish to distinguish turns to the categoriality of *relation:* an action is said to be moral, and morally good or bad, because it is related to another action or to some other state of affairs which follows from it. In this group we have teleological, utilitarian, and consequentialist moral theories, those that explain the goodness or badness of an action by appealing to that in view of which the act is done, or to that which is the outcome of the action. This kind of moral theory would claim that the moral character of a behavior is constituted by the categorial form of relation rather than that of judgment. One action is good because it leads to, or is done in view of, greater happiness or greater relief of distress; another action is bad because it leads to, or is done in view of, some unhappiness or displeasure or some undesirable condition.

In summary, then, there are two kinds of moral theories, the judgmental and the relational. Each of them locates the substance of moral behavior in a categoriality that informs human behavior. The judgmental moral theories, the deontological and the axiological, claim that an action is first constituted as moral when it becomes involved in a moral judgment: this or that action is judged to be an instance of this or that moral category, or it is judged to be in accordance with or in violation of this or that moral rule. The relational moral theories, the teleological, utilitarian, and consequentialist, claim that an action is first constituted as moral by its reference to the goal or the outcome in view of which it is done.

The categoriality in question, whether judgmental or relational, is articulated by the moral agent or by the moral evaluator, not by the moral theorist. The moral theorist points out what it is in the action itself that makes the action to be moral. The moral theorist is not the one who first introduces moral categorialities; he merely describes and clarifies them. He points out the thinking at work in the minds and actions of those who are engaged in the moral performance. It is the categorial form, the moral thinking, that establishes a human performance as a moral action.

Now each of the two kinds of moral theory I have described has a serious problem associated with it. The first, the judgmental kind of theory, cannot show where the moral categories, rules, and values come from. Although we can make inferences and applications once the categories and rules and values are there, we do not seem able to establish them themselves. This means that we can be rational *within* the context of the categories, rules, and values, but that we cannot be rational *about* the categories, rules, and values themselves. We seem to be forced to appeal to moral intuitions, to custom and social convention, or to a simple perception of values. The second kind of moral theory, the relational, cannot explain the moral goodness or badness of the goals or the outcomes of the actions, nor can it show how such goals and outcomes can generate moral obligations. It cannot explain how a moral point of view is introduced into human life by the fact that certain desirable goods issue from what we do.

I suggest that these difficulties arise because the nature of moral thinking is not adequately clarified by the two kinds of moral theories we have distinguished. Moral categorialities are not exhausted by the two forms we have described, by moral judgment and moral relation. These two forms have a place in moral action, but they are not basic enough to explain what moral action is. We must introduce another kind of moral thinking. And because Husserl has done so much to clarify the nature of categoriality in general, I think he can help us in supplying what is needed to give a more adequate account of moral thinking.

2

As Husserl shows in *Logical Investigations*, we articulate what we experience into various categorial objects: into states of affairs, facts, relations, collections, universals and their instances, and the like. Husserl observes that we can intuit such articulated categorial objects. Thinking is not merely a rearrangement of concepts in our minds but a registration of the various states and relations in which things can be presented and intended by us. We can, for example, register and present the "being together" of the house and the tree, when we say "the house and the tree," and we can register and present the "being red" of the car when we say, "The car is red." When we do this, when we accomplish categorial intuitions, we do not simply absorb sensuously what is around us; we do absorb, but we also articulate. We differentiate and identify.

The culminating part of *Logical Investigations*, section 2 of Investigation 6, deals with the categorial form of predication, of articulating an object into subject and predicate. But Husserl also provides an analysis of a more simple identification. He describes what happens when we simply recognize, say, Hans as Hans or Berlin as Berlin. This is less that the achievement of predication, but it is nevertheless a form of thinking. In fact the more articulated categoriality of predication is rooted in this simpler form of thinking, the kind that occurs when we just identify or recognize an object as itself. This kind of thinking is simple identification, and Husserl explores it in his analysis of empty intention and fulfillment in section 1 of Investigation 6.

Now I would suggest that the moral categorialities we have discussed above, the categorialities of judgment and of relation, can also be grounded upon a more elementary form of moral thinking, on a type of fundamental moral identification. When the categorialities of moral judgment and relation are thus based on this more fundamental kind of thinking, they receive a philosophical clarification that resolves the difficulties that seem endemic to them. The categories, rules, values, goals, and outcomes will no longer seem to dangle from nowhere, they will no longer seem to be unexplained, simply given, and almost arbitrary. Thus I want to use the philosophical resources Husserl has given us to provide an escape from the bad alternative of either deontologism or teleology that has marked recent ethical theory.

3

I maintain that what makes human behavior into moral action is a special kind of thoughtful identification. It can be described as follows. I perform a moral transaction when I do something that is good or bad for you, and identify it, *insofar as it is good or bad for you*, as my good or bad. In other words, I perform a moral transaction when I want to do *this* precisely insofar as it is good or bad for you; or when I avoid *that* precisely insofar as it is good or bad for you. For example, you are hungry and I give you some food. Being fed, as being good for you, is identified and brought about as my good. It is not just that you are being fed; it is also not just that your being fed is somehow beneficial for me; it is that *as* being good for you, your being fed becomes good for me. I want and bring about your being fed insofar as it is good for you. There is, so to speak, a kind of laminated identification that occurs here. I recognize this activity as good for you, and *as such* I want it and recognize it as good for me. Your good, *as* your good, becomes *my* good. Or, in another kind of moral transaction, I may want and recognize a bad that I do for you as being, as such, good for me: your losing your job, *as* bad for you, is wanted, achieved, and recognized by me as good for me. In such a case I am being cruel or harmful to you. In either case, whether I am being kind or cruel, whether I am doing good to my friend or harming my enemy, it is the thoughtful dimension, the complex identification, that provides the categorial form that turns mere behavior into moral transaction. This categorial form is what establishes the difference between a nonmoral human performance and a moral action.

A moral action therefore is made into a moral action by two things: by a behavior of some sort, which works as a substrate; and by the categorial identification that I have described, which works as the form. To be moral agents we must initiate a performance, but we must also understand and identify the performance in a certain way. The identificational form, this special pattern of recognition, is more basic in what we could call *moral ontology* than are the categorial forms of judgment and relation that, in other moral theories, are said to constitute the substance of a moral performance. Indeed the judgmental and relational forms presuppose this identificational categoriality.

4

I would like to amplify my description of a moral transaction. The recognitional form I have introduced—my doing and taking what is good or bad for you, as such, as my good or bad—is a categoriality that permeates a concrete performance. It is not a mere mental intention. Something has to be done. To be moral agents, we have to initiate something, we have to crease the world. The categoriality modifies how something worldly is presented to us. The categoriality is placed outside, it is not just somehow in the mind. In this respect the moral categoriality resembles the categorialities Husserl describes in *Logical Investigations.* They too are not just forms or categories in the mind but are articulations and structures that permeate the objects we experience and that modify how these objects are presented and intended. The approach I have provided thus makes moral behavior more of a public, manifest phenomenon, not something accomplished in an intention or in an interior act of willing.

Furthermore, my analysis shows that moral behavior is essentially interpersonal, that it is a transaction, since I as a moral agent take the good of someone else formally as my good. My actions are first made to be moral by virtue of this intersubjective identificational structure, not by virtue of conforming or disconforming to a rule, value, moral category, or goal. Even the virtues and vices that seem to be purely personal or self-directed, such as temperance and intemperance, or fortitude and cowardice, are established as moral by this structure, since in such actions we become related to our own selves—our present and our future selves—in a moral way. If we act temperately we perform an action that is good for us, and, as such, we take it as our good; we want and we do the action as good for ourselves if we are indeed acting out of the virtue of temperance. In these self-regarding virtues and vices, in temperance and intemperance, fortitude and cowardice, there is a kind of reflexivity that is analogous to our relationships with other persons. We act toward ourselves as toward another, and we become either friends or enemies to ourselves.

My claim therefore is that a human performance is made to be not merely a nonmoral event but a moral transaction by the special categoriality that informs it. I not only hand some food over to you; this handing over becomes kindness because as good for you it is taken as my good. I not only bump into you; this bumping becomes an insult or a cruelty because as bad for you it is taken as good for me. Only when this moral form is present does a moral relationship between you and me become established or adjusted. Only through this form am I established as generous or cruel, are you established as a beneficiary or as someone who has been harmed, and are you justified in being grateful or resentful for what has happened.

In the case of malevolent moral actions, the primary instance is the one in which I accomplish what is bad for you and do so directly as good for me. This occurs in acts of cruelty, insult, revenge, ridicule, and the like. These are the paradigm cases of malevolent moral transaction. Very many cases of doing injury, however, are not as direct as this; often harm is done not out of direct malevolence but because the action in question is somehow useful for me: I assault you not because I hate you but because I want your money; I calumniate you not out of revenge but in order to get your job. But even in such cases of utilitarian malice, the form we have described is what makes the action moral, because your bad still becomes good for me: not directly, but as a means to some benefit that I want. My transaction is still malevolent, but in a different way.

And in a more positive vein, gifts are an instance of a special kind of benevolence. Most good actions are prompted by needs that emerge in our situations. Someone is hungry, confused, tired, saddened, or wounded. The urgent substrate calls for a form of benevolence and if our character as agents is good we will respond appropriately. But giving a gift is not controlled by a necessary good. It is not prompted by what is needed. It is a form of benevolence that searches for a substrate in which it can realize and express itself. The form, not the substrate, comes first.

The introduction of the form of moral identity opens up for us the possibility of a moral life. There are countless different ways in which I can take your good or bad formally as my own, and in which you and others can do the same for me. Acts of gratitude and revenge, generosity and envy, loyalty, betrayal and forgiveness, reconciliation and hatred, are only some of the structural variations possible in this interaction. What happens in this domain—what we do and what is done to us—are the most important things in our lives with one another. It is through the human actions constituted by the form of moral thinking that we establish, confirm, and change the human relationships without which we could not be what we are, and there is no human happiness or grief more arresting than the kind that occurs in this domain.

5

Let us then suppose that the recognitional form that I have described is indeed the element that makes an action to be moral, that it is what changes nonmoral behavior into a moral transaction. We can now ask the question of how this categorial form is related to the two other categorialities we discussed earlier, the categoriality of moral judgment and the categoriality of practical relation, of doing one thing in view of another. I have claimed that these two forms of practical thinking are grounded on the form of a moral transaction; how is this the case?

The structure of a moral transaction—identifying the good or bad of another, as such, as my own good or bad—is analogous to the structure of a perceptual recognition. And just as simple perception does not engage the issue of meaning as forcefully as do the articulations that are built upon perception, so too the moral transaction does not yet raise the question of what exactly I am doing in taking this good or bad as my own. The form of a moral transaction moves my behavior into the domain of morals, but it does not itself classify what I am doing and does not articulate whether I am acting rightly or wrongly, whether what I am doing is praiseworthy or blameworthy. To draw the analogy with the case of cognition, perception alone is not fully elevated into the kind of meaning and the kind of justification that is reached in the further categorial articulations of predication, collection, measurement, and the like.

In other words, the moral transaction needs to be evaluated, and it is evaluated in the further categorialities of judgment and relationship. These two categorialities bring out the meaning of the moral performance. For example, if in a particular circumstance I take this good of yours, as such, as my good, then I, you, and the others will all go on to judge my action in the light of the moral maxims, categories, rules, exemplars, and exhortations that our moral tradition provides. We will say, for example, that it was a cowardly action, or a generous act with a touch of

envy, or an ambitious action, or one worthy of an Achilles, or
a Napoleonic action. These judgmental categories have themselves originally issued from countless moral transactions in the
past; they are the moral memory of our world; they are there to
help us bring out the meaning of our actions and to make our
moral actions truly good. But our actions can be so evaluated
only "after" they are first made to be moral and good or bad, not
by this deontological judgment, but by the recognitional form
of moral thinking. The judgment articulates what the actions already are.

Moral relativity, the fact that moral values, categories, emphases, and paradigms can differ from one culture to another, appears more pronounced when we focus on the categories used in
moral judgments and neglect the concrete moral performance,
the action that is constituted as moral by the form of a moral
transaction. Cultural differences in ethics appear to be almost
unbridgeable if we remain only with the abstract formulations
of moral traditions (and this, of course, is what academic and
anthropological analyses of cultures tend to do). If we go beyond moral abstractions toward the concrete moral performance,
toward the substantial moral action, there is a far greater possibility of appreciating, even across cultural lines, the goodness or
the badness of what is being done by one agent to another.

Furthermore, in contrast to moral abstractions, the concrete
moral transaction is always individualized and situated, but it does
not become arbitrary. To understand how I as agent can be taking your good or bad as such as my own good or bad, one must
comprehend the particular circumstances at the moment of action, the alternative courses of action that, realistically, might
have been followed, who the agent is and who the target is, what
has gone on before between them, and so on. Only then can one
tell how and why this is a good or a bad for both the agent and
the target. And yet, despite this situatedness, the good or bad is
objective and not arbitrary; it is what is indeed possible here and
now, it is what is called for by this situation at this time and place.
The form of a moral transaction thus account for both the in-
dividualizing and the objectifying of a moral performance. Just
as Husserl's account of perception and thinking clarifies both
the objective and the subjective dimensions of knowledge and

experience, so this form accounts for the objective and subjective aspects of moral experience and recognition.

We have shown how the deontological form, the form of moral judgment, can be grounded on the form of a moral transaction. The relational form, the kind that is the center of emphasis in teleological or utilitarian moral theories, also brings out the meaning of a moral transaction. It is a further articulation that registers what has occurred in a moral performance. However, it works by exploiting the peculiar temporal structure of moral action: when we act, we do not always simply do what we are doing now. We are not exhausted in the present of our behavior. Instead of just doing *this*, we may be doing *this* for the sake of *that*. And what follows later will often shed light on what we are doing now; it will let our present action show up more vividly for what it is in itself. The scope of our action can be so expanded that a kind of duality emerges that is peculiar to human behavior. *This* and *that*, what is done *now* and what will follow *then*, the action and its purpose or the action and its consequences are distinguished and yet joined in the unity of a complex performance, and the full meaning of what we are doing now, the full meaning of *this*, can only be seen in relation to *that*, to what will follow *then*. These are possibilities inherent in human performance. Therefore another way of evaluating what we are doing is to see what it is done for and what issues from it. The purpose and consequences can reveal the character of what we have done. This relational form of moral thinking, along with the deontological form of moral judgment, is another way of showing the ethical meaning of what we are doing; but again the teleological form presupposes that the action in question has already been constituted as a moral transaction. The relational form merely brings out what has already been accomplished. It does not originally establish the action as moral.

Therefore, just as the forms of predication and relation are founded upon simple identifications, so also are the forms of moral judgment and of moral relatedness founded upon what we have described as the simple form of a moral transaction. It is this simple form—the categorial form of taking what is good or bad for you, as such, as being good or bad for me—that moves us into the domain of morals; it is the kind of thinking that first introduces reason into desire and aversion, that allows us to see goods and bads not only as they seem to us, but as they are for others, and that allows us to begin asking whether what seems to be good for me is really good or not.

If we recognize this moral categoriality as the substance of moral action, it becomes clear that there never is a serious problem about whether and how a human being needs to be persuaded to adopt the moral point of view. We have no choice about adopting the moral point of view. We exist morally not by virtue of a decision, but by virtue of the fact that we share a world with other agents, and that what seems good to us will usually also show up as good or bad to others, that as good or bad for others it can be good or bad for us, that there can consequently be both conflicts and harmonies in the intersection of our goods and bads, and that we as agents can appreciate the intersection of our goods and bads with those of others. That space of intersection is the space in which we act. There is no more a problem about how we enter into the moral point of view than there is a problem about how what I perceive from this angle can also be perceived from another angle by someone else. That is the way things are, and that is the way we are. The moral point of view is simply another expression of our ability to think and to identify things and goods across various perspectives. It is an expression of our rational being and of our being with others. We can, of course, be mistaken about the various goods and bads and about how they intersect. Things that are bad may seem good to us, and things that are good may seem bad. There is always the problem of distinguishing the real meaning from the mere appearance in morals, and moral education consists in being helped to become insightful in such matters. But to be or not to be moral is not itself a matter of choice; we are moral by the way we exist with others.

6

We have distinguished and discussed two levels of thinking in moral conduct. The first level involves the simple form of moral identification. The agent takes the good or bad of the

target, as such, as his own good or bad. This categoriality makes
conduct to be moral as opposed to nonmoral. The second level
or moral thinking contains the categorialities of judgment and
relation, which bring out the meaning of the moral action. In
them we determine what kind of action is going on. On this
second level we bring the categories, rules, and paradigms of our
moral tradition to bear on what has transpired between agent and
target, and we consider what the purposes and outcomes of the
action have been. By using judgmental and relational forms, we
articulate whether the action was moral or immoral, praiseworthy
or blameworthy. But we can move on toward a third level of moral
thinking. We can go beyond meaning and introduce a question
of truth. This issue will have repercussions on what we accomplish
on the first two levels of moral categoriality.

The question of truth can be raised in two different ways. First,
when an evaluation, a moral description, of an action has been
made, we can go on to ask whether that evaluation was correct
or not, whether the attribution of this or that meaning to the
act was true or false. Someone draws another person into dubi-
ous financial practices and declares, "I'm only loosening him up,
getting him to look out a bit for himself, to make a profit here
and there"; but a more perceptive commentator might say, "No,
you're making him dishonest." The meaning given to the action
by the agent is rejected as false. His judgment about the action
is denied and said to be not true. In other cases, of course, the
original assessment may be confirmed as true. The point is that
one is not just attributing a sense to the action and evaluating
it, but discussing the truth or the falsity of the attribution and
evaluation. The issue of truth is raised.

But, second, we can also ask whether the category our moral
tradition gives us is itself truly good or bad. We can question the
truth, not of the application of a category, but of the category
itself. If cannibalism is practiced in a particular society, the moral
tradition may have a category for it as praiseworthy such as, "eating your enemy to absorb his strength," and this category will
be applied to particular performances to express their meaning.
But a question can be raised whether this is a moral term for
the *truly* praiseworthy. Here the question of truth is not about
the correctness of a particular application of a term, but about

the term itself as a moral category. Is this term the expression of something truly morally good or bad, as we have taken it to be? Is this custom or law, this way of behaving, truly good or bad, as we have taken it to be? Is this moral category, is this practice genuinely good or bad?

This issue of the moral truth or falsity of a moral category is the issue of the difference between nature and convention in morals. At this point there arises the distinction between what is good or bad by custom, convention, or law, and what is good or bad by nature. Sometimes the inherited moral category will become manifest as unnatural or against nature, but sometimes it will be confirmed as true, as in accordance with nature and the morally genuine. But the issue of its truth or falsity has been raised and the distinction between nature and convention has been drawn. This distinction introduces a further set of moral categorialities that supplement and penetrate those we have seen on the first two levels of moral categoriality, the level of moral transaction and the level of moral characterization.

Furthermore, although the distinction between nature and convention occurs in regard to a moral term, the distinction is triggered by the application of that term to particular cases. It is in "living out," say, cannibalism that human agents begin to appreciate that the practice is not in conformity with the beings and relationships involved in it. They begin to appreciate that this is no way for people to be related to one another. Something in the thing asserts itself as not subsumable under this practice and this moral category; the category does not fit what it is supposed to fit. The distinction between nature and convention does not arise through a kind of abstract description of alternative ways of acting, but through thoughtful action itself and the identifiability and differentiation that arise in action. The distinction between nature and convention is made when we go back to actual moral transactions, to concrete cases of an agent's taking the good or bad of another as such as his own good or bad, when we go back to a moral transaction that has been shaped by the practices of our moral tradition and evaluated by its categories. The meaning of the action has been articulated, but now the truth of that meaning gets called into question: the action itself calls the convention into question. The action may ultimately confirm the convention, but it also may show that the convention is against nature. Such a questioning and denial of a convention occurs when someone disobeys a law he considers unjust, as a way of showing the injustice of the law; he appeals to nature against convention not by abstract argument but by action, by using the action to show the incoherence of the convention.

Thus the contrast between nature and convention does not emerge in a comparison of two abstractions called *nature* and *convention*, nor in the comparison of two abstract descriptions of behavior, one of which would give the natural features of the action while the other would provide the conventional characteristics. The contrast arises rather in a concrete performance, when a convention is blended with a moral transaction, but when the blend does not "take," when the action refuses to be described as the convention describes it, and when the action shows the convention to be morally incoherent. Thus the actual moral transaction is the place in which a contrast between nature and convention is first made. The moral transaction, constituted by the categorial form we have described, is the origin even for the difference between the natural and the conventional.

In summary, (1) the form of a moral transaction establishes a human performance as moral as opposed to nonmoral; (2) the forms of judgment and relation bring out the meaning of the moral performance and allow us to distinguish between the moral and the immoral, the praiseworthy and the blameworthy; and (3) we can go on to ask (a) whether the moral category or moral meaning attributed to the action has been correctly attributed, whether the attribution is true or not, and (b) whether the category or meaning itself is a moral category of the truly good or bad, whether as a moral convention it is or is not according to nature. These three levels in moral thinking are analogous to three levels that can be distinguished in cognition: (1) the level of perceptual identification or recognition; (2) the level of predication, relation, and other categorialities, the level of articulated meaning; (3) the level of the truth of the categorialities articulated in (2).

In closing, I would like to point out a limitation in what we have done in this paper. A philosophical analysis such as the one we have carried out, a study of the form of manifestation and the form of being of moral behavior, does not as such makes us morally good or bad. Only our actions, only what we do makes us into a particular kind of agent. But our philosophical analysis can disclose what it is in us that makes us to be moral agents at all; and this understanding, although not strictly a moral good, has another kind of goodness all its own. It is a philosophical good. I hope that in achieving this understanding, if indeed I have succeeded in doing so, I have accomplished not only something good for myself, but something good for you as well. If I have done so, however, my accomplishment will not have been a moral transaction. I will not have acted morally toward you, nor you toward me. Instead, we will have accomplished a philosophical clarification, an activity that neither of us does alone, but that we achieve together.

13
What Is
Moral Action?

> "He is devoted to you in his way," said
> Miss Ridley.
> "I daresay a cat does the right thing to
> a mouse in its way."
> "Doing things in your own way is not
> really doing them," said Megan.
>   I. Compton-Burnett,
>   *The Present and the Past*

I wish to clarify, philosophically, what a moral action is. The best way to proceed in this venture would be to exhibit a moral performance and to reflect on it. What I have to say could be said much more effectively if I were able to comment on something that occurs publicly before me and my audience, that is, if I could do more than speak in general and in the abstract.

But as I prepare this lecture I know that I cannot count on a moral exchange happening just when I am to deliver the lecture.

An earlier version of this paper was presented as the Suarez Lecture at Fordham University on April 2, 1987. In having the paper published I wish to retain the form it had as a lecture because I think the centrality of actual performances

It is most unlikely that at precisely *that* moment—at this moment now, while I read these words to you—some moral performance would be transacted in the full view and with the full understanding of my audience and me: some act of cunning revenge or tactful gratitude, of tender benevolence or furious insult. No, it would be too much to ask fortune to place such an example before us at the exact moment it is desired.[1]

I have no alternative but to take the issue in hand myself and, by my own efforts, to bring an example to my mind and yours. I cannot do this by doing something moral myself, since I am to be engaged in a situation that requires only that I speak, not that I act. Furthermore, there will, most likely, be nothing in the situation in which I speak that will call for an action, and without the appropriate setting no action is possible. Anything that I might do as a contrived performance would be a pretense at action, not a genuine deed. Nor can I depict an action to you in its concreteness by presenting a drama or running a film, since the time needed to establish the characters, set the circumstances, and stage the transaction would leave us with no time to philosophize about what has taken place. We would be engrossed by the enactment and would have to forgo thinking about it.

If I am to bring a concrete action before you, I can do so only by talking about one, by describing one. And this of course is to bring the action before you in its absence. A few words will have to suffice to establish the characters and set the circumstances, a few more words to describe the action itself. What I have to say will be no more than a simple pencil drawing, a few lines that seem as nothing whether compared to the staged depiction or to the bodily presence of the event. Much has to be left to your imagination.

---

in moral philosophy can be better expressed in that way, and also because the change from a spoken to a written form can occasion an interesting study of perspectival, hermeneutical shifts, as I try to show in note 1. The paper presents the theory of moral conduct that I developed at greater length in my book, *Moral Action: A Phenomenological Study* (Bloomington: Indiana University Press, 1985), and in two essays: "Moral Thinking," above, ch. 12; and "Knowing Natural Law," below, ch. 14.

1

Ralph is a bachelor. Conflicts at his job have worn him down. He has lost his nerve, he is ill and depressed. He happens to have an appointment with Norman, his dentist and friend, who asks him about the general state of his health and soon hears the whole story of Ralph's ordeal. Norman soon realizes that much of Ralph's distress stems from loneliness, from the pressure of living alone at a time when he needs help. He suggests that Ralph come to live for a while with him and his family. Ralph does so. He lives with them for a month, and with their help he is much better able to deal with his conflicts at work and with his other problems. His life is put on a steadier course.

What Norman and his family did was a moral transaction. Ralph is grateful for what was done, and gratitude is the response to benevolence. Gratitude is, we might way, the appropriate perception of benevolence. It is the way the target of the benevolence, the beneficiary, recognizes what has been done. Ralph's gratitude is a kind of warrant for us *that* a moral performance has occurred.

But what makes Norman's action to be a moral action? What makes it different from an action without moral quality? Suppose that Ralph had rented a room in a boarding house and through the conviviality of the other boarders managed to get over his nervous isolation. The owner of the house, in renting Ralph the room, did not become engaged in a moral transaction. Ralph would consider himself lucky that he moved into the house, but strictly speaking he would not be morally grateful to the man who rented the room to him. There would be no change in the moral relationship between Ralph and the owner, but there is a change in the relationship between Ralph and Norman because of what was done. What accounts for this difference? What is there in a moral exchange that is not found in other human exchanges?

Before trying to answer this question, let us observe that benevolent actions, or what we would call good moral actions, are not the only kind we must discuss. A malevolent transaction is a moral action too. A moral action can be morally good or morally bad. The special difference that constitutes a moral act as moral must be able to account for both the good and the bad. What we are looking for is what puts human behavior into the domain of morals as such. We wish to determine what places a human action into the "game" of morals, whether the action be judged to be good or bad.

I will therefore sketch in words another moral exchange besides the one that occurred between Ralph and Norman. Let us add a concrete instance of maleficence to the benevolence we have described.

Sidney is working hard for advancement in his career. Just when the crucial promotion is within reach, just as he is about to get what he has always wanted, Arthur reveals Sidney's secret. It was something that was done a long time ago, something of which Sidney has often repented. He lived in fear that it would someday become known. Arthur learned about the secret through the long-standing rivalry between their respective families, and just at the right moment, at the time when it would do the most devastating and irreparable damage, Arthur reveals the secret to the local gossip, who by the very inclination of his nature quickly makes it known to everyone. Sidney's career is destroyed.

What makes this to be a moral exchange? Why does Sidney bear resentment toward Arthur, and why have he and Arthur been established, by the action, as morally related, as offended and offender? What makes this case different from one in which, say, a clerk happens to discover and reveal the damaging information during a routine check? If only this had happened, the effect on Sidney's career might well have been the same; his career night well have been just as decisively destroyed. Sidney would then have considered himself unlucky, but he would not have been henceforth morally related to the clerk as the one offended to the offender, nor would he bear resentment toward the clerk. In fact, even in the exchange between Sidney and Arthur, Sidney does not bear the same resentment, the same moral response, toward the gossip as he does toward Arthur, who "did" something to him more explicitly than the gossip did. What makes this action moral?

A moral action is constituted as such by a special identificational form. An action is a *moral* action because it is identified by the agent in a special way. A particular human performance is established as, say, a benevolent action, because what is done is appreciated, by the agent, as good for someone else, and it is wanted and accomplished precisely as good for that other person. Norman appreciates company and conversation here and now as good for Ralph; he knows that Ralph needs this and that it will be good for him; and he wants and accomplishes it precisely as good for him. As good for Ralph, it becomes good for Norman. It is because of this identificational form that the behavior becomes a moral transaction and does not remain a morally indifferent exchange. It is because Norman wanted and did something as good for Ralph, that Ralph becomes constituted as a beneficiary and responds with gratitude.

An analogous recognitional form establishes a performance as a malevolent moral action. Arthur appreciates the disclosure of Sidney's secret as bad for Sidney, as dreadfully bad for him. And Arthur wants and accomplishes this event precisely as bad for Sidney. As bad for Sidney, it becomes Arthur's good. Because of this recognitional form, a moral transaction, an act of cruelty or of revenge, has been enacted between Arthur and Sidney.

2

Let us state this more formally. A performance becomes a moral performance when it becomes wanted and done, or unwanted and averted, precisely as good or bad for the target of the action. As good or bad for the target, it becomes good or bad for the agent. It is this identificational form, this categoriality, this thoughtful recognition, this style of "taking . . . as . . . ," that changes a bodily performance into a moral transaction. The identificational form changes a handing over into a generous giving, it changes a shove into an insult, it changes an act of feeding someone in a restaurant into an expression of gratitude, it changes denting someone's car into a mean-spirited act of revenge. Adapting a word used by Husserl, I would like to introduce the term *moral categoriality* to name this recognitional form, the form that constitutes a moral transaction.[2]

By *categoriality* Husserl means the formal articulation we achieve in an object when we let the various parts of the object be differentiated and recognized as parts. In a perception, for example, we might first simply see a shiny, whitish patch; then we may register the patch as ice; then we may take the ice as slippery and dangerous. The simple, precategorial sensibility of a shiny white patch becomes articulated into a categorial object, one that we might express as, "This slippery patch of ice is dangerous." A categorial object is an object infected with syntax, and the categoriality of the object lies in the syntactic form the object takes on.

There is a categoriality proper to moral thinking and moral conduct. It is the form of someone else's good or bad being taken, and done, as my own good or bad. In this categorial form the various parts of the good, and the various slants the good presents, are articulated and registered. Such moral categoriality is specifically human. It is also a rational accomplishment. It is the introduction of moral thinking into human desires and aversions. When we become capable of exercising such moral categoriality, we become established as moral agents. This moral form, this categorial identification is what opens up the logical space in which terms such as resentment and gratitude, pity and pardon, indignation and forgiveness, blame and praise, and other terms that express moral uptake acquire their meaning. This identification-form puts us into the domain of morals.

Various objections to my analysis come to mind. One objection might be formulated as follows: "Arthur injured Sidney by revealing his secret. But surely the reason why the revelation was a moral transaction lies not in any complicated form such as you describe, not in any categoriality, but rather in the fact that Arthur freely decided to reveal the secret. It was an act of Arthur's will, a decision, that made his performance moral. His act of free choice, together with the intention he had at the time, made the revelation to be not merely an unlucky accident but a moral transaction."

But this objection misplaces the central and primary accomplishment in moral action. It assumes that the substance of a moral performance lies in a decision that precedes the public behavior. The public behavior, in this understanding, would only *issue* from the act of the will; the public behavior would be the outcome of a choice. But in fact the substance of the moral action is in the performance itself. Sidney is injured when the secret is revealed. The public event is what changes the moral relationship between Sidney and Arthur. Arthur may have made up his mind at an earlier time to reveal the secret, but this making up of his mind is only a kind of anticipation of the deed. We should understand the decision in relation to the performance, not the performance in relation to its anticipation.

To place the substance of a moral action in the internal act of the will is to etiolate the moral action, to make it far too much a private episode rather than a transformation or rearrangement of the way things are in the world. There are such things as decisions, and we do sometimes make up our minds to act before we perform, but such thoughtful changes in us must not be seen as ends in themselves; they are the beginnings which end in public performances, they are the anticipations of morally formed behavior, the initial stirrings of action. They are faint inceptions and not the climax of action. They are the empty intendings of which the actions themselves are the fulfillments.

The substance of a moral transaction lies therefore not in a thought or in an intention or in an act of willing, but in thoughtful behavior, in an embodied performance which, as good or as bad for another, is done or averted as the agent's good or bad. It is the thoughtful form that makes the performance moral, but of course the form needs the performance as its embodiment and expression.

The form of a moral transaction can be realized in innumerable ways, and there are countless variations and nuances in the manner in which I can take your good or bad, as such, as my own good or bad. Let us mention a few examples from Shakespeare: Iago's fanning of Othello's suspicion: Edgar's protection of his blinded father Gloucester; Maria's deception and humiliation of Malvolio; Macbeth's slaughter of Macduff's wife and children; the shepherd's preservation of Perdita; even Hamlet's refusal to kill Claudius while he is praying (Claudius's good, the salvation of his soul, is taken as Hamlet's bad and is averted); so much variety of performance, so many vivid transactions, yet in all of them the same formal pattern, with the agent taking the good or the bad of his target as his own good or bad. And moral actions, constituted by this form, do not occur only as momentous actions that are worthy of being displayed in a drama. They occur on the small scale as well: the person seated next to you rudely steps on your foot while he makes his way to his seat, so you then stick chewing gum onto his coat. This nasty action is moral: you take and do what is bad for your neighbor as your good.

The form of a moral transaction is an elementary form of thinking. It is the installment of reason into our likes and dislikes. It allows us to live beyond our own immediate desires and aversions and it introduces a special kind of transcendence into our pursuit of the good. Through this form we become capable of appreciating something as good or bad for another; but more than this, through this form we become capable of accomplishing or averting something as good or bad for another. The form allows us not only to appreciate but also to do. The form is so simple that it is usually overlooked in philosophical analyses of moral conduct, just as the simple recognition of an object as being the same in many perceptions is often overlooked in studies of the more amplified forms of predication and relation. Moral categoriality is one of those forms that make all the difference, that open a new dimension, but that are so taken for granted that we hardly notice their presence and their achievement. We usually get caught up in issues found within the space opened by the moral form and overlook what generates the space itself. Furthermore, the form not only constitutes an action as moral, it also constitutes us as morally responsible, as agents that can be morally praised or blamed for what we do. It is the initial form of moral reason.

3

My philosophical use of the moral form, the form of taking the good or bad of another as one's own good or bad, can give rise to another objection. Someone might say, "Issues of temperance and fortitude are among the most common topics discussed in morals. Indeed Aristotle mentions them as the first examples of virtuous and vicious behavior in book 3 of the *Nicomachean Ethics*. But when we act self-indulgently or temperately, or when we act with rashness, cowardice, or courage, we do not seem to be related to the good or bad of another. We seem to be related to our own selves. Does your moral form, your moral categoriality, apply to temperance and courage?"

In response to this objection, I assert that in issues of temperance and fortitude we take a kind of distance to ourselves, and we become either friends or enemies to ourselves. If Helen performs temperate actions—if she eats the right food in the right amounts, for example—her actions are temperate not just because they happen to be the healthy thing to do, but because she does them as healthy, as good for her own self, and as the way of being moderate in regard to appetite. She does not just do the right action; she does it as good for herself. Only if this further categoriality is added to the healthy performance is the performance changed into a moral action. And the intemperate action, which is a kind of malevolence or enmity toward oneself, is constituted when something that is bad for you is taken as your own good; when smoking, which is bad for Helen, is wanted and chosen and done, when it is taken as her own good.

Thus the formal interplay of goods and bads can take place within our own selves. We are such beings that we can be harmonized or divided within ourselves, we can be friends or enemies, benevolent or malevolent, to ourselves. What makes it possible for us to be like this is precisely the distance to ourselves that is generated when reason is introduced into passion and thoughtful identifications take place that are more complicated than the identifications that our desires and passions alone can achieve.

My analysis of moral action bears an affinity to one of Aristotle's teachings in the *Nicomachean Ethics* and can, I think, be confirmed by what he writes. It is often said that Aristotle deals with ethics and not with morals as we understand morals. But the difference between ethics and morals should not be exaggerated, and I would suggest that what I have described as the domain of morals is treated by Aristotle under one of his definitions of justice in book 5, chapter 1, of the *Nicomachean Ethics*.

In that chapter Aristotle makes a distinction between particular justice, which is one virtue among many, and justice in a more general sense, the justice which can be equated with the whole of virtue. Particular justice is the virtue that makes us seek fair distributions and corrections; it keeps us from being grasping and from seeking more than our share. Justice in the more general sense is the virtue of obeying the law, and since the law orders the whole of our ethical life, a person who is law-abiding will, if the laws are as they should be, cultivate all the virtues.

Now Aristotle says that justice as lawfulness does not only perfect us in our individual activity; he says that such justice is "complete virtue, but not simply, but toward another, *pros heteron*" (1129b26–27).[3] The specific feature of general, legal justice is its involvement with other agents. Aristotle says such justice is complete virtue "because one who possesses it can exercise his virtue toward another and not only in himself; for many can exercise virtue in their own affairs, but cannot do so in matters relating to another" (1129b31–1130a1). He goes on to state that "for this same reason justice, alone of the virtues, seems to be 'another's good,' because it is [directed] toward another; for it does what is advantageous to someone else. . . ."(1130a3–5).

I would suggest that what Aristotle describes as justice in this general sense, justice as lawfulness and as equivalent to the whole of virtue, is similar to what I have described as "the moral." The point in common is the orientation toward another: the just man wants to do the good of another, the unjust man is willing to do what is bad for another; the just man takes and does the true good of another as his own good, the unjust man will take and do the bad of another as his own good. If such general justice is virtue entire, then the "toward another," the *pros heteron*, brings about a completion of ethics and sheds light on all the other virtues. The involvement with others is a form that fulfills all the particular virtues.[4]

In his analysis in the *Nicomachean Ethics*, Aristotle works gradually toward justice as the completion of virtue. He reaches justice only in book 5. What I have tried to do in invoking the "toward another" as constitutive of morals is to begin with such justice as the measure and standard of behavior, and to analyze the being of moral conduct in terms of it.

4

After this comparison of my analysis with that of Aristotle, I would like to draw another comparison, a comparison between my description of moral action and the analysis of morals provided by Adam Smith in *The Theory of Moral Sentiments.*[5] Smith describes our various moral sentiments and considers sympathy to be the most important and most fundamental of them all. He then says that sympathy itself, as well as all the other moral sentiments, is made possible by a special ability that we enjoy. He says that our moral sentiments come into being because we are able to place ourselves, in imagination, in the situation of someone else. We change places, in fancy, with another person.[6] Smith repeatedly refers to "that imaginary change of situations."[7] Sympathy and all the other moral sentiments depend on this displacement. Because we can displace ourselves imaginatively into the situation of another, we can sympathize with the resentment or gratitude of that other person, we can praise or blame what he does, we can share in his fear and hope.

The imaginary change of situation is something like a presentational or categorial form. It allows us to live a human life in common with others. According to Smith, it establishes us as moral beings. Is it the same as the moral categoriality that I have described? I think not, and I think there are two important differences between Smith's concept of imaginative displacement and my concept of moral form.

First, Smith describes moral sentiments, whereas I have tried to describe moral actions. Smith admits that moral actions issue from moral sentiments, but his analysis rests chiefly with the sentiments. The actions seem to be established as moral by the sentiment that precedes or accompanies them, not by the understanding that informs them. Indeed much of his analysis is directed toward the spectators of human behavior, to the ones who respond with approval or disapproval, with the appropriate sentiments, whereas my analysis is centered on the transaction itself and on the understanding of the agent who initiates this transaction. In analyzing moral sentiments, Smith describes the

penultimate in moral conduct, whereas I have tried to describe
the ultimate, the climax and the actuality of conduct itself, not
what precedes it or what responds to it. This is one difference
between Smith's analysis and mine.

Another difference is that I appeal to a form of thinking, to a
categoriality, as constitutive of morals, whereas Smith appeals to
a form that belongs in the imagination and with the sentiments.
It seems to me that he does not give enough weight to the rational aspect of moral conduct. It is true that one should not simply
rationalize human agency; desires, sentiments, and ethical perceptions must be given their proper place, and Smith's analysis
of them rings true as far as it goes. Moreover, his description of
"that imaginary change of situation" as the foundation of moral
sentiments is a recognition of something almost like a moral categoriality, something almost like a form of moral thinking. But
the imaginary displacement does not reach moral thinking. It
is less than the kind of recognition that makes a particular behavior of mine to be good or bad for me insofar as it is good
or bad for you or for another. Smith's analysis remains with the
peripherals of moral conduct and misses its center.

An illustration of how different Smith's analysis of human action is from mine can be found in his description of what we
praise or blame when we evaluate someone's conduct. He says
there are three possibilities:

> Whatever praise or blame can be due to any action, must belong
> either, first, to the intention or affection of the heart, from which
> it proceeds; or, secondly, to the external action or movement of the
> body, which this affection gives occasion to; or, lastly, to the good or
> bad consequences, which actually, and in fact, proceed from it. These
> three different things constitute the whole nature and circumstances
> of the action, and must be the foundation of whatever quality can
> belong to it.[8]

Having distinguished the three components of action, Smith excludes the last two as candidates for what we praise or blame:
"That the two last of these three circumstances cannot be the
foundation of any praise or blame, is abundantly evident; nor
has the contrary ever been asserted by any body."[9] In particular,
he sees no difficulty in dismissing the public behavior:

> The external action or movement of the body is often the same in the most innocent and in the most blameable actions. He who shoots a bird, and he who shoots a man, both of them perform the same external movement: each of them draws the trigger of a gun.[10]

He will conclude that only the intention or the sentiment from which the action proceeds can be the object of praise and blame.

Smith describes the bodily action as though it were only bodily, as though it were the corpse of an action. The action is said only to "proceed" from the intention and sentiment or to be merely "occasioned" by them. In contrast, in my description the action is seen to be informed by the categoriality and the understanding of the agent. The categoriality and the understanding qualify the behavior and make the behavior to be the agent's own. They make it his action and they make it a live action. They also make the action to be one of a certain kind. Drawing the trigger of a gun must be described as part either of shooting a bird or of shooting a man, and if it is part of shooting a man, then it can be part of the agent's taking the harm of another as his own good.

The reason it is possible for us to add a new dimension to the theory of moral sentiments and to take into account the thoughtful, categorial aspect of moral agency, is that we are lucky enough to have inherited a much more adequate philosophical discussion of human thinking than Adam Smith had at his disposal. In Husserl we have a description of categorial form that does justice to the publicity of thinking. Husserl's analysis of intentionality allows us to see categorial formations as part of the being of things; things are seen as presentationally shaped by the categorials in which they are articulated. Husserl's descriptions avoid the excesses of both rationalism and empiricism, as well as the deficiencies of the Kantian philosophy of mind that followed, chronologically, the thought of the Scottish moralists. Husserl's thought is often applauded for its discussion of prepredicative experience, for its analysis of corporeality, or for its description of the life-world that underlies science, but his analyses of the more formal aspects of experience, his analyses of categorial form and structure, deserve far more study and exploitation than they have received. His descriptions, in the *Logical Investigations*, of identity-synthesis, recognition, predication, and categorial form constitute a radical innovation in philosophy, and my discussion of the categorial form of moral action is but an application of his thought to the domain of human conduct.

5

In the rest of my paper I wish to discuss further the categoriality, the kind of thinking, associated with moral action. I will do so by responding to a third objection that might be raised against the analysis I have given. Someone might say, "Your moral categoriality is not sufficient to account for all the aspects of moral thinking. In particular, it does not seem to account for questions concerning the truth of a moral transaction. Suppose I take and do someone's good formally as my own good; can I not be mistaken in my assessment of what is my neighbor's good? And even when I try to be malevolent, I may be mistaken in my assessment of what is to my neighbor's disadvantage and I may accidentally help him instead of doing him harm. Your form of moral action seems to have nothing to say about truth and error in human action."

The issue of truth is indeed a further issue, one that has not been addressed in my description of moral conduct. But it does come after the issue of what makes an action to be moral. In fact we can distinguish several levels in the issue of truth. The first level is that of the truth or falsity of the material part of the performance. I may attempt, say, to help someone by giving him food, but it turns out that he is diabetic and the food I give him makes him sick. I am in error concerning the material part of the action. This is a question of premoral truth or falsity.

On a second level, I may be right or wrong about the moral predicate that applies to what I have done. I may claim that I am helping someone by, say, getting him out of trouble, but in fact I may be doing it in such a way as to make him cowardly or dishonest. *I* may call the action benevolent, but another person may call it inducement to treason. In this case there is no argument about the material character of what has been done, but there is a question about how we are to classify the action morally. What kind of moral action is it? Is it true that it is an act of dishonesty? Or is it true that the action is a clever but honest escape?

When we try to describe the moral nature of what has been done, when we try to specify its moral kind, we make use of the moral predicates that our community has developed and keeps in store: terms such as *murder, cruelty, irreverence, treason, cowardice,* and *bellicosity;* or terms such as *gratitude, piety, courage, temperance,* and *justice.* And when we apply such terms we use them as predicates, and we engage what I would like to call the categoriality of judgment. The judgment is meant to be true; it is meant to state what the action really is. And it is true that such judgmental categoriality accomplishes more than does the categoriality that establishes the action as moral in the first place. The moral categoriality, the agent's taking the target's good or bad as his own good or bad, remains, so to speak, naive and simple. It remains in the domain of immediate appearances. It has not yet fully activated the truth or falsity of the appearances; it has not yet explicitly confirmed whether the appearances are genuine. For this reason, the judgmental categoriality, which does do such things, accomplishes more than the original moral categoriality can accomplish.

However, had the moral categoriality not done its work, there would be nothing for the judgmental categoriality to be about. Only because the action has already been constituted as a *moral* action is it possible for us to raise the further question about what *kind* of moral action it really is. The judgmental categoriality does do more, but it does not do everything, and in particular it does not first establish the action as moral. That achievement is the work of the form of a moral transaction.

And because the moral categoriality is a categoriality, a form of thinking, it sets us on the road to truth. It engages not just mere appearance but a pretense at the true or genuine appearance. Because I take someone's good or bad as my own good or bad, I begin to submit myself to the question whether the good or bad really is as it seems to be. Categoriality inevitably engages truth; logical form of any kind commits us to determine whether what seems to be is genuinely so. The judgmental categoriality therefore follows naturally after the moral categoriality, just as predication follows naturally after the more simple identifications we make when we just recognize individuals. Moral categoriality does not only put us into the "game" of morals; as categoriality it also puts us into the "game" of truth. We want to pursue good and avoid evil as *truly* good and *truly* evil.

In responding to the last objection raised against my analysis, I have discussed two levels of the issue of truth: the truth of the material aspect of moral actions, and the truth of the moral predicates that are to be applied to actions. There is a third level of truth that I will mention only briefly. It is also possible, and sometimes necessary, to turn to the moral predicates themselves that are found in our moral community, and to ask whether they are genuine, whether they really should have the positive or negative character they are thought to possess. In this case we argue not about a particular action and what sort of action it is, but about a kind of action, about a type of moral behavior. We do not ask whether this particular action should receive this or that predicate, but whether the predicate itself truly is as it seems to be. We might, for example, argue about the morality of slavery, or piracy, or usury, or abortion. It is in such controversies that the distinction between what is good or bad by nature and what is good or bad by convention or custom comes into view. This is a further aspect of moral reasoning, but once again this kind of controversy can arise only because something far more elementary has occurred, only because human actions have been constituted as moral in the thick of human exchanges; and they are constituted as such by the form of a moral transaction, by the initial installment of moral reasoning into human desires and aversions.

Moral philosophy must therefore always return to human action as its theme. For that reason, the concrete examples I used to begin my paper, the stories about Norman and Ralph, and Sidney and Arthur, were more than rhetorical devices or aids in making my argument clear. They, and other actions like them, are what our moral discussion must always ultimately be about. Moral truth begins and ends in what is done.

14
Knowing
Natural Law

It is of theoretical and of practical interest to examine how natural law is made known to us. Theoretically, such an examination helps us in thinking about being; we come to see that being permits the emergence of the human estate. We are shown how we come forward as agents, how we come to recognize a difference between the good that is proposed to us by our customs and laws, and the good that is good in itself. We are, in fact, scarcely there as agents until this distinction dawns on us, until we recognize that moral goods can be distinct from what our laws and customs show forth. The distinction may arise in respect to goods that are materially the same—caring for one's children, for example, may be customary and legal as well as being good in itself—but we come to appreciate that things can be good in two different ways. The display of these two forms of the good is what lets us become responsible as agents. In our discussion of natural law, therefore, we will not try to show how some particular moral good is known to be good by nature; we will try to study the emergence of the contrast between the good that becomes good by agreement and the good that is good in itself, and we will study the agent who is established by this difference.

But we cannot speak about what is good without remembering that we are the ones for whom it is good. We ourselves are the agents we propose to examine, and we cannot stop being them. Our discussion therefore has practical importance. We will not focus on any particular controversial issue in natural law, but we will try to clarify what it is to be concerned about things that are good in themselves and not good just by reason of convention or use. If we can clarify this, we may help ourselves in the contest that no one of us can escape for as long as we live, the struggle to avoid being caught by illusion in regard to the most important things. None of us can be disinterested in this. For none of us wants just to *know* that there can be a difference between what is good and what only seems to be so, whether the seeming is generated by our customs and laws or by our own inclinations; we want, finally, to *do* what is good in itself and to become good ourselves. Even when we just speculate about the human good, therefore, we cannot forget that it is something that we, inevitably, must also worry about.

1

How do we come to know the natural law? We find out about a positive law by being told about it. We can be informed that the laws of this country do or do not permit you to cross someone's property, that this action is murder and that action is manslaughter, that we must pay this or that amount in taxes, or that elections take place according to such and such a procedure. Because the word *law* is used in *natural law*, we may feel that the natural law is shown to us in a similar way, that is, that someone knows what the natural law is and tells us about it. If we follow the classic statement that natural law is accessible to human reason, we may still feel that our reason acts autonomously when it articulates this law, that it behaves rather like the law expert who can tell us what the positive laws are. We may suppose that we learn the essentials of human nature by reason and then derive our moral obligations from what we know; our moral philosophy appears to rest on our epistemology, anthropology, and metaphysics. It seems that we make the natural law available through an independent intellectual activity, and that we make positive laws and customs available through another independent intellectual activity, through jurisprudence or the study of comparative law. The two kinds of laws seem to be correlated to two kinds of rational enterprises, and we may, at the end, try to join the two by comparing various positive laws with the law of nature.

In such a description, the natural and the positive laws are joined after both are elaborated, and the natural may be used to criticize the conventional. But such an approach starts very far from the beginning. Before the natural and the positive can be separately presented, there must be a union between them; in fact, in the beginning, there is no explicit recognition that there are two moral dimensions. In the beginning human actions expand in the way things are customarily done. Human wants and human pleasures are first exercised in response to the good as people are brought up to seek it in the community in which they live. The good is not seen as conventional, because the difference between the conventional and the natural is not yet displayed. From the beginning there will be differences between what we would like to do and what we are told we ought to do, but these are conflicts between inclination and custom, not between the natural and the conventional. Furthermore, the mere exposure to foreign customs and laws is not enough to make us aware of the natural good, nor do we necessarily need such alien contacts to distinguish between the natural and the customary.

How then does the sense of what is good or bad by nature arise? It occurs primarily in an immediate, particular criticism of the customary behavior within which one lives. Someone gradually appreciates that something we all do really ought not be done, not just because some other people do not do it, or because we do not want to do it, but because it is simply wrong. Or someone gradually appreciates that something we do not do should really be done, not because other societies do it, but because it is simply good. We are always saturated by custom and by something at least similar to laws, and it is in the thick of such ordered behavior that this differentiation between the established and the natural emerges. If infants are exposed, or captured enemies are cannibalized, it may occur to some persons that somehow or other this should not be done. The sense that it should not be done may evolve over time, as the opinion of one person is confirmed by the agreement of others. Such a divergence between what is done and what should be done occurs in regard to particular activities and in regard to concrete events; it does not occur first as an insight into a general moral principle, and the individual case need not be seen as an instance of a universal rule; nor need the moral perceiver see the activity as wrong simply because he would not want it done to himself. Generalizations like these are not the beginning of moral judgment. Instead someone recognizes that there is something wrong going on here in this sort of action. The behavior builds itself up as wrong as we see how it works in its consequences, how it modifies those who perform it, how it affects those upon whom it is practiced. The primary moral phenomenon takes place in the accumulation of particular acts and in the larger embedding of those acts. An act is not wrong just because of its consequences, but the consequences help show the act for what it is, just as the fruits of a tree help show the tree itself.

The sense of a natural good or evil thus occurs primarily in criticism of what is done. What is good by nature asserts itself as a cancellation of what has been proposed as good by custom, just as, analogously, material nature emerges when the instrumental breaks down and the recalcitrance and insistence of things in themselves are affirmed. Nature is displayed in contrast with what we have been used to. Moreover, the emergence of natural law in the thick of established customs and rules may be episodic and may vary in intensity. There may be a rather clear conviction, for example, that what is done in regard to sick infants is wrong; and that the way captives are treated is wrong; and that certain ritual practices may be degrading. Or there may arise suspicions that something or other might need to be changed in regard to the way food is distributed, or in the way the sick are cared for. The moral imagination, the presentation of a way of acting different from the way that is in place, always works in the thick of things, and it suggests a possibility that can be done in the circumstances that prevail. There has to be a concrete option, not a mere abstract critique, and the option has to be visible as better than what is done. This visibility is contrastive; the better behavior is not displayed as good just by a deduction from premises, but by being seen against what else can be done. Certain kinds of improvement are possible in the midst of certain circumstances; not everything is possible everywhere.

Moreover, the improvements that the moral imagination proposes are themselves made truly possible by the inherited customs that are being criticized. A new pattern of behavior must be styled by the behavior that precedes it. It will therefore be easy for a stranger to condemn certain practices in a particular community, but difficult for him to introduce a better way of acting. For example, Alexander Solzhenitsyn has voiced many criticisms of American customs and institutions, and many of his comments may well be true; but it is hard to conceive of him showing positively how Americans should act. He is not sufficiently part of the weave of American society, not sufficiently shaped by its customs, to be able to adjust it this way or that in view of what is the natural good. Only someone formed with a people can indicate, concretely and effectively, what its next steps should be.

The sense of natural law does not arise therefore all at once in a kind of cultural trauma, a sudden realization that we live in conventions and that there is a nature behind the conventional. The natural good or bad is constantly played off, in stronger and weaker ways, against what people do as a matter of course. Someone insists on different behavior because it would be "better." The improvements may deal with important matters or with slight ones; they may be proposed clearly and decisively or only tentatively, to see whether they will indeed be better or not. They may be changes that are quite new or they may attempt to revive earlier behavior that has been abandoned; they may invoke other customs in the community that seem at odds with the action being criticized; or they may attempt to imitate the behavior of other people.

But who is capable of perceiving that something is wrong in the way things are done? Who possesses the power not only to imagine a better way of acting, but even to see that there is something to be corrected in what is normally done? Who can appreciate that there is a moral issue in the customs in which we live? It can only be someone who is a good man. Aristotle says that we ourselves are responsible for moral appearances, and this is nowhere more true than in the emergence of a distinction between what is good by custom and what is good by nature.[1] Sheer speculation will not provide us with principles against which we can criticize established practice. The moral perception of good men in the thick of things is necessary. And the just and prudent man is needed not only in the emergence of natural law, but also after the disclosure of natural law has become a prominent feature of our moral conversation. Even then virtue and prudence are needed to comprehend the impact of the naturally good and bad, to understand what moral terms mean, to have a sense of what issues in our current society are in need of criticism, to be able to judge what is possible and what is appropriate in our situation.

This means that everybody's opinions about moral matters are not equal, that statistical surveys do not tell us what is naturally right or wrong, and that we must keep in mind who is speaking when a proposal is made concerning the possibilities of human behavior. It also means that we must be concerned about being good ourselves not only for our own sake but so that we will be able to say publicly what should be done. We cannot avoid engaging our character in our public moral discourse. And we have our character not simply by virtue of words and ideas, but by virtue of the actions we have performed, first under the guidance of others, then gradually on our own. Likewise the most effective moral persuasion is not in verbal arguments but in patterns of behavior that show the possibility of being good and that criticize, by contrast, the established custom or law. The good activity has to be displayed and the natural thus brought into distinction, over time, against the conventional. But this can be done only within the background of a massive agreement in regard to many of the activities we share.

Furthermore, it is not the case that human nature is first cognitively recognized and then made to be a basis for practical guidance. Rather, the essence of the human being is displayed as we experience human nature functioning well, that is, when we see how it can be good. The good and the natural are disclosed together. We do not, for example, first learn some necessary facts about family life, like the fact that children are dependent on their parents for many years, and then deduce practical conclusions from these facts, like the obligation of parents to care for their children and the obligation of children to respect their parents. Instead we learn what family relationships are when we see them functioning well. We then see what it is for children to depend on their parents. Good families show what the possibilities of family life are. The good and the obligatory are disclosed when the nature is disclosed; the essence involves the excellent.

To illustrate this, let us draw an analogy with athletics and take advantage of that perplexing and provocative similarity that exists between sportsmanship and morals. Suppose we tried to find out what a particular sport is by reading the rule book and by reading a description of the motions the players are supposed to go through in the game. Such a sheer cognitive knowledge of the "essence" of the sport would not give us any indication of what a good player is like. We would have no idea of what counts as a good performance—how many tries a good goalie can block, how many runners a good catcher can throw out, how many points a champion can score—and we certainly would not have any practical directions to give to the players. We must experience the game being played, and being played well, if we are to know what an excellent player is like. Even the nature of the game is not truly displayed until the game is seen being played well. Only then do we truly know what an offense and a defense are, why a score is an achievement, why one player can emerge as a hero and another as a flop. In sum, only then do we know why the game is played, why it is a sport and not random physical exercise. Only then do we have the substance of the game. Human nature and moral behavior are something like this. Goodness in action is not supplementary to the human essence. The theoretical definition of human nature is not achieved prior to the display of human activity in its excellence; rather the theoretical definition is derived from the human being acting well.

2

The attempt to display the good in itself through sheer cognition, apart from moral sensibility and practice, is a feature of rationalistic approaches to ethics. Kant's moral philosophy is an example of this.[2] Kant says we discover our moral obligations by trying to make a particular form of conduct into a universal law for mankind. If such a universalization would make human life impossible, we know we have run into an action that is forbidden. I may wish to lie or steal, but I realize, by the test of generalization, that if everyone were to lie or steal, human life would be impossible. Such a way of determining right and wrong is very different from the recognition of the good and the bad in the thick of things. Kant appeals to the compelling force of reasoning, not to moral perception.

We can and we will criticize Kant's approach, but before doing so we must first acknowledge something good in it. Kant brings out the fact that when we begin to argue about moral issues, when we leave the immediacy of a situation and begin to formulate moral issues in speech, we inevitably must generalize and we must begin to see ourselves as somehow the same as other people. Kant helps us remember that as immediate and as thick as a situation might be, it always has essential features that can be brought to reasoning. And this elevation of a situation into reasoning also displays us, the agents, as being like the rest of men. *The* self-deception in moral experience is the thought that we have loosened ourselves from the human condition, that what holds for others does not hold for us. The self-deception is shown to be deception when we try to argue for what we have done. An action that is vicious cannot withstand the penetration of reason. We get caught in a net of contradictions, even to our own mind, if we try to argue for something that is wrong. Thus the relentless universalizing power of reason makes us condemn ourselves. This entrapment of vice by reason is vividly brought out by the Kantian theory.

But Kant makes the rational test for morality into the ground for morality. What helps to show us the goodness or badness of an action is taken to be the basis for its goodness and badness. Kant confuses a proof "that" something is good or bad with a proof "why" it is so. And because the reason why he says things are right and wrong is that they are necessary for human life, there is something utilitarian about his ethical theory. Certain actions are right or wrong because of something beyond them, not because they simply are a good or a bad actualization of the human agent, not because we simply should or should not *be* the way these actions are. It would seem, in Kant's moral philosophy, that if human life could somehow be preserved when a putatively bad action is universalized—perhaps by adding other actions or adjustments to it, by checks and balances, or by devising a new sort of society—the action would no longer be bad.

These are some of the objections one might raise to Kantian moral doctrine, but there is a more basic objection which applies not only to his teaching but also to that of others. Kant suggests that we determine moral obligation by turning, primarily, to abstract reasoning. He finds nothing compelling or obligatory in moral sensibility as such. Only the necessitating force of reason instills a prohibition or a command into behavior. This move into abstract argument implies that the person who reasons about morals loses his engagement in situations. He becomes more and more the simple thinking mind, scrutinizing moral proposals for consistency, and less and less the agent who is supposed to determine what the best course of action is in the circumstances in which he finds himself. This movement to sheer thinking is pushed to an extreme in the theory of justice proposed by John Rawls.[3] Rawls wants to get beyond particular social conventions and to reach rules of distribution and arrangement that must hold in any society. He wishes to nullify the pressures of self-interest and to guarantee true objectivity on the part of the persons thinking about what is truly just, the just in itself. To do all this he imagines, and calls upon us to imagine, something he calls "the original position," in which we are to assume "that the parties are situated behind a veil of ignorance." He says that in this position "no one knows his place in society, his class position or social status; nor does he know his fortune in the distribution of natural assets and liabilities, his intelligence and strength, and the like. Nor, again, does anyone know his conception of the good, the particulars of his rational plan of life, or even the special features of his psychology."[4] The parties who take up the original position, Rawls says, are then to think out patterns for social distribution that will ensure that no one is severely disadvantaged. They will be motivated to do so by a residual self-interest, since they do not know what position they themselves will be in when the veil of ignorance is removed.

In the moral theories of both Kant and Rawls, we are given a method that is supposed to determine for us what the good and the bad, or the just and the unjust, are in themselves. A method is something that any person can employ and it is primarily a procedure for thinking. Hence anyone who learns the method will be able to generate moral objectivities and will be in a position to criticize actual customs and laws. This way of training people to be morally objective is different from the ethical education we described earlier, in which we are to cultivate moral habits and perceptions, so that the good in itself becomes the good for us, and we are made able to determine what is the good thing to do in the thick of things. In such ethical activity, who we are makes all the difference; but in learning a technique, who we are does not matter. It is more important to master the method than to have a certain kind of character. Hence Rawls postulates moral appraisers who do not know who they themselves are and what their own conception of the good is, whereas Aristotle, when discussing the moral circumstances we might be ignorant of, says, "No one could be ignorant of the agent; for how could he be ignorant of himself?"[5]

In the original position, "we" can exercise only our minds in a mathematical calculation of the distribution of goods. The personal pronouns hardly apply—we become something like a separated moral agent intellect common to all men—and the only thing left of desire is the wish not to be disadvantaged. As a thought experiment Rawls' description is intriguing, but is it an account of how our obligations can be displayed to us? Kant does not go to the extremes that Rawls attains; Kant does not postulate the same anonymity of the moral appraiser, and he also discusses issues, like lying and suicide, beyond those of distributive justice. But his attempts to handle moral issues by appealing to reason first and foremost involves the same neglect of character that we find in Rawls.

3

We have emphasized the importance of character as a source for moral perception and we have stressed the significance of the agent, situated in the thick of things, as involved in the disclosure of what is naturally good and obligatory. We have admitted that rational argument can serve negatively as a test for the good and the bad. But is this diminished role of reason sufficient? Does reason not do more than this in disclosing natural law? In differing with the rationalist extremes of Kant and Rawls, have we not moved to another extreme, to one that puts all the moral weight on ethical intuition and sensibility? For example, in examining an action we often ask by what principle the agent justifies what he has done. And ethicians and casuists have often referred to deductions from natural law; certainly they must have been on the track of some true moral phenomenon.

There are deductions from natural law, but the most basic and the most interesting movement of such deductions is not from a codified premise to a particular conclusion. It is a movement in the other direction, moving upwards from below, from a particular action that is morally prominent to a wider premise that clarifies the immediate action. We begin with a moral fact, whether good or bad: this man giving food to that man is doing good; that man revealing secrets about someone else is doing bad. Or, to consider an action only about to be performed, I can either give medical assistance to this wounded person, or I can take his watch because he is helpless; in the first case I would do good, in the second I would do bad. Now a "deduction" from natural law means to expand my moral appraisal of this particular action. It is to let a more general description of the action emerge beyond the material components of what is done. It is to articulate a rational moral form for the action. This action is then said to be good because it is an instance of helping the helpless, and people who are unable to care for themselves should be assisted. That action is bad because it is a case of betraying a secret, and secrets should be respected; or it is a case of stealing, and the property of others should not be taken from them. There is no moral action, good or bad, that cannot be so illuminated and expanded by being seen in its generalizable form.

Moreover, the action can be generalized to a higher and higher level. Taking the man's watch can be seen as theft, or as violating the principle of property (which can be done in other ways besides stealing), or as violating the very general principle of "to each his own." If we push the generalization far enough we might find that revealing a secret and thereby damaging someone's reputation may be "the same" as stealing a man's watch, because both violate the primary principle of natural law, *suum cuique.* And we are all familiar with the idea that the more basic the principle of natural law, the more self-evident it is supposed to be; the more derived, the less self-evident. There are controversies as to what self-evidence means in this context, and perhaps we can clarify what it means by turning the issue around: we assume not that we somehow have the most general principles first and then descend to the inferior, less clear regions; but that we begin with the moral fact—that I clearly should or should not do *this*—and work up to the more general principles, not by a kind of empirical induction, but by letting the moral fact, which is evident and compelling on its own, engage and display the more general principle.

For our purposes, the most interesting step is not any one of the moves between a less general and a more general principle, but the move between the immediate moral fact and any moral generality. The moral fact can be described without using any morally evaluative terms. Suppose I am with people who are nearly starving and am sufficiently fed myself; and suppose I take food from them to gratify my appetite. I can describe this action in simply material, nonevaluative terms: "I am taking food from desperately hungry people simply to satisfy my taste." And I can then add that this action would be bad. Now once I move up the ladder of moral generality, I would find myself making statements like, "Murdering is wrong," or "Greed is wrong," or "Stealing is wrong." At this higher stage the statements begin to look like moral tautologies. We start talking about stealing or murder, and not about a material performance. We start saying that murder is wrong and stealing is wrong, and we fall into the usual arguments about what is to count as murder and what is to count as stealing. There are legal positivists who follow Hobbes's belief that "what is to be called theft, what murder, what adultery, what injury in a citizen, this is not to be determined by the natural, but by the civil law."[6] But we seem to be forced into such stipulated self-evidence because we approach these moral terms in an *a priori* way, starting from the top of our moral argument and working down, rather than beginning with the moral fact and working upward. If we begin with the moral fact we more obviously begin with something good or bad by nature, not by decree. To take this food from these people now is bad, no matter what any sovereign may say. It is bad in its immediate material reality. The evaluative term *bad* is added as a predicate to the material description of the act; it is not analytically contained in the subject, as it is in the statement, "Murder is wrong." When we add terms like *murder* or *stealing* to our description of what is going on, we give reasons why the act is bad or good; but there is no "why" until there has been a "that," and the most elementary "that" is not expressed in a sentence like, "I am murdering this person," but in a material description like, "I am taking necessary food from a helpless, starving person, for my own gratification."

Because the description of such material facts does not immediately involve words like *murder* or *stealing*, there is built into the moral experience of such facts the possibility of criticizing custom and positive law. No matter what custom, law, and legal definition may say, *this* action is bad (or, correlatively, it is good, despite their saying it is bad). I as an agent know it is bad or good. Under no law or custom should *this* be done, or *that* be left undone. Moreover, the force of this knowledge comes from the nature of the thing being done, not from opinions people have about it. It is not because everyone everywhere would say this is bad or good that it is so. Marsilius of Padua, for example, is mistaken when he describes certain rights as natural "because in all regions they are in the same way believed to be lawful and their opposites unlawful."[7] I do not judge this action to be naturally good or bad because of common human consent but because I know *this* could not be bad or good, no matter what people think. There will of course often be general agreement about a good or bad action, but there may be disagreement as well. And the moral agents or perceivers must be relatively good and decent people to judge correctly about the goodness and badness of particular actions. A vicious person might not recognize wickedness in taking food from the hungry, even though, as we have seen, he would not be able to justify his action if he tried to give a rational accounting for it.

In any concrete action there are an indefinite number of circumstances surrounding what is done, but it is possible to highlight what counts as essential in the performance. The action is taking food from hungry people, or it is protecting someone

from a person who is trying to inflict harm, or it is giving cloth-
ing to someone who is suffering from exposure. We as agents
involved in such actions may intend to perform the act as we
describe it to be, but it is not intention that makes the act what
it is. Whether we like it or not, we are taking food from someone
who is hungry. The material elements and relationships in the
situation make up the nature of the action. Our intention is a
recognition of what we are doing rather than a determination of
it. And we know the action is bad or good not because we intuit
a moral quality in it, but because we appreciate what the thing
before us is and what it ought to be.

Now when we apply a word like *murder* or *stealing* or *generosity*
to an action, we do two things. First, we move into an abstraction.
We consolidate those essential features, the material elements of
the action that were there before the value-laden term was im-
posed, and we now take the individual case as an instance of
a general category. And, secondly, we introduce a term that is
moral in itself. When we deal with the material action, the killing
or the taking or the giving, we have to add a moral predicate to
the fact; we say this killing is bad, this taking is bad, this giving
is good. But when we move into terms like *murder* or *stealing* or
generosity, the moral predicates become folded into the name of
the action. Murder or stealing do not need predicates to be registered as wrong, they are wrong internally; and generosity does not
need a predicate to be stated as right, it is right internally. Murder and stealing are defined as unjustified killing or taking, and
generosity is defined as virtuous giving. Consequently the value-
laden terms are always paired off against corresponding material
terms: *murder* is always paired off against *killing*, *stealing* against
taking, *generosity* against *giving*. Our move into an abstraction is
therefore also a move into an internally moral category.

And then we may begin to ask ourselves what we have done to
the neutral term to make it into the moral one. What have we
done to killing to make it murder, what have we done to giving to
make it generosity? So long as we remain on the level of abstractions, this question never gets resolved. Only when we engage the
particular moral action that supports the abstractions, only when
we engage the action whose moral predicate becomes folded into
the abstract term, do we reach the substance of morality and the

material that gives the abstractions their life. This is true even in regard to the very first principles of morality, the principles that good is to be done and evil avoided, and that each man is to receive what is his due. We do not begin by learning these principles and then finding ways to apply them; such a procedure would constitute ethical rationalism. Moral thinking works the other way around. We act in response to the good and the bad in particular situations, and we come to formulate the truth that the good and the bad are always an issue for us, and that we never eliminate the issue of justice, so long as we are acting as human agents. The first principles of natural law are not a beginning for deductions but a perpetual engagement that we can never circumvent. The principles of natural law thus do stand behind particular acts, but never in such a way as to deprive the concrete action of its moral prominence and substantiality.

The particular action in its materiality is where the human agent exists. He does not exist in abstract considerations, and the attempt to live a moral life just in thinking is bound to take all the weight, solidity, and resistance out of morals. The human agent is actualized in a situation in which he must do something, in which he is to bring about a change that would not have occurred if he had not decided to act. What he chooses to do is made possible by the articulation he makes of his situation, by what he sees as good or bad, morally desirable or morally repellent, in what is before him. The agent masters his situation not by a cognitive possession of principles, but by being himself a kind of light and measure. Only his character keeps him from the deceptive interpretations of vice or the sluggish blindness of moral indifference, which does not even recognize that moral issues have arisen in the circumstances around him. To be able to respond to the natural law—indeed to let it become actual as law, to show by one's actions what can be done, and thus to make others see what should be done—is to be a certain kind of person: not one who simply conforms to things set down, but one who lets the good appear, to himself and to others, in what he does.

Notes

Picturing

1. On *pairing* as a special kind of perception and on its role in our awareness of other minds, see Edmund Husserl, *Cartesian Meditations*, trans. by Dorion Cairns (The Hague: Nijhoff, 1960), §51.

2. On mirrored reflections and pictures, see Hans-Georg Gadamer, *Wahrheit und Methode*, 2d ed. (Tübingen: Mohr, 1965), pp. 131–134. Jacques Lacan has emphasized the importance of mirrored reflections of ourselves in the establishment of our own body image and in the subsequent development of the self and its ego functions. Seeing one's body reflected as a whole and recognizing it as one's self, seeing a view of a living body and appreciating it as the same mass of mobility and affection one is beginning to pattern, experiencing the same motions from the inside and at a distance, is a consolidation that precedes and permits further emotional and cognitive syntheses; the *stade du miroir* occurs as early as the sixth month of life and brings about a sense of the self which is a condition for such experiences as the Oedipal identifications and conflicts. See "Le stade du miroir comme formateur de la fonction du Je," in *Ecrits* (Paris: Editions du Seuil, 1966), pp. 93–100.

3. Gertrude Stein, *Lectures in America* (New York: Random House, 1962), pp. 96–97.

4. Ibid., p. 98.

5. James Boswell describes a party in honor of David Garrick, held, in a room in which Garrick's portrait was present, some time after his death: "The very semblance of David Garrick was pleasing" (*The Life of Samuel Johnson* [New York: Random House (n.d.)], p. 971).

6. In serious forms of mental illness the sense of one's self as imitator can be lost: "The boundaries between self and object become undifferentiated and the patients seem to believe that if they do what the doctor does they thereby become the doctor" (Elizabeth R. Zetzel and W. W. Meissner, *Basic Concepts of Psychoanalytic Psychiatry* [New York: Basic Books, 1973], p. 209). In dreams the imagining self is almost entirely put to sleep.

7. See Theodor Conrad, *Zur Wesenslehre des psychischen Lebens und Erlebens*, Phaenomenologica 27 (The Hague: Nijhoff, 1968), pp. 1–41. On the imagination of future possibilities of action, see Ibid, pp. 48–49. Conrad observes that sometimes we remain firmly in control as we plan our future actions by going through them deliberately in imagination; at other times we relax our control and slip into passive reverie. In the first case the imagining self remains prominent, in the second case the imagined self predominates. The concept of the displacement of the self is developed by Husserl and elaborated along many different directions in his analyses of inner time-consciousness.

8. Gilbert Ryle, *The Concept of Mind* (London: Hutchinson, 1949), p. 247.

9. Ibid., p. 248.

10. Ibid., pp. 249, 248, 273. In the chapter entitled "Imagination" in *The Concept of Mind*, Ryle is careful to distinguish looking at pictures from activities like imagining, remembering, theatrical acting, the acting in children's games, and pretending, but he does not sufficiently notice differences among these latter activities themselves. For example, he tends to equate theatrical performances with pretending (p. 250). Also, he talks about a genus of "seeming to perceive" and says that looking at photographs and imagining are two species of it (p. 254). But the "seeming to perceive" in looking at photographs is very different from that in imagining; there is no displacement of the self in looking at pictures.

11. See Theodor Conrad, *Zur Wesenslehre des psychischen Lebens und Erlebens*, p. 19. Furthermore, the possibility of conceptual thinking is based not on perception alone, but on the interplay between perception and imagination. A conceptually articulated object is one that is appreciated as invariant when imagined and perceived. The self is the kind of being that can enact such displacements without losing its identity; in fact, its identity as a self is developed and maintained precisely in such self-differentiation, not only in imagination but also in remembering,

recognizing, repeating things, understanding other persons, and the like. *Versetzung* is not something merely added to a self; it helps constitute the self.

12. See C. S. Lewis, *An Experiment in Criticism* (Cambridge: Cambridge University Press, 1961), pp. 52–53: "I am probably one of the many who, on a wakeful night, entertain themselves with invented landscapes. . . . But I am not there myself as explorer or even as tourist. I am looking at that world from the outside. A further stage is often reached by children, usually in co-operation. They may feign a whole world and people it and remain outside it. But when that stage is reached, something more than mere reverie has come into action: construction, invention, in a word *fiction*, is proceeding."

13. Andreas Lommel, *Shamanism: The Beginnings of Art*, trans. by Michael Bullock (New York: McGraw Hill, 1967), p. 16: "The hunter saw in the picture of an animal its soul-force, its spiritual being, and believed that by painting pictures he could capture and influence its force. Among the Australian aborigines—who remain today at the level of the early Stone Age hunters—rock-paintings depicting animals and plants are, every year, not repainted but touched up, so that new, powerful 'souls' may go out from them and take on new bodies." The aboriginal identification of pictures with forces of life betrays, of course, a primitive's inability to come to terms with differences among kinds of presencing. However, Lommel's own remarks about things like "ideas," "images of one's own psyche," "ego," "world," etc. (v.g., pp. 11–12) betray another kind of misunderstanding of presences, one that can be called psychologistic; he takes such presences as entities in the psyche of the person who has them. For further examples of picturing, see Lommel's other book, *Masks: Their Meaning and Function*, trans. by N. Fowler (London: Paul Elek Books, 1972), in which he distinguishes between masks used in embodiment and masks used for disguise.

14. The special character of icons is related to Christian belief in God and in the Incarnation. The Christian God is not a thing in or a part of the world and therefore cannot be imaged in himself, but in the Incarnation the Second Person of the Trinity has become present as a part of the world, as a human being. An icon of Christ is a depiction of the person of Christ, who is God made man; it is not an attempt to portray the man Christ (therefore physical and psychological characteristics are eschewed), but the man Christ as united to and transformed by the divine nature. Icons of saints, furthermore, are also hieratic and avoid sentiment and corporeal realism; they are meant to portray the man or woman as transformed by grace and as serving as an epiphany of grace to the world. See Leonid Ouspensky and Vladimir Lossky, *The Meaning of Icons*, trans. by G. E. H. Palmer and E. Kadloubovsky (Boston: Boston

Book and Art Shop, 1969), pp. 35–50, 69–70. I am grateful to John Botean and Timothy Quinn for discussions and references concerning iconography.

15. See Robert Sokolowski, *Husserlian Meditations: How Words Present Things* (Evanston: Northwestern University Press, 1974), p. 26.

16. On naming, presence, and absence, see Robert Sokolowski, *Presence and Absence* (Bloomington: Indiana University Press, 1978), ch. 3; also Plato *Sophist* 234B: "And so we recognize that he who professes to be able by virtue of a single art to make all things will be able by virtue of the painter's art to make imitations which have the same names as the real things" (trans. by Fowler, in Loeb Classical Library).

17. The Lincoln Memorial in turn has, of course, a picture or statue within itself, so that when we picture the Memorial we may have a picture of a picture. We can also remember or imagine a picture; "A name on being mentioned reminds us of the Dresden Gallery and our last visit there: we wander through the rooms, and stand before a picture of Teniers which represents a picture gallery. If we suppose that pictures of the latter would in their turn portray pictures which on their part exhibited readable inscriptions and so forth, we can measure what interweaving of presentations, and what mediations in regard to the objects grasped, can truly be set up" (Husserl, *Ideas: General Introduction to Pure Phenomenology*, trans. by W. R. Boyce Gibson [New York: Macmillan, 1931], §100; translation modified).

18. See Plato *Sophist*, 240B: "*Stranger:* That which is like, then, you say does not really exist, if you say it is not true. *Theaetetus:* But it does exist, in a way. *Str.:* But not truly, you mean. *Theaet.:* No, except that it is really a likeness. *Str.:* Then what we call a likeness, though not something existent (*ouk on ara ontōs*), is still existent (*estin ontōs*)?" (trans. by Fowler, in the Loeb Classical Library; translation modified).

19. On oneness and diversity as more primitive than being as being, see Robert Sokolowski, *Presence and Absence*, ch. 15; and "Ontological Possibilities in Phenomenology: The Dyad and the One," *Review of Metaphysics* 29 (1976), pp. 691–701, where these phenomenological issues are related to Plato's doctrine of the One and the Indeterminate Dyad.

2

Quotation

1. See Nelson Goodman, "On Some Questions Concerning Quotation," *Monist* 58 (1974), pp. 294–98. V. A. Howard, in "On Musical Quotation," *Monist* 58 (1974), p. 310, speaks of "replication-plus-reference" as characterizing direct quotation.

2. See John Searle, "What Is an Intentional State?" *Mind* 88 (1979), p. 85. Also "Intentionality and Method," *Journal of Philosophy* 78 (1981), pp. 726–27.

3. On registration and reporting, see Robert Sokolowski, *Presence and Absence* (Bloomington: Indiana University Press, 1978), pp. 7–9; and *Husserlian Meditations* (Evanston: Northwestern University press, 1974), pp. 32–42.

4. Of course, instead of going to see for myself, I can just turn to some other and greater authority than the person I have quoted, to someone in whom I have greater trust. On the basis of what he says, I can disquote and merely state, as true, what I have been quoting. In such a case I do not appeal to my own registrations but to more authoritative reports. And along another modality, I may quote someone else as a way of making a point for which I do not want to take responsibility at the moment; as Freeman Dyson says, "It's easier to say these things by quoting others." See Pamela Weintraub, ed., *The Omni Interviews* (New York: Ticknor and Fields, 1984), p. 363.

5. See Kenneth Mark Colby, "Modeling a Paranoid Mind," *The Behavioral and Brain Sciences* 4 (1981), p. 519: "Cooperating people, engaged in purposeful dialogue, do not converse in riddles or in isolated sentences. Their dialogues are largely clear in meaning and show great referential continuity."

6. Willard V. O. Quine, *Word and Object* (Cambridge: MIT Press, 1965), p. 221.

7. Ibid., p. 212.

8. A complicating factor, which we have not mentioned, is the pressure exerted on the person we quote by his opponent or "interlocutor." A full quotation would have to take that pressure into account: the person we quote does not just say what we quote but says it in response to what someone else has said.

9. See Machiavelli, *The Prince*, ch. 11.

10. Although there can be quotation in music, there is no such thing as a reference to or a naming of another melody.

11. The line from Eliot is from *Little Gidding;* the music for the ballet *Le spectre de la rose* is by Carl Maria von Weber, with orchestration by Hector Berlioz. On Eliot's line and the allusion, see Helen Gardner, *The Composition of Four Quartets* (Oxford: Oxford University Press, 1978), p. 202. The piece by Claude Debussy is *Preludes*, bk. 2, no. 7. In his Prelude no. 9 of the same book, entitled *Hommage à S. Pickwick, Esq., P.P.M.P.C.*, Debussy quotes, and does not merely allude to, "God Save the King." I am grateful to Edward Kasouf for these examples from Debussy.

12. Descartes, *Meditations on First Philosophy*, in *The Philosophical Works of Descartes*, trans. by E. Haldane and G. Ross (New York: Dover, 1955), vol. 1, p. 171.

13. Ibid., pp. 156, 157.

14. Ibid., p. 149.

15. Ibid., pp. 189–90, 198–99.

3
Making Distinctions

1. James Boswell, *The Life of Samuel Johnson* (New York: Random House [n.d.]), p. 19.

2. Ibid., pp. 956, 1032, 1119.

3. What we describe as making and dwelling on distinctions is what Hannah Arendt calls *thinking*. She distinguishes such thinking from judging in *The Life of the Mind*, 2 vols. (New York: Harcourt, 1977), vol. 1, pp. 92–97, 193. It would be interesting to relate the making of distinctions to the achievement of the logical structure of reversibility, which Piaget sees as essential to conceptual thought. Reversibility has two forms, negation (or inversion) and reciprocity, the first being used in concrete acts of classification, the second in concrete acts of relating. Only at the age of about eleven or twelve can children begin to combine both forms in logical operations; but making distinctions seems to engage both forms of reversibility. See Jean Piaget, *Genetic Epistemology* (New York: Columbia University Press, 1970), pp. 22–30, 39–40; Bärbel Inhelder and Jean Piaget, *The Growth of Logical Thinking from Childhood to Adolescence* (New York: Basic Books, 1958), pp. 105, 133-34, 335. The "involved," pragmatic use of language by children is described by Hans Furth in *Piaget for Teachers* (Englewood Cliffs, N.J.: Prentice Hall, 1970), pp. 56–71.

4. The distinction is made by Michael Gosman in an unpublished essay, "Ezra Pound's Literary Theory and Poetic Techniques."

5. In a letter to Boswell, Johnson writes, "His disposition towards you was undoubtedly that of a kind, though not of a fond father. Kindness, at least actual, is in our power, but fondness is not; and if by negligence or imprudence you had extinguished his fondness, he could not at will rekindle it" (Boswell, *Life of Johnson*, p. 1012).

6. John Henry Newman, "Faith and Doubt," in *Discourses Addressed to Mixed Congregations* (New York: Longmans, 1906), p. 231.

7. See Robert Sokolowski, "Humanistic Studies in the Social Work Curriculum," *Social Thought* 4 (1978), pp. 39–43. The craft of a teacher

consists in presenting and controlling imaginary cases in such a way that a strategic distinction is achieved by the students who listen to him. The immediate context is important in such teaching; one cannot safely rely on mechanical means, on records, videotapes, or even on writing, to make distinctions.

8. John Le Carré, *The Looking Glass War* (New York: Bantam, 1965), p. 7.

9. Lionel Trilling examines the literary and historical development of this new moral "appearance" in *Sincerity and Authenticity* (Cambridge: Harvard University Press, 1971). The development of the notion is related, of course, to social and political, as well as to ideological changes, and at the deepest level it is related to shifts in being, in presencing and representation. Ch. 2 of part 1 of Sartre's *Being and Nothingness* discusses authenticity and bad faith; see also Schubert M. Ogden, *The Reality of God* (New York: Harper and Row, 1963), p. 11.

10. One might say that most philosophical arguments are not about the reality or unreality of a particular term or thing (like *the world* or *a priori categories of the mind*) but about whether or not a particular distinction should be entered at all. We have stated that historical developments may lead to unreal distinctions, but certainly not all historical developments do so. Some are legitimate; some distinctions can be reached only after others have been made. How do we distinguish "true" from "false" developments? This is the issue of the historicity of distinctions. A historicist interpretation of distinctions would simply rest with the fact that certain distinctions are held by certain people at a certain time; it would not try to judge between those that "are" and those that "are not." Or at best it would say that some distinctions found in the past are still maintained by us, so they still "are," while others are not accepted; however, we ourselves are merely the inhabitants of another historical period. Clearly such a historicist reading does not treat distinctions adequately. We cannot discuss the historicity of distinctions in this chapter, but would observe that the problem of distinctions is a fruitful way through which to approach hermeneutics. It provides more resources, and engages more directly the issue of truth, than does the use of meaning or language alone.

11. Besides overdistinguishing and underdistinguishing, we might also err by making an irrelevant distinction. The terms distinguished do not apply to the issue before us, or they apply to one of the genera located above the species we are confronted with. However, irrelevant distinctions are not as interesting philosophically as the two ways of erring we examine in the text. And just to add a brain-teaser to our analysis, the following distinction is not so obviously true, nor are its

terms so clearly opposed to each other, as might appear at first sight: "Fruits are not vegetables."

12. George E. Vaillant, *Adaptation to Life* (Boston: Little, Brown, 1977), p. 63.

13. T. S. Eliot observes that "there is a close analogy between the sort of experience which develops a man and the sort of experience which develops a writer," and describes the identification that can occur between a writer and an author from the past. In this experience, a young writer "may be changed, metamorphosed almost, within a few weeks even, from a bundle of second-hand sentiments into a person" ("Reflections on Contemporary Poetry," *Egoist* 6 [July 1919], p. 39).

14. Vaillant, *Adaptation to Life:* "But our adaptive mechanisms are given to us by our biological makeup, by internalization of people who loved us, and from other sources as yet unidentified" (p. 28). "The importance of internalized people seemed to outweigh sociological factors" (p. 70). Vaillant speaks of the "by-product of successful identifications with other people" and "suitable models for identification" (pp. 88–89). See also William F. Lynch, *Images of Hope: Imagination as Healer of the Hopeless* (Notre Dame, Ind.: University of Notre Dame Press, 1974), p. 61: "An essential problem of all human life is to become separated-out (to become myself) without separation."

15. On *Versetzung*, see Theodor Conrad, *Zur Wesenslehre des psychischen Lebens und Erlebens* (The Hague: Nijhoff, 1968), pp. 1–41; Robert Sokolowski, "Picturing," ch. 1, above; Eduard Marbach, *Das Problem des Ich in der Phänomenologie Husserls* (The Hague: Nijhoff, 1974), pp. 111–20, 288–90, 299, 307–10, 335–38; Edmund Husserl, *Zur Phänomenologie der Intersubjektivität,* 3 vols. (The Hague: Nijhoff, 1973), vol. 1, pp. 288–320 (p. 299: "Die phantasierte Erscheinung fordert ein Ich, und zwar gerade mich"), and vol. 3, pp. 514–18.

16. The need to be in contact with concrete circumstances is what makes it so difficult to try to deal with problems at a distance or far in the future; we feel we should do something but cannot imagine what ought to be done.

17. See Robert Murphy, *Diplomat among Warriors* (New York: Doubleday, 1964), p. 432: "Perhaps history will demonstrate that the free world could have intervened to give the Hungarians the liberty they sought, but none of us in the State Department had the skill or the imagination to devise a way." An example of the other extreme, an excess of imagination, can be found in the case of General Giraud, who was brought out of Vichy France to help in the Allied invasion of northern Africa. Eisenhower reports in *Crusade in Europe* (New York: Doubleday, 1948), pp. 99–100: "It was quickly apparent that he had come out of France

laboring under the grave misapprehension that he was immediately to assume command of the whole Allied expedition." Giraud also thought there should be an immediate invasion of the French mainland. Clearly, he had spent time projecting these possibilities, imaginatively, before he left France to meet Eisenhower. Michael Oakeshott, in *On Human Conduct* (Oxford: Clarendon, 1975), gives "imagining a satisfaction" (p. 34) an important role in human action. He speaks of an agent "who is able to imagine [his situation] different from what it is and can recognize it to be alterable by some action or utterance of his own; and when alternatives present themselves to his imagination, he must be able to choose between them" (p. 36). "Deliberating is not merely reflecting in order to choose, it is also imagining alternatives between which to choose" (p. 43). He speaks of ranges of choice in which an agent is "limited only by the virtuosity of his imagination" (p. 43).

18. See Edmund Husserl, *Experience and Judgment*, trans. by J. Churchill and K. Ameriks (Evanston: Northwestern University Press, 1973), §86–87; *Phänomenologische Psychologie* (The Hague: Nijhoff, 1962), §9; *Cartesian Meditations*, trans. by D. Cairns (The Hague: Nijhoff, 1960), §34. For an analysis and other references, see Robert Sokolowski, *Husserlian Meditations* (Evanston: Northwestern University Press, 1974), ch. 3.

19. Yves R. Simon, *Philosophy of Democratic Government* (Chicago: University of Chicago Press, 1951), pp. 1–71.

20. See Plato *Republic* 7.522C–525A; the finger can be seen as both large and small, or soft and hard, and this existence in opposition is what summons the intellect to determine what the large and the small, or the soft and the hard, are; but they can be defined only after their opposition is recognized as necessary.

21. At the risk of specifying these relationships too exactly, we might say that it is the imagined me that makes the tentative confinement of the genus to one of its species, and the imagining me that realizes that such a confinement cannot be carried out because it cannot be integrated with what I have experienced (the "I" is what is the same in both the imagining and the imagined me). In dreams or in emotional distress, this controlling distance is lost; the imagining me is not displaced sufficiently from the imagined, and the confusion cannot be dealt with. The Platonic dialogue is an appropriate literary form for working out distinctions; the reader must displace himself into several interlocutors. Does the reader identify himself with Socrates in a way different from the way he identifies himself with Socrates' conversationalists?

22. Saul Kripke, "Naming and Necessity," in *Semantics of Natural Language*, ed. by D. Davidson and G. Harman (Boston: Reidel, 1972), p. 321; Peter Strawson, *Individuals* (London: Methuen, 1959), pp. 63–86 (see

his remarks on his own method, pp. 85–86); Gilbert Ryle, *The Concept of Mind* (London: Hutchinson, 1949), pp. 248-49; Richard Rorty, "The World Well Lost," *Journal of Philosophy* 69 (1972), p. 657; Hannah Arendt, *The Human Condition* (Chicago: University of Chicago Press, 1958), pp. 236–43; Plato *Republic* 5.463C–E; Aristotle *Politics* 1.4.

23. The use of imaginative variation is found everywhere in philosophical writing because philosophy is generally concerned with bringing out necessities. An appropriate way of doing "metaphilosophy" is to determine what genus the imaginative variation is trying to sustain, what confusion it is trying to overcome, and what species are being distinguished in order to avoid the concentration of the genus into only one of its species. Among the examples cited in the last footnote, for instance, Arendt is engaged in showing that the genus *reaction to others' actions* has to encompass both *holding them to what they have done* and *releasing them from what they have done*. She does this by imaginatively constricting the genus to the first species and showing that the uncertainty that accompanies all human action, the unforeseen consequences all action entails, would render us incapable of acting if we could not hope for forgiveness should things go wrong. (One might dispute whether she interprets forgiveness properly; we are here concerned only with the formal structure of her argument.) In his essay, Rorty argues against the notion of alternative conceptual schemes. His argument implies the fact that the genus *language* necessarily involves as species something like *opaque* and *transparent* or *untranslatable* and *translatable*. In the passage we quote he imagines the possibility of constricting *language* to one of these species—the *opaque* or the *untranslatable* or even the *unrecognizable*—and the constriction is seen to be unacceptable on its face. The notion of alternative conceptual schemes would involve the possibility of such a constriction, and Rorty's imaginative proposal is a move in his argument against that notion.

24. Despite his use of relation in explaining how being can be said in many ways (*Metaphysics* 4.2.1003a33–b19), Aristotle is unsympathetic with Plato's attempt to get beyond substance to a kind of "relatedness" that lets substances be. See Robert Sokolowski, *Presence and Absence* (Bloomington: Indiana University Press, 1978), p. 173.

25. Edmund Husserl, *Die Philosophie der Arithmetik* (The Hague: Nijhoff, 1970), p. 119.

26. Edmund Husserl, *Ideas*, trans. by W. R. Boyce Gibson (New York: Macmillan, 1931), §24, translation modified.

27. Edmund Husserl, *Formal and Transcendental Logic*, trans. by D. Cairns (The Hague: Nijhoff, 1969), p. 10; see also §69–79. One of the strongest statements Husserl made on the theme of distinctions can

be found in the introduction he drafted in 1913 (with some revisions in 1924) for a new edition of the *Logical Investigations:* "For more than three decades my entire work has taken place in immanent intuition; with unparalleled efforts I have learned to see and keep projections (*Einlegungen*) out of what I see. I see phenomenological distinctions, in particular distinctions of intentionality, as well as I see the distinction between this white and that red as pure data of color" (*Introduction to the Logical Investigations*, ed. by Eugen Fink, trans. by Philip J. Bossert and Curtis H. Peters [The Hague: Nijhoff, 1975], p. 57, translation altered).

28. See Sokolowski, *Presence and Absence*, ch. 15.

4

Explaining

1. A good example of a merely apparent "one" that is really an accidental unity of two distinct things can be found in Elie Kedouri, *Nationalism* (London: Hutchinson, 1960), p. 89. Kedouri observes that nationalism is sometimes identified as a politics of the right, sometimes as a politics of the left. In either case, he says, "this conjunction . . . is a fortuitous accident." To state this in the terms we have been using, if one were to probe the being of an entity called *right-wing* (or *left-wing*) *nationalism*, one would not come to any axioms for this thing as a whole. Nationalism may in fact be right-wing or left-wing but it is not essentially so.

2. See Yves R. Simon, *The Tradition of Natural Law*, ed. by Vukan Kuic (New York: Fordham University Press, 1965), p. 72: "In philosophy, also, complete rigor requires that every concept be analyzed into its components up to the level of the indefinables. One reason why philosophy rarely exists in a perfectly rigorous and scientific condition is that the complete analysis of a philosophical term is an operation involving such strain that few people can stand it. A philosopher who cares to have any readers must generally stop short of the indefinables, just when he has reached a level where the reader experiences a feeling of sufficient clarity. If intellectual training is sound, this feeling is dependable, and if it is unsound, not much can be done anyway."

3. There is an interesting parallel between retrospective and prospective explanations and pseudo-explanations:

Retrospectively, we explain a phenomenon (1) by giving the cause that preceded it ("This car was damaged by that explosion") and is other to it. However, (2) sometimes we give what seems to be an antecedent cause but really is an elaboration of the form of the phenomenon in question; this occurs when we tell a legend that clarifies the nature of the thing being discussed.

Prospectively, we can explain a phenomenon (1) by giving the *purpose* for which it is done ("Dick is shoveling the snow so that Jane can go shopping"). There is a definite otherness between the event and its purpose, just as there is a definite otherness between a phenomenon and the cause that precedes it. However, we also can explain an event prospectively (2) by giving the *end* that is maturating within it, the end by which the event is defined: a child's faltering steps are *walking* in its incipient phases, and *adolescence* is definable as "incipient adulthood." Now we may give a pseudo-explanation by treating the end as though it were a purpose. We may speak as if the purpose of toddling were walking, as if the purpose of adolescence were maturity, as though toddling and adolescence were chosen in view of walking and maturity, as though the latter were distinctly other to the former. But although a purpose is other to that which is chosen for it, an end is really immanent in its event. The final cause is a version of the formal cause. To treat the end as a purpose is like treating a form as the outcome of a choice. (I am grateful to Francis Slade for his remarks about the difference between purpose and end.)

5

Timing

1. If we place a yardstick down five times against a wall, the sum of the placements measures another whole, the wall. We have measured the wall, not the placements, although we have counted the placements. Simply counting five turns of the hourglass would be like summing the placements of the yardstick without equating them with anything.

2. See G. J. Whitrow, *The Natural Philosophy of Time* (New York: Harper and Row, 1961), p. 175.

3. Isaac Newton, *Principia*, trans. by Motte-Cajori (Berkeley: University of California Press, 1966), vol. 1, p. 6: "Absolute, true, and mathematical time, of itself, and from its own nature, flows equably and without relation to anything external, and by another name is called duration."

4. See Adolf Grünbaum, *Philosophical Problems of Space and Time* (Boston: Reidel, 1973), p. 42: "The number of times which a given body B will contain a certain unit rod is a property of B that is not first conferred on B by human operations."

5. My description of clocking motion depends on Aristotle *Physics* 4.10–14, as interpreted by Wolfgang Wieland, *Die aristotelische Physik* (Göttingen: Vandenhoeck and Ruprecht, 1962), pp. 322–29.

6. Grünbaum admits the objective and "physical" reality of the relations of earlier and later or before and after, but claims that the now or the present, as well as the future and past, are mind-dependent or "psychological," and that therefore becoming (as opposed to process or motion) is mind-dependent. See "The Status of Temporal Becoming," in *The Philosophy of Time*, ed. by Richard M. Gale (Garden City: Doubleday, 1967), pp. 322–53; also *Philosophical Problems of Space and Time*, pp. 314–29. Aristotle likewise said that time, as the measure of motion, is mind-dependent and that before and after belong to motion independently of mind (*Physics* 4.14.223a22–29). The major difference between Grünbaum and Aristotle lies in what each takes awareness or the mind to be. Grünbaum fails to recognize awareness as intentional or presentational. He takes it as an effect brought about by an external cause, not a presentation of anything except itself and its own reactions. Consequently there is really only self-awareness. Hence he says the present or the now is just a feature of awareness, not something belonging to what one is aware of. According to Aristotle the mind presents and counts motions, so in registering a present motion it is involved in something beyond itself. The difference between Grünbaum's position, which is shared by many other writers, and the position represented in this essay, is based not primarily on the concept of time but on the concept of consciousness. Strangely, Grünbaum seems to imply that the only discourse that is about objective, physical reality is discourse about what is absent to us and not discourse about what is actually presented.

D. H. Mellor's *Real Time* (New York: Cambridge University Press, 1981) is an attempt to show that tenses are not real. Mellor distinguishes between tenses and dates and observes that the same temporal interval can be identified by a tense and by a date, but that tenses and dates differ since "dates are fixed and tenses are not" (p. 22). He uses our mundane identification of temporal units as an ultimate criterion of which units are real. The translatability of tenses into dates, and the contradictions that attend the purely objective use of tensed expressions, make him deny the reality of tenses. It seems to me that Mellor does not analyze dates and tenses in terms of their presentational or intentional differences, as I have attempted to do in this essay by distinguishing between clock and calendar time. Only such a presentational or phenomenological analysis will get to the final differences in time and tense, since time and tense are essentially related to presencing. And only by getting to such final differences will we be able to preserve, philosophically, the reality of both time and tense.

7. Aristotle *Physics* 4.11.219a14–21. See Robert Sokolowski, *Presence and Absence* (Bloomington: Indiana University Press, 1978), pp. 122–24.

8. The form "before and after" functions much as the form "object and feature," which can apply to something bodily present to us and articulated, but which works also when we speak about the same object in its absence. In fact the form of object and attribute permits us to speak about the object in its absence, because the crisp differentiation between the context we are in and a context we are not in but are talking about is made possible by linguistic, logical, and ontological syntax; by the breaking up of a distinct subject and predicate, noun and verb, object and feature. Until this syntactical distinction occurs, there is only one global "context," without differentiation. See Sokolowski, *Presence and Absence*, ch. 2, "Nouns, Verbs, and Contexts."

9. Evelyn Waugh, *Brideshead Revisited* (Boston: Little, Brown, 1979), p. 180.

10. See the title of Husserl's book on time, *Towards the Phenomenology of the Consciousness of Inner Time: Zur Phänomenologie des inneren Zeitbewußtseins*, ed. by Rudolf Boehm (The Hague: Nijhoff, 1966). Husserl examines not just inner time, but the consciousness of inner time.

11. Henry James, *The Wings of the Dove* (New York: Random House, 1937), ch. 29, pp. 258–59.

12. See Robert Sokolowski, "Picturing," ch. 1, above, pp. 16–21. "Making Distinctions," ch. 3, above, pp. 77–81.

13. Thomas Hobbes *Leviathan* 1.2; *The Elements of Law* 1.3.1.

14. Present, past, and future are irreducibly three. Before and after are two. Now and then are two but potentially three, because the then can be either elapsed or anticipated.

15. Incoherences can arise if we take *the present, the past, the future*, or *now* as names of motions or events. It would be wrong, for example, to say that the future is after the present or that the past is before the future. (See Adolf Grünbaum, "Are Physical Events Themselves Transiently Past, Present, and Future? A Reply to H. A. C. Dobbs," *The British Journal for the Philosophy of Science* 20 [1969], p. 145: "The past and the future can be characterised as respectively earlier and later than the present.") It is subsequent *motions* that are after, and prior motions before, the present motion; the future is not after the present any more than my right is to the right of me, or my front is before me. It would also be incoherent to say that a later now is later than earlier ones (Grünbaum says this in *Philosophical Problems of Space and Time*, p. 316). A motion or an event can be later than others, but now is not a motion or an event.

16. T. S. Eliot, *Four Quartets*, "East Coker," last line.

17. Mircea Eliade, *Myths, Dreams, and Mysteries* (New York: Harper and Row, 1967), p. 30. See also A. W. Reed, *Aboriginal Legends: Animal*

Tales (Sydney: A. H. and A. W. Reed, 1978), p. 7: "Both men and animals were part of an endless Dreamtime that began with the deeds of totemic ancestors. Their deeds are part of life, and men are part of animals, as animals are of men . . . . In these Dreamtime tales, men and animals may change from one to the other, or share the form and nature of both." Reed speaks of "those who live close to nature in the ever-present Dreamtime." My thanks are due to Andrew Murray for bringing Reed's work to my attention.

18. Some peculiarities of succession are mentioned by Husserl in *Zur Phänomenologie des inneren Zeitbewußtseins*, pp. 370–71.

19. G. J. Whitrow, *The Natural Philosophy of Time*, p. 292: "Time is not itself a process in time . . . . The happening of an event is not itself a further event."

20. It is what, in Husserlian terminology, we might call "the form of inner time-consciousness" (as opposed to "inner time-consciousness"), but we wish to avoid the intensely introspective tone of Husserl's terms. He once speaks of it as "Vorstufe der Zeit als Koexistenzform" (MS, C, 7, I, p. 17; see Klaus Held, *Lebendige Gegenwart* [The Hague: Nijhoff, 1966], p. 116). Husserl also often refers to this as the form of *nunc stans*. See Held, pp. 112–18, 123–37. Other passages in Husserl's manuscripts in which this form is mentioned are: C, 2, I, p. 15 ("stehendes und bleibendes Urjetzt als starre Form"); C, 3, III, p. 25, p. 29, p. 36; C, 7, I, p. 14; C, 7, II, p. 16; C, 10, p. 24 ("mein urtümliches Nicht-Ich as Urform der Zeit"); C, 15, pp. 2–3; C, 16, p. 17; C, 17, III, p. 15. A special question related to the form of succession is how we as persons and human beings identify with "our" form of succession. I wish to thank John Brough for help with this essay.

6

Measurement

1. For some examples taken at random, see the diagram for prey selection proposed by J. P. Ewert, "Behavioral Selectivity Based on Thalamotectal Interactions," *The Behavioral and Brain Sciences* 7 (1984), p. 337; and the diagram for behavior generation proposed by Graham Hoyle, "The Scope of Neuroethology," ibid., p. 373. In an essay entitled "Perceptual-Motor Processes and the Neural Basis for Language," Michael A. Arbib provides a diagram for visually directed grasping, another for optic flow, and another for prey selection (see *Neural Models of Language Processes*, ed. by M. A. Arbib, D. Caplan, and J. C. Marshall [New York: Academic Press, 1982], pp. 530–51).

2. On Edmund Husserl's concept of idealization, see his *Crisis of European Sciences and Transcendental Phenomenology*, trans. by D. Carr (Evanston: Northwestern University Press, 1970), pp. 23–24. See also Robert Sokolowski, *Husserlian Meditations: How Words Present Things* (Evanston: Northwestern University Press, 1974), pp. 77–79. It is not just physical objects that become idealized in the exact sciences. Even something like an information processing machine, and the very processing of information, are pushed toward idealized forms when they are scientifically studied. See Charles H. Bennett and Rolf Landauer, "The Fundamental Physical Limits of Computation," *Scientific American* 253 (July 1985), pp. 48–56. In economics we have such things as the perfect competition model: its idealization is perfect decentralization, "the complete absence of conscious control by anyone over the plans of others" (Harold Demsetz, *Economic, Legal, and Political Dimensions of Competition* [New York: North Holland, 1982], p. 8). A very interesting example in which the measuring process itself becomes idealized can be found in Rachel Wallace Gardner, *Modern Logic and Quantum Mechanics* (Bristol: Adam Hilger, 1984), p. 80: "We can therefore assume that measurements are nondisturbing, just as we shall assume that they can be performed arbitrarily quickly, so that no evolution of the system takes place." And, "One assumes that measurements are performed ideally quickly, so that no evolution takes place, and also with ideally little disturbance" (pp. 84–85).

3. On the relationship between measurement and Husserl's notion of idealization, see Robert Sokolowski, "Exact Science and the World in Which We Live," ch. 7, below, pp. 164–70.

4. The Cartesian and Kantian notion of an inner conscious world contrasted to an outer world, with mental constructs as devices to organize and predict our sensations, is very common in the philosophy of science. For an especially vivid instance, see the work of Eugene P. Wigner; for example, "Two Kinds of Reality," in *Symmetries and Reflections* (Woodbridge, Conn.: Ox Bow Press, 1979), pp. 188–89. Another instance can be found in the concept of mind proposed by Karl R. Popper and John C. Eccles; see their volume, *The Self and Its Brain* (New York: Springer International, 1981), p. 327.

5. We should note that the theory does not describe the diagram that may be associated with it; rather, the theory describes that which the diagram is a diagram of: the object measured in the internal measurement system.

6. See Henry Margeneau, "Philosophical Problems Concerning the Meaning of Measurement in Physics," in *Measurement, Definitions, and*

Theories, ed. by C. W. Churchman and P. Ratoosh (New York: John Wiley and Sons, 1959), p. 164: "If observation denotes what is coercively given in sensation, that which forms the last instance of appeal in every scientific explanation or prediction, and if theory is the constructive rationale serving to understand and regularize observations, then measurement is the process that mediates between the two, the conversion of the immediate into constructs via number or, viewed the other way, the contact of reason with Nature." The current search for proton decay is a large-scale, extremely complex experiment prompted by recent grand unified theories that predict such decay. No proton decay has yet been found, but the theoretical considerations—considerations based on internal measurement systems—strongly suggest that it should be found.

7. Thomas S. Kuhn, "Measurement in Physical Science," in *Quantification*, ed. by H. Woolf (Indianapolis: Bobbs-Merrill, 1961), p. 39.

8. See Bradley E. Schaefer, "Gamma-Ray Bursters," *Scientific American* 252 (February 1985), p. 52.

9. For their generous help in this essay, I am grateful to Richard Hassing, Nicholas Metropolis, and Tom Palmer.

7

*Exact Science
and the World
in Which We Live*

1. Edmund Husserl, *The Crisis of European Sciences and Transcendental Phenomenology*, trans. by David Carr (Evanston: Northwestern University Press, 1970). References to *Crisis* appear in parentheses in the body of the present chapter, as will references to *Ideas*, i.e., Husserl's *Ideas Pertaining to a Pure Phenomenology and to a Phenomenological Philosophy*, bk. 1, trans. by F. Kersten (The Hague: Nijhoff, 1982).

2. Karl Marx: *Capital*, trans. by S. Moore and E. Aveling (New York: Random House, 1906), part 1, ch. 1, sec. 2, pp. 48–54.

3. Ibid., sec. 4, p. 84: "This division of a product into a useful thing and a value becomes practically important, only when exchange has acquired such an extension that useful articles are produced for the purpose of being exchanged, and their character as values has therefore to be taken into account, beforehand, during production."

4. Thomas Hobbes, *Leviathan*, ed. C. B. Macpherson (Baltimore: Penguin, 1968), ch. 20, pp. 252–53. Harold Macmillan makes a comment

that expresses the political problem of exact science. Speaking about Walter Bagehot, Macmillan says: "He wrote about 'political economy,' a very good phrase, because it meant that economics was about people, the art of the possible. Now we have got this extreme form of mathematical economics which doesn't appear to be about anything in particular. But the old phrase meant exactly what it was intended to mean. It was the art of governing people in accordance with certain laws which appear to have shown themselves to be of value to organized humanity" (*The Economist* [30 December 1978], p. 11).

5. Aristotle *Metaphysics* 3.2.996a20–b1.

6. See Burton H. Klein, *Dynamic Economics* (Cambridge: Harvard University Press, 1977), p. 218: "Regulatory agencies desire an environment with little or no uncertainty." P. 219: "Under conditions of strong uncertainties, competition is the best form of regulation. Without imposing risk, how can the best available alternatives be found?" P. 254: "A better understanding of the dynamics involved in dealing with a greater degree of uncertainty may be the single most important issue to be resolved in the social sciences." See also pp. 99–101, 210–12, 226–27, 205–55.

7. On indeterminacy as an ontological foundation for human action, see Aristotle *Nicomachean Ethics* 3.1.

8. I wish to thank Richard Hassing and Jorges Bellet for suggestions on earlier drafts of this chapter.

8
*Exorcising
Concepts*

1. Ferdinand de Saussure, *Cours de linguistique générale*, ed. by C. Bally and A. Sechehaye (Paris: Payot, 1962), p. 98.

2. Ibid., p. 28.

3. See Gilbert Ryle, "Are There Propositions?" in *Collected Papers* (London: Hutchinson, 1971), pp. 122–38; the essay originally appeared in 1930.

4. John Searle, *Intentionality* (London: Cambridge University Press, 1983), p. 230.

5. Frege argues strongly against the reduction of thoughts to subjective, mental ideas. His solution is to place them neither among material objects nor among ideas, but in a new realm, and he too posits this domain not because he experiences it but because he is forced by argument to do so: "A third realm must be recognized" (see "The Thought:

A Logical Inquiry," trans. by A. M. and Marcelle Quinton, *Mind* 65 [1956], p. 302). My chief concern in this essay is to argue against concepts as mental entities, so I do not discuss Frege's third realm as such; however, if I can show that conceptual mental entities need not be posited, I will also have shown that a subsistent third realm need not be posited either. Or, to put it another way, I will have clarified what Frege is getting at when he feels the need to postulate a third realm.

6. De Saussure, *Cours de linguistique générale*, p. 144.

7. To hear *what* is said *about* the thing is to engage the structure Aristotle names in his phrase, *ti kata tinos*.

8. See Gottlob Frege, "On Sense and Reference," trans. by M. Black, in *Translations from the Philosophical Writings of Gottlob Frege*, ed. by P. Geach and M. Black (Oxford: Blackwell, 1960), pp. 56–78.

9. See Aristotle *Metaphysics* 4.4.1006a21, b7–9.

10. Philippe Forget, ed., *Text und Interpretation* (Munich: Fink, 1984).

11. See Robert Sokolowski, *Presence and Absence* (Bloomington: Indiana University Press, 1978), ch. 13.

9
Referring

1. Leonard Linsky has emphasized that it is not expressions themselves but the users of expressions, the speakers, that establish reference, and that they do so in a context; see his *Referring* (Atlantic Highlands, N.J.: Humanities Press, 1967), pp. 116–17. See also Peter Strawson, "On Referring," in *Logico-Linguistic Papers* (London: Methuen, 1971), p. 8: "'Mentioning', or 'referring', is not something an expression does; it is something that someone can use an expression to do."

2. Donald Davidson, "Reality without Reference," in *Inquiries into Truth and Interpretation* (Oxford: Clarendon, 1984), p. 220.

3. See Robert Sokolowski, *Presence and Absence* (Bloomington: Indiana University Press, 1982), pp. 5, 27–31.

4. On the exclamatory, see Sokolowski, *Presence and Absence*, pp. 33–36.

5. On idealization and Husserl's understanding of it, see Robert Sokolowski, "Exact Science and the World in Which We Live," ch. 7, above, pp. 156–59.

6. See Gian-Carlo Rota, "The Barrier of Meaning," *Letters in Mathematical Physics* 10 (1985), pp. 97–99.

7. Strawson calls this characterization the "descriptive meaning" of an expression used in reference; see "On Referring," p. 21.

8. Gottlob Frege, "Comments on Sense and Meaning," in *Posthumous Writings*, trans. by Peter Long and Roger White (Chicago: University of Chicago Press, 1979), p. 119: "What in the case of a function is called unsaturatedness, we may, in the case of a concept, call its predicative nature." See also "Concept and Object," in *Collected Papers on Mathematics, Logic, and Philosophy*, ed. by Brian McGuinness (New York: Blackwell, 1984), p. 187 n. 11; also "Function and Concept," ibid., pp. 146–47.

9. On predicates as not having reference, see David Wiggins, "The Sense and Reference of Predicates," in *Frege: Tradition and Influence*, ed. by Crispin Wright (New York: Blackwell, 1984), p. 134.

10. On the predicate as never ceasing to be predicational even when made into a grammatical substantive (*red* being made into *redness*), see Edmund Husserl, *Formal and Transcendental Logic*, trans. by Dorion Cairns (The Hague: Nijhoff, 1969), p. 203: "In following up the sense of the substantivized adjective, we are led back to the original adjective." See also appendix 1, pp. 309-10.

11. Aristotle *Metaphysics* 7.3.1029a20–30. On the meaning of this passage in Aristotle, see Robert Sokolowski, "Matter, Elements, and Substance in Aristotle," *Journal of the History of Philosophy* 8 (1970), pp. 276–77.

12. There are many other aspects of reference that can be pursued: (1) When a speaker targets a referent, he emerges as a speaker and his addressee surfaces as an audience, but the term used in reference does not refer to either the speaker or the hearer. What sort of indication does the term make of speaker and hearer, and how does this indication differ from reference? (2) There is always some context for a reference, but the terms used to refer to an object do not refer to the context. By definition a context is not a text, a background is not a theme. How do words used in reference indicate their context? (3) There can be interesting fragmentations of a single reference, through subordinate clauses and subordinate statements. The persistence of a reference through such fragmentation is different from the persistence of a theme through many features. In the latter a reference is made once and allowed to accumulate manifestations continuously. In the former the reference becomes restated intermittently and may be modified or fragmented; I may begin by talking about Sally and then refer to her job, then speak of her house, then talk about her when she was in college. She remains the ultimate referent, but as fragmented into her job, house, and college years. (4) The speaker, the one who achieves reference, can take on various forms: sometimes the speaker is clearly identifiable, sometimes anonymous, sometimes unknown. How are we

established as addressees for a speaker when we find a piece of paper with a sentence written on it? Is there a speaker for mechanical speech, such as the kind that tells you your weight or informs you on the telephone of the state of your bank account? Are the words "uttered" by such machines used to establish reference?

10
Grammar
and Thinking

1. A crucial thought-experiment in distinguishing pictographs from pictures—a crucial imaginative variation in intuiting these eidetic structures—consists in trying to show how an array of pictures differs from a sequence of pictographs. Why is an array of pictures, such as a group of photographs on a wall, not as such a pictographic statement? One difference seems to lie in the following: there is no necessary sequence in reading the group of photographs, but in a pictograph one *must* go from one particular element to another and the temporal sequence is significant; if you were to read the pictograph in another sequence it might convey a different message. If this is a legitimate difference between pictographs and pictures, it would indicate an essential connection between grammar and time, between syntax and temporal sequence. Still other thought-experiments would involve comparing a pictographic sequence with the order of images in, say, a triptych, a series of stained-glass windows depicting the life of a saint, and the succession of images in films such as *Ivan the Terrible* and *Barry Lyndon*.

2. One of the most interesting marginal cases of vagueness occurs when a speaker who thinks vaguely nevertheless happens to say something that is illuminating. He may say something that is far more than he can really think. But for this event to occur, the speech must be heard by someone who can think distinctly about the issue in question. Only then is the "brilliant-but-lucky" remark registered for what it is. A dabbler in science, for example, may hit on a formulation that a real scientist may find to be just what is needed; a student who is struggling with the material may say just the right thing at a critical moment. Such statements occur out of vagueness, out of a wobbly and inadequate grasp of the material. They do not occur out of ignorance, because the ignorant speaker would not possess enough words with which to approach the issue; and they do not occur out of knowledge, because then they would not be considered lucky.

11
Tarskian Harmonies
in Words
and Pictures

1. E. H. Gombrich has described the contribution the viewer must make to see a picture correctly; the viewer must project an interpretation if he is to recognize the image for what it is. See *Art and Illusion: A Study in the Psychology of Representation* (New York: Pantheon, 1960), pp. 53, 195, 205. Such projection may require training; we may have to learn how to "read" cubist paintings or Egyptian figures. However, learning of this sort presupposes the ability to recognize pictures as such, the knowledge that we should see this thing not as a thing in itself but as an image. It is hard to imagine how we could convey the idea of a picture to someone who claimed to know not at all what pictures—or at least imitations—were. It is hard to imagine someone who claims not to be able to take anything as a picture. The notion of images seems to be with us from the beginning; words, images, mimicry, and perceptions seem to differentiate themselves together from a more primordial state. It is not as though we could first achieve words and then use them to get the notion of pictures or imitation across. On "reading" a picture correctly and on "holding a picture together," see the remarks made by John M. Brealey, chairman of the Department of Paintings Conservation at New York's Metropolitan Museum of Art, in the profile written about him by Calvin Tomkins ("Colored Muds in a Sticky Substance," *New Yorker* [March 16, 1987], p. 44; see p. 53: "Suddenly, the picture was readable again").

2. On things taken as the meanings of words, see Robert Sokolowski, "Exorcising Concepts," above, ch. 8, pp. 177–79.

3. Although we have to turn away from a picture when we move to the thing itself, it is not the case that the picture vanishes totally when we move to the object. Pictures are not throwaways. The picture's afterglow affects how we will see the thing. As E. H. Gombrich says, "For this is the secret of a good caricature—it offers a visual interpretation of a physiognomy which we can never forget and which the victim will always seem to carry around with him like a man bewitched" (*Art and Illusion*, p. 344). Of course, this effect of image upon original does not occur only in regard to caricatures: nature begins to look different after landscape painting, and kings become more regal thanks to the painters at court. The image captures the essence of the original and allows that essence to "body forth" more vividly in the original itself.

4. On the prepredicative and predicative, see Edmund Husserl, *Experience and Judgment*, trans. by J. Churchill and K. Ameriks (Evanston: Northwestern University Press, 1973), pp. 27, 71–236.

5. See Alfred Tarski, "The Concept of Truth in Formalized Languages," in *Logic, Semantics, Metamathematics*, 2nd ed. (Indianapolis: Hackett, 1983), pp. 152–278; "The Semantic Conception of Truth," *Philosophy and Phenomenological Research* 4 (1944), pp. 341–75; "Truth and Proof," *Scientific American* 220 (1967), pp. 63–77.

6. See Tarski, "The Semantic Conception of Truth," pp. 348–51.

7. See Tarski, "Truth and Proof," p. 68.

8. See Tarski, "Truth and Proof," p. 67; "The Concept of Truth in Formalized Languages," pp. 164–65.

9. See Tarski, "The Semantic Conception of Truth," p. 348.

10. See Karsten Harries, *The Broken Frame: Three Lectures* (Washington: The Catholic University of America Press, 1989), pp. 67–75.

11. On grammatical elements as signals, see Robert Sokolowski, "Grammar and Thinking," above, ch. 10.

13
*What Is
Moral Action?*

1. Temporal horizons shift in interesting ways when I change from (1) preparing these remarks for delivery in a lecture, to (2) actually stating them before an audience, to (3) preparing them for an essay to be (4) interpreted by readers. The hermeneutic contexts become radically different and the "now" changes in the four situations. I was alone as I originally wrote the words ("now$_1$"), but when I lectured, I and my audience were together in a single context ("now$_2$"). I became a public presence. Furthermore, because I was there as the speaker, I could react to the situation and could modify what I said in order to adapt it to what was going on. I was able to control the interpretation to some degree. But when I "now$_3$" as a writer use the same words I once prepared for an audience, those same words that I once spoke to an audience, I return to solitude, and I know that you at some time ("now$_4$", while you are reading) will also be alone as you achieve your interpretation. I cannot be there to accommodate my words to your context. At that time we shall be bodily separated but united in the achievement of one and the same meaning, interpreted through all these contexts. You will appreciate what you read as the same as what I once declared before a group of listeners, and you will even see through the speech-situation to the time

("now$_1$") when I first wrote the lecture. The speech-situation, which was once the final, actual context, becomes relativized and profiled within new contexts, the contexts of the various readers, who will be in many different places. The various "nows" become nested within one another.

2. On Husserl's notion of categorial form, see my essay, "Husserl's Concept of Categorial Intuition," *Phenomenology and the Human Sciences*, supplement to *Philosophical Topics* 12 (1981), pp. 127–41. On the application of categoriality to morals, see Robert Sokolowski, *Moral Action: A Phenomenological Study* (Bloomington: Indiana University Press, 1985), pp. 1–6.

3. The passages from Aristotle are taken from Ross's translation, with extensive emendations.

4. The most conspicuous difference between Aristotle's analysis and mine consists in the following: I claim that the form of acting "toward another" works even in the case of private, individual virtues such as temperance and courage, but Aristotle seems to limit his concept of justice to actions that are explicitly directed toward others. However, in bk. 5, ch. 11 of the *Nicomachean Ethics*, he does concede that "by metaphor and by resemblance" (1138b5–6) there is a kind of justice within an individual, a justice that consists in the proper ordering of the various parts of the soul under the guidance of reason. And earlier, in ch. 1, he indicates that the law does attempt to form such virtues as bravery, temperance, and gentleness (1129b19–25). Furthermore, Plato is quite willing to admit that justice can be found in the individual soul, not just metaphorically but literally and in the primary sense. In the *Republic*, Socrates asserts that justice "does not lie in a man's external actions, but in the way he acts within himself, really concerned with himself and his inner parts. . . . He orders what are in the true sense of the word his own affairs well; he is master of himself, puts things in order, is his own friend . . ." (443C–D; Grube translation).

The reason there is some difference between Aristotle's analysis and mine is that Aristotle presents virtue and justice as they appear politically and ethically, as they are political and moral phenomena, whereas I am trying to uncover the form of presentation, the way of being manifest, that is proper to moral agency. Getting to this level of analysis highlights the similarities in all moral behavior, whether public or private. Plato is also interested in the primary differentiations of morals, in the first sorting out of justice, and so my remarks more obviously conform to his teaching.

Another difference between my analysis and Aristotle's is that his general justice is also legal justice, the virtue of the law-abiding man, whereas my description does not invoke a legal dimension. I need primarily the "toward another" as constitutive of morals, not the dimension of civic law. But even here one can find a similarity. Moral categoriality involves something analogous to law; the interplay of the good and bad of another with my own good or bad has something of the obligatory about it. I ought to respect the good and eschew the bad of another. Civic law draws on this prelegal obligation and receives some of its moral force from it.

5. Adam Smith, *The Theory of Moral Sentiments*, ed. by D. D. Raphael and A. L. Macfie (Oxford: Oxford University Press, 1976).

6. Ibid., 1.1.1, pp. 9–13.

7. Ibid., 1.1.4, p. 19.

8. Ibid., 2.3.intro., p. 92.

9. Ibid.

10. Ibid., pp. 92–93.

14
Knowing
Natural Law

1. Aristotle *Nicomachean Ethics* 3.5.1114b1–3: "If each one is somehow the cause of his own habit of being (*hexis*), he will also be the cause of the appearance (*phantasia*) as well." See also William W. Fortenbaugh, who comments on passages in the *Eudemian Ethics* (1229b21–26, 1230a31) and says: "To the coward what is not formidable appears formidable, and what is slightly formidable appears exceedingly formidable. For the rash person appearances are reversed. But to the courageous man things appear as they really are. . . ." Then he says, "What courage does is to insure a correct perception of a particular situation" ("Aristotle's Conception of Moral Virtue and Its Perceptive Role," *Transactions and Proceedings of the American Philological Association* 95 [1964], p. 78).

2. Immanuel Kant, *Foundations of the Metaphysics of Morals*, trans. by Lewis White Beck (Indianapolis: Bobbs-Merrill, 1959), p. 39: "Act only according to that maxim by which you can at the same time will that it should become a universal law."

3. John Rawls, *A Theory of Justice* (Cambridge: Harvard University Press, 1971). On the relationship between Rawls and Kant, see Robert Paul Wolff, *Understanding Rawls* (Princeton: Princeton University Press, 1977), pp. 101–16.

4. Rawls, *A Theory of Justice*, pp. 136–37.

5. Aristotle *Nicomachean Ethics* 3.1.1111a7–8.

6. Thomas Hobbes, *De Cive*, VI, sec. 16.

7. Marsilius of Padua, *Defensor Pacis*, trans. by Alan Gewirth (New York: Harper and Row, 1956), discourse 2, ch. 12.7.

Index